Survival

GLOBAL POLITICS AND STRATEGY

Volume 60 Number 6 | December 2018–January 2019

'May embarked on a process for which the country had not been prepared, then failed to boost her electoral mandate, and was then left moving forward with a divided government, a febrile parliament and a confused country. This led to a strategy of incremental capitulation.'

Lawrence Freedman, Trump and Brexit, p. 11.

'[McCain] often overcommitted to politicians in transitional countries that turned out to be undemocratic or corrupt. But he believed fervently that it wasn't good enough to strengthen the West at its core.'

Kori Schake, A Patriot's Farewell, p. 183.

'The left behind … feel, understandably, that they have a right to remain in the communities they have always considered home … This kind of thinking may make some sense in moral terms, but the American capitalist economy is not known for emphasising morality. Rural decline – and its political companion, rural rage – will likely be with us for some time to come.'

David C. Unger, Book Reviews, p. 222.

T0332587

Survival

GLOBAL POLITICS AND STRATEGY

Volume 60 Number 6 | December 2018–January 2019

Contents

On the cover
UK Prime Minister
Theresa May arrives
at the European Union
summit in Brussels on
14 December 2017.

On the web
Visit www.iiss.org/
publications/survival
for brief notices on
new books on Europe,
the United States, and
Counter-terrorism and
Intelligence.

***Survival* editors' blog**
For ideas and
commentary from
Survival editors and
contributors, visit
www.iiss.org/blogs/
survival-blog.

Strategic Shifts

Good Intentions

Review Essays

Book Reviews

Closing Argument

Survival

GLOBAL POLITICS AND STRATEGY

The International Institute for Strategic Studies

2121 K Street, NW | Suite 801 | Washington DC 20037 | USA
Tel +1 202 659 1490   Fax +1 202 659 1499   E-mail survival@iiss.org   Web www.iiss.org

Arundel House | 6 Temple Place | London | WC2R 2PG | UK
Tel +44 (0)20 7379 7676   Fax +44 (0)20 7836 3108   E-mail iiss@iiss.org

14th Floor, GBCorp Tower | Bahrain Financial Harbour | Manama | Kingdom of Bahrain
Tel +973 1718 1155   Fax +973 1710 0155   E-mail iiss-middleeast@iiss.org

9 Raffles Place | #51-01 Republic Plaza | Singapore 048619
Tel +65 6499 0055   Fax +65 6499 0059   E-mail iiss-asia@iiss.org

Survival Online www.tandfonline.com/survival and www.iiss.org/publications/survival

Aims and Scope *Survival* is one of the world's leading forums for analysis and debate of international and strategic affairs. Shaped by its editors to be both timely and forward thinking, the journal encourages writers to challenge conventional wisdom and bring fresh, often controversial, perspectives to bear on the strategic issues of the moment. With a diverse range of authors, *Survival* aims to be scholarly in depth while vivid, well written and policy-relevant in approach. Through commentary, analytical articles, case studies, forums, review essays, reviews and letters to the editor, the journal promotes lively, critical debate on issues of international politics and strategy.

Editor **Dana Allin**
Managing Editor **Jonathan Stevenson**
Associate Editor **Carolyn West**
Editorial Assistant **Jessica Watson**
Production and Cartography **John Buck, Kelly Verity**

Contributing Editors

Gilles Andréani	Bill Emmott	Hanns W. Maull	Steven Simon	Ruth Wedgwood
Ian Bremmer	John A. Gans, Jr	Jeffrey Mazo	Angela Stent	Lanxin Xiang
David P. Calleo	John L. Harper	'Funmi Olonisakin	Jonathan Stevenson	
Russell Crandall	Erik Jones	Thomas Rid	Ray Takeyh	
Toby Dodge	Jeffrey Lewis	Teresita C. Schaffer	David C. Unger	

Published for the IISS by
Routledge Journals, an imprint of Taylor & Francis, an Informa business.

About the IISS The IISS, a registered charity with offices in Washington, London, Manama and Singapore, is the world's leading authority on political–military conflict. It is the primary independent source of accurate, objective information on international strategic issues. Publications include *The Military Balance*, an annual reference work on each nation's defence capabilities; *Strategic Survey*, an annual review of world affairs; *Survival*, a bimonthly journal on international affairs; *Strategic Comments*, an online analysis of topical issues in international affairs; and the *Adelphi* series of books on issues of international security.

SUBMISSIONS

To submit an article, authors are advised to follow these guidelines:

- *Survival* articles are around 4,000–10,000 words long including endnotes. A word count should be included with a draft. Length is a consideration in the review process and shorter articles have an advantage.
- All text, including endnotes, should be double-spaced with wide margins.
- Any tables or artwork should be supplied in separate files, ideally not embedded in the document or linked to text around it.
- All *Survival* articles are expected to include endnote references. These should be complete and include first and last names of authors, titles of articles (even from newspapers), place of publication, publisher, exact publication dates, volume and issue number (if from a journal) and page numbers. Web sources should include complete URLs and DOIs if available.
- A summary of up to 150 words should be included with the article. The summary should state the main argument clearly and concisely, not simply say what the article is about.
- A short author's biography of one or two lines should also be included. This information will appear at the foot of the first page of the article.
- *Survival* has a strict policy of listing multiple authors in alphabetical order.

Submissions should be made by email, in Microsoft Word format, to survival@iiss.org. Alternatively, hard copies may be sent to *Survival*, IISS–US, 2121 K Street NW, Suite 801, Washington, DC 20037, USA.

The editorial review process can take up to three months. *Survival*'s acceptance rate for unsolicited manuscripts is less than 20%. *Survival* does not normally provide referees' comments in the event of rejection. Authors are permitted to submit simultaneously elsewhere so long as this is consistent with the policy of the other publication and the Editors of *Survival* are informed of the dual submission.

Readers are encouraged to comment on articles from the previous issue. Letters should be concise, no longer than 750 words and relate directly to the argument or points made in the original article.

ADVERTISING AND PERMISSIONS

For advertising rates and schedules

USA/Canada: The Advertising Manager, Taylor & Francis Inc., 530 Walnut Street, Suite 850, Philadelphia, PA 19106, USA Tel +1 (800) 354 1420 Fax +1 (215) 207 0050.

UK/Europe/Rest of World: The Advertising Manager, Routledge Journals, Taylor & Francis, 4 Park Square, Milton Park, Abingdon, Oxfordshire OX14 4RN, UK Tel +44 (0) 207 017 6000 Fax +44 (0) 207 017 6336.

SUBSCRIPTIONS

Survival is published bi-monthly in February, April, June, August, October and December by Routledge Journals, an imprint of Taylor & Francis, an Informa Business.

Annual Subscription 2018

Institution	£505	$885	€742
Individual	£144	$243	€196
Online only	£442	$774	€649

Taylor & Francis has a flexible approach to subscriptions, enabling you to match individual libraries' requirements. This journal is available via a traditional institutional subscription (either print with online access, or online only at a discount) or as part of our libraries, subject collections or archives. For more information on our sales packages please visit http://www.tandfonline.com/page/librarians.

All current institutional subscriptions include online access for any number of concurrent users across a local area network to the currently available backfile and articles posted online ahead of publication.

Subscriptions purchased at the personal rate are strictly for personal, non-commercial use only. The reselling of personal subscriptions is prohibited. Personal subscriptions must be purchased with a personal cheque or credit card. Proof of personal status may be requested.

Dollar rates apply to all subscribers outside Europe. Euro rates apply to all subscribers in Europe, except the UK and the Republic of Ireland where the pound sterling rate applies. If you are unsure which rate applies to you please contact Customer Services in the UK. All subscriptions are payable in advance and all rates include postage. Journals are sent by air to the USA, Canada, Mexico, India, Japan and Australasia. Subscriptions are entered on an annual basis, i.e. January to December. Payment may be made by sterling cheque, dollar cheque, euro cheque, international money order, National Giro or credit cards (Amex, Visa and Mastercard).

Survival (USPS 013095) is published bimonthly (in Feb, Apr, Jun, Aug, Oct and Dec) by Routledge Journals, Taylor & Francis, 4 Park Square, Milton Park, Abingdon, OX14 4RN, United Kingdom.

The US annual subscription price is $842. Airfreight and mailing in the USA by agent named Air Business Ltd, c/o Worldnet Shipping Inc., 156-15, 146th Avenue, 2nd Floor, Jamaica, NY 11434, USA. Periodicals postage paid at Jamaica NY 11431.

US Postmaster: Send address changes to Survival, C/O Air Business Ltd / 156-15 146th Avenue, Jamaica, New York, NY11434.

Subscription records are maintained at Taylor & Francis Group, 4 Park Square, Milton Park, Abingdon, OX14 4RN, United Kingdom.

ORDERING INFORMATION

Please contact your local Customer Service Department to take out a subscription to the Journal: **USA, Canada:** Taylor & Francis, Inc., 530 Walnut Street, Suite 850, Philadelphia, PA 19106, USA. Tel: +1 800 354 1420; Fax: +1 215 207 0050. **UK/ Europe/Rest of World:** T&F Customer Services, Informa UK Ltd, Sheepen Place, Colchester, Essex, CO3 3LP, United Kingdom. Tel: +44 (0) 20 7017 5544; Fax: +44 (0) 20 7017 5198; Email: subscriptions@tandf.co.uk.

Back issues: Taylor & Francis retains a two-year back issue stock of journals. Older volumes are held by our official stockists: Periodicals Service Company, 351 Fairview Ave., Suite 300, Hudson, New York 12534, USA to whom all orders and enquiries should be addressed. *Tel* +1 518 537 4700 *Fax* +1 518 537 5899 *e-mail* psc@periodicals.com *web* http://www.periodicals.com/tandf.html.

The International Institute for Strategic Studies (IISS) and our publisher Taylor & Francis make every effort to ensure the accuracy of all the information (the "Content") contained in our publications. However, the IISS and our publisher Taylor & Francis, our agents, and our licensors make no representations or warranties whatsoever as to the accuracy, completeness, or suitability for any purpose of the Content. Any opinions and views expressed in this publication are the opinions and views of the authors, and are not the views of or endorsed by the IISS and our publisher Taylor & Francis. The accuracy of the Content should not be relied upon and should be independently verified with primary sources of information. The IISS and our publisher Taylor & Francis shall not be liable for any losses, actions, claims, proceedings, demands, costs, expenses, damages, and other liabilities whatsoever or howsoever caused arising directly or indirectly in connection with, in relation to or arising out of the use of the Content. Terms & Conditions of access and use can be found at http://www.tandfonline.com/page/terms-and-conditions.

The issue date is December 2018–January 2019

The print edition of this journal is printed on ANSI conforming acid-free paper.

Trump and Brexit

Lawrence Freedman

In early 2017, at gatherings of the globalist elite, a new word could be heard – 'Trumpandbrexit'. It captured the idea that the two shocking events of the previous year – the Leave victory in the UK referendum on membership in the European Union and Donald Trump's victory in the 2016 US presidential election – were part of a single mysterious phenomenon that the elite was ill-equipped to understand. Trumpandbrexit appeared as a popular revolt against their most cherished values: multilateralism and international cooperation, liberalism and human rights, open borders and free trade. As the US and UK had historically been two of the most energetic promoters of those values, the rebuff was both distressing and unfathomable. Might Trumpandbrexit be the vanguard of a movement threatening all that had been achieved in the Western world since 1945?

This elite feared that the nationalist virus might spread. In 2015, Chancellor Angela Merkel of Germany had accepted that putting up barriers to those desperate to flee the wars of the Middle East and North Africa was unconscionable, but also probably futile. The resultant surge of migration into EU territory had galvanised rightist parties. It was not inconceivable that these parties might win elections in all parts of Europe. In 2017, the challenge was beaten back first in the Netherlands, then France and, somewhat less convincingly, in Germany. But it was hard to ignore the harsher tone that had entered into the politics of many countries, and that in some cases intolerant nationalists were in power or getting closer.

Lawrence Freedman is Emeritus Professor of War Studies at King's College London.

Survival | vol. 60 no. 6 | December 2018–January 2019 | pp. 7–16   DOI 10.1080/00396338.2018.1542795

The phenomenon could be dramatised as an existential struggle across the Western world between the liberal and illiberal, the global and the parochial, the open and the closed, and the broad-minded and the mean-spirited. It pitted the optimism of big cities against the pessimism of small towns. But presenting the struggle as one between the enlightened and the bigoted, lamenting the ease with which populist demagogues had beguiled those from the poorer, less educated, less travelled and more elderly sections of society, risked patronising and caricaturing these people, and missed the complexity of the phenomenon and the contingent and unique features of the different national settings. Popular grievances were expressed in a variety of ways, in some cases via the far left instead of the far right. Most importantly, there were good reasons for people to be cross. Many had been left behind by the transformational economic changes of recent decades and were then badly hit by the financial crisis of 2008 and its aftermath. They saw the wealthy as benefiting from cheap immigrant labour and from the low interest rates that boosted the value of their assets. Levels of inequality were as bad as ever.

The wellsprings of Trump and Brexit did show similarities. These lay not only in migration and the financial crisis, but also in the US and UK's fraught collaborations on the 'war on terror' and the endless wars in Afghanistan and Iraq. There was even the shared figure of Nigel Farage, who had made his career pushing the case for Leave in the UK and who turned up in 2016 as a confidant of Trump. But the differences were also significant.

Trump won an election, and with a Republican Congress was able to pursue an agenda that was true to his instincts. Subsequent elections could produce reversals of some of his policies even if their effects lingered. Brexit, by contrast, involved a simple in–out proposition. The Leave camp mounted two quite separate campaigns – an official one going for the higher political ground and Farage's playing on fears of yet more immigrants. Both offered reassurances to uncertain voters that the Leave proposition was far less radical than it might appear. The Leave victory was therefore quite different from Trump's. It reflected a disgruntled mood but not a coherent philosophy. After the vote, the most enthusiastic Leavers could not claim a mandate for any particular sort of Brexit. Some insisted that 17.4 million people had voted for a sharp break with all EU institutions and practices no matter what. Others argued that, in practice, the ties were bound to stay close, and that the country was merely giving itself a bit more freedom of manoeuvre without cutting itself off from all mutually beneficial trading relations.

British confusion

Compounding this lack of underlying clarity on the meaning of the project was the speed with which the political class embraced it. Sensing the extent of popular anger, it was loath to dismiss the result as an aberration and work immediately to overturn it. Not respecting this exercise of democracy risked aggravating public cynicism. In retrospect, a new and different debate was now needed, focused not on what had just happened, but on what needed to be done to implement the result of the referendum. Looking forward, this debate might have been informed by a realistic appraisal of the complexity of the task and the range of issues that must now be addressed, set against not only the interests of the UK but also those of the remaining 27 members of the EU.

This debate did not arise for a number of reasons, but the main one was the uneasy consensus behind the project. Those in charge were divided on its meaning, on a spectrum from the hardest to the softest versions, and so was the opposition. Seeking a definitive answer to the question of what it was all about risked opening up divisions and alienating supporters. Though both leaders of the two main political parties supported Remain, they were both always lukewarm in this position. Labour leader Jeremy Corbyn was on record rejecting the EU as a restraint on a proper socialist platform. Theresa May, as home secretary, had tried to cut back on migration and was aware of the limits on what she could do while the UK was still a member of the EU's single market. She became prime minister mainly on account of her rivals' self-destruction, and was not seriously challenged on how she saw the project being taken forward. Her slogan 'Brexit means Brexit' was a means of reassuring Leavers that she would not let them down, and of asserting her authority over the Conservative Party, but its banality underscored the lack of clear, agreed objectives and principles informing the project. Both parties described desirable outcomes while ducking questions of whether they were at all negotiable, as if pointing out legal and technical difficulties were bad form and self-defeating. The administrative class in particular saw their task as largely one of damage limitation. Some ardent Remainers were still in key positions in both the cabinet and shadow cabinet. Accordingly, the consensus encompassed varying degrees of enthusiasm and high degrees of blandness.

May tried to give herself more authority over the process by calling an election for May 2017, intended to strengthen her parliamentary majority. Despite starting with a 20% lead over the Labour Party, a lacklustre campaign left her without a majority at all, in power only with the assistance of Northern Ireland's Democratic Unionist Party – a dependency that became increasingly important as the border between the North and the Republic of Ireland became an increasingly vexed issue. May's political weakness affected every stage of the subsequent negotiations with the EU, as she could take very few risks. Her compromises had to be tentative and on occasion were withdrawn. To make matters worse, she had called the election just after invoking Article 50 of the Lisbon Treaty, starting the clock on the UK's withdrawal. Two years later, on 29 March 2019, the UK would be out of the EU with or without an acceptable withdrawal agreement unless the 27 remaining members agreed to extend the deadline.

The EU was fed up with British demands

Invoking Article 50 lost the UK whatever leverage it might have had to shape the course of the negotiations. This catered to the preference of the EU, which held that there could be no negotiations with the UK prior to this formal step. Negative referendums in other countries had been followed by efforts to find concessions and then new votes that yielded more positive results, but the UK referendum appeared too momentous to be handled in this way. Moreover, the EU had already been through some unsatisfactory negotiations with May's predecessor, David Cameron, prior to the announcement of the referendum, and was reluctant to entertain more special pleading. In short, it was already fed up with British demands, especially after negotiated opt-outs from the euro and Schengen, and budget rebates. Brussels also wanted the UK out before the May 2019 elections for the European Parliament.

The American election was also a factor. In other circumstances, the US government would have seen such disunity in Europe as a major problem and worked to help broker a solution. But Barack Obama's presidency was coming to an end. Trump supported Brexit and was generally hostile to the EU. This coloured the stances of European leaders. They tended to see Trump and Brexit as part of the same phenomenon, which encouraged a strong stand against both. They wished to keep their distance from Trumpism and demonstrate to Britain that if it wanted to leave the EU it would be on the EU's terms. Elections had to be respected and the American and British governments dealt with, but there was no need to appease them.

If May had not been in such a hurry to get the process started, orderly and substantive discussions of possible ways of taking the issue forward might still have been possible because then there would have been pressure on the EU to help move the process along. More time would also have enabled the UK to work out exactly what leaving the EU would mean in practice. Instead, May embarked on a process for which the country had not been prepared, then failed to boost her electoral mandate, and was then left moving forward with a divided government, a febrile parliament and a confused country. This led to a strategy of incremental capitulation, edging towards a position that the EU could accept, hoping she might be offered something in exchange to make it look more like a substantive negotiation, trimming each concession to avoid triggering an unmanageable parliamentary revolt. The strategy became more fraught as its logic became apparent, although it lasted longer than many might have expected. It required shifting the choice from what Britain wanted to what Britain could get, with an alternative of no deal at all.

Meanwhile the EU held together. Leavers looked for signs of splits among the EU27, hoping that their predictions that the Union was about to fall apart would come true sooner rather than later. The EU certainly had big problems to address, not least the developing tensions with countries such as Poland and Hungary, and the risks posed by the Italian government to the eurozone. But Brexit made little difference to how these issues would unfold, and they gave the UK no leverage. It was not terribly difficult for the 27 to stay united and let the lead negotiator, Michel Barnier, do the best he could. Few in the EU blamed problems in the negotiations on the European Commission. Most saw them as the result of a lack of realism on the UK's part. Some might have had a grudging admiration for the British trying to honour a democratic vote with a magnificent stubbornness. Others just assumed the country had taken leave of its senses.

Divided and bored

Even with a strong majority, May would have struggled with the essential contradiction at the heart of the UK position. From the start she stressed two aspects in particular – taking the UK out of the jurisdiction of the European Court of Justice and ending freedom of movement. Whatever some Leavers said about the great trading opportunities away from the EU, migration was the issue that had most animated voters and with which May herself had the greatest sympathy. It was the area in which David Cameron had sought relief from the EU prior to the referendum. The problem was that ending freedom of movement meant no longer being part of the single market, just as the desire to negotiate trade deals separate from the rest of the EU meant leaving the customs union. To the business and financial communities, that meant inevitable economic harm. The single market, which had been energetically promoted by Margaret Thatcher's government during the 1980s, had contributed to Britain's recent prosperity and the country's ability to present itself as a global hub.

The UK government understood that some migration was necessary and that trade was good. This set it on a path of what the EU saw as 'cherry-picking' – that is, seeking to secure as many benefits as possible of the single market and customs union without accepting the full package of European Court of Justice jurisdiction and freedom of movement. Strictly speaking, this was an issue for post-withdrawal, and a transition period was agreed during which the future trading arrangements with the EU would be set. Awkwardly for the British (and to a degree for the EU), the Irish border had to be settled as part of the withdrawal agreement. Dublin insisted on maintaining an open border as agreed under the Good Friday Agreement.

As this is the UK's only land border, the issue raised questions that might have been left for the transition. If border checkpoints were not to be set up and Northern Ireland not separated from the rest of the UK, it was hard to see how something close to the single market and customs union could be avoided. This of course was anathema to the hardline Leavers.

Throughout 2018, May tried to find a formula that would feel like an actual Brexit while building in a realistic transition period to iron out the details of a future trading relationship and avoid disrupting too many lives, whether of EU citizens living in the UK or UK citizens living in the EU. As she tried to find the formula, she struggled against the somewhat unimaginative EU approach of waiting for UK proposals and then finding them wanting. The main problem lay in a country that was divided on the issues of principle while progressively bored with the technical matters of negotiation. It was hard for voters to express a preference for 'Norway minus' or 'Canada plus' as visions for the future, and unclear whether May could get a parliamentary majority behind any deal. The Labour Party wanted to force another election, although it was not clear they would improve on their 2017 position. Remainers, frustrated with Labour's equivocation, increasingly organised around demands for a second referendum; the only reason to suspect a different result was the hostile reaction of Leavers to the very idea.

Meanwhile, the clock was ticking and the prospect of the country simply crashing out of the EU without any withdrawal agreement growing, with the potential for a huge economic and political crisis. This would affect the rest of the EU, although the UK would suffer most. While most of the withdrawal agreement had been drafted for some time, the fixation on the Irish border problem meant that many of its other provisions were left largely unscrutinised. Some of the ministers from the Leave camp charged with responsibility for the negotiations left when it was clear that May was prepared for a softer Brexit than they wished. When released from cabinet responsibility, they were conspicuously unable to come up with a credible alternative, doing little more than demanding a tougher negotiating stance.

Assuming the UK manages to extract itself from the EU, the Remainers will stress the damage done to the country's standing and the many inconveniences to which UK citizens are subject. Of course, they may well be joined by Leavers lamenting that the project had been betrayed or ineptly handled. If somehow the country – as a result perhaps of a second referendum – decided to reverse its position and stay in, the Leavers would be in full told-you-so mode, as either the drive for an ever-closer union resumed, or the EU became more fractious and dysfunctional because of nationalist objections to continued migration and the restraints of the eurozone. In counterpoint, Remainers might highlight the damage inflicted on Britain's ability to influence events by three chaotic years.

*   *   *

Trumpism and Brexit were never the same. Both were symptomatic of divided countries, but Trump was associated with clear policy preferences that his victory allowed him to carry through. In the end, his victory reflected a stage in the normal political cycle. The referendum mandated a more detached relationship between the UK and the EU, but left unclear how detached and in precisely what areas. The idea behind the referendum was to settle the European issue in British politics once and for all, but all it achieved was to escalate the issue to a new and more vexatious level and stoke arguments and recriminations likely to continue for years to come.

Another obvious difference between Trumpism and Brexit was that, whereas Trump has relished his chance to disengage from a whole range of international treaties and obligations, and has taken pride in his ability to upset allied governments, May needed all the international support she could get to make Brexit happen and then forge new trading relationships. In 2017, she tried to get close to the newly elected Trump, but on successive issues – Jerusalem, Iran, climate change – she has sided with other European leaders. The president's slogan was 'America First'; the prime minister's was 'Global Britain'. Post-Brexit Britain was not going to be strong enough to demand consideration from others. It was going to have to work hard to demonstrate that whatever happened with the EU, it would be a good citizen elsewhere – for example, in the UN and NATO. Yet in one respect Trump and Brexit did seem to be part of the same phenomenon. These two countries had, in their times, been world leaders. But even before Trump's ascendance, the US was tiring of that role and the UK was increasingly unable to marshal the resources required to play it effectively. As the Brexit debate raged, there was a separate but related one about whether Britain really could – or should – be considered a major military power anymore. France and Germany are found together at summits on Ukraine or Syria, while the UK is absent.

Since 1962, the British establishment has been pondering Dean Acheson's jibe that it had lost an empire and failed to find a role. The special relationship with the US was one remedy, and London's determination to be central to almost any international initiative was another. 'Global Britain' carries the implication that the UK is still a country to be reckoned with. But there was always another answer to Acheson: that the country did not need a role. Surrounded by water and protected by its own nuclear deterrent, well away from the world's worst trouble spots, the UK arguably could dispense with leadership positions and making extraordinary exertions to address other people's problems. Trump claimed to be about Making America Great Again, although he seemed to mean that to be in the sense of economic and military strength rather than any concrete achievements. UK foreign policy has tended to depend on a big joint project with the US – the Second World War, the Cold War and its end, globalisation and then the war on terror. If there are to be no more great projects shared with the US, then the UK will have little to latch on to. An alternative might have been some sort of shared leadership role in Europe, but that was also ruled out. Nobody said so explicitly, and all British politicians might deny the inference, but one interpretation of Brexit was that it represented a moment when Britain decided to retire from greatness and lead a quieter life.

Europe's Defence: Revisiting the Impact of Brexit

François Heisbourg

In April 2016, the editors of *Survival* invited me to write an article on the potential impact on European security of a 'Leave' vote on the occasion of the referendum, which was to be held in the United Kingdom on 23 June. The piece was duly published a few days before the vote.[1] With an eye on the schedule of Britain's effective departure from the European Union, currently set for 29 March 2019, the editors came back to me for a revised assessment. The challenge here is not simply to update a forecast, a comparatively straightforward process, but also to reflect on the lessons to be drawn from the departures between what was projected in 2016 and what has occurred since then.

The view from 2016

I made two basic points before the referendum and both remain apposite today. Firstly, defence is not caught in a web of intertwined national and supranational competencies: the UK has had only a limited commitment in the EU's narrowly based and essentially intergovernmental Common Security and Defence Policy, and it avoided giving any European dimension to the Franco-British Lancaster House Treaties in 2010.[2] Thus, there is no European omelette here to unscramble in case of a Brexit.[3]

Secondly, Brexit would unleash a trifecta of political forces – *souverainisme*, federalism and separatism – which, separately or in combination, would

François Heisbourg is Special Adviser to the Fondation pour la Recherche Stratégique and Chairman of the IISS.

Survival | vol. 60 no. 6 | December 2018–January 2019 | pp. 17–26   DOI 10.1080/00396338.2018.1542796

have far-reaching consequences for a post-Brexit Britain's security and defence choices. In mid-2016, the risks flowing from *souverainisme*, as opposed to a revival of federalism or integrationist tendencies, appeared to be paramount. With the election of an integrationist president and National Assembly in France in 2017, the relative strength of these factors has changed. However, the long-term future of the EU remains far from settled. The bottom line holds: 'a British exit from the European Union … would certainly not remove Britain from Europe's troubles'.[4]

Rumsfeldian metrics

In 2002, Donald Rumsfeld, then the US secretary of defense, famously distinguished three orders of knowledge when questioned about US intelligence on the transfer of Iraqi weapons of mass destruction to terrorist groups. There were 'known knowns' and 'known unknowns' – that is, things we know we do not know. He added that there were also 'unknown unknowns' – things we don't know we don't know.[5]

At the time of the Brexit referendum, one of the more important known unknowns was the meaning the British government would give to leaving the EU. This was made clear in Prime Minister Theresa May's 'Plan for Britain' speech on 17 January 2017, which excluded continued membership of both the single market and the customs union.[6] May, by triggering Article 50 of the Treaty of European Union ten weeks later, also made it known that the date of the UK's eventual exit from the EU would be 29 March 2019. Neither of these self-limiting decisions was mandated by the referendum.

Outside the UK, three known unknowns were resolved in a no less surprising manner. Firstly, in September 2016, the EU27 adopted a unified stance that rapidly proved immune to British attempts at slicing and dicing.[7] They feared that Europhobic sentiment would be encouraged if Britain were seen as being able to 'cherry pick'. Thus, forecasts of *souverainisme*, including my own, served as self-denying prophecies. Secondly, in November 2016, the unexpected election of Donald Trump as president of the United States immediately prompted changes in European attitudes toward defence and security policy. Thirdly, and no less surprisingly, in spring 2017 a pro-European president and National Assembly were elected in France.

Unknown unknowns have also had their impact. Contrary to the EU's expectations, Britain's much-admired civil service, with its outsize influence in European affairs, did not play a central role. This was part of the broader failure of the British government to act as a coherent negotiating partner over the course of more than a year after the referendum. Indeed, it remains to be seen whether it will be able to do so at all. The UK general election held in June 2017 was another surprise, all the more unforeseeable since the 2011 Fixed-term Parliaments Act had been enacted to hinder such elections. The election's razor-thin outcome has made the Tory-led government beholden to Northern Ireland's Democratic Unionist Party (DUP), which has strong views on the Irish border – one of the most sensitive and difficult issues of the Brexit negotiation.[8]

Unknown knowns

Rumsfeldian metrics, while perhaps useful in categorising levels of knowledge for managerial purposes, are of little help in understanding the past. Trump's election or the DUP's stranglehold were only knowable *ex post facto*. Yet in forecasts of the impact of a Leave vote, one of the most consequential failures has flowed from a category that is conspicuously absent from Rumsfeld's array: things for which the knowledge was readily available but which remained unknown. These are the unknown knowns.

The most prominent unknown known was the full width, depth and intricacy of the links established between each member state of the EU and the EU as a whole, and with other member states. During the referendum campaign, as part of their narrative of taking back control, the Leavers denounced this web of mutually binding commitments. Conversely, the Remainers insisted on the mutually beneficial nature of these ties, which were often of British inspiration, such as the single market. Yet neither camp appeared to possess a full grasp of the deeper truth of their own campaign propaganda – namely, that the ties binding the EU together are not only numerous but organic. Had anybody outside of narrow and divided niches of expertise appreciated the deep resonances of antibiotics and animal-health regulations, the supervision of nuclear power plants, the Irish border and air transport, to cite but a few issues, they might have at least approached the referendum with greater care. Likewise, May probably would not have so readily excluded both the single market and the customs union in early 2017.

This lack of understanding of the macro-level consequences of micro-level issues also impacts security and defence. One 'small' example: there may be no tariffs in aerospace, but with the UK moving out of the single market and the customs union after the post-2019 transition period, regulatory rules of origin will kick in, gumming up cross-English Channel value chains. By June 2018, the accumulation of such considerations led Airbus – Europe's largest aerospace company with both civil and military products – to state that it could be forced to 'reconsider its footprint in the country, its investments in the UK and its dependency on the UK'.[9]

The lesson for analysts and policymakers is clear: more effort will have to be put into cross-disciplinary, broad-spectrum, fine-grained analysis, in order to produce knowledge and understanding of issues that straddle the borders between strategic, political, economic, societal and regulatory areas of study and decision-making. If this sounds difficult and cumbersome, that is because it is. However, the downstream costs and difficulties of not doing so in a timely manner are plain to see.

Given the changes that have occurred inside and outside of Europe since 2016, and in view of our painfully and belatedly acquired understanding of the general consequences of Brexit, three areas are especially crucial: transatlantic relations, the nuclear question and the Europeanisation of defence.

The transatlantic dimension

One could argue, as I did, that the existence of NATO, of which most EU states are members or close partners, would contribute to the constructive management of post-Brexit defence relations.[10] The election of Trump has cast doubt on this assumption. Although the United States, with the strong support of the Department of Defense, increased rather than reduced its European footprint in 2017, the president's mercantilist (not to say mercenary) approach to Alliance relations has made NATO more difficult to sell to the US public. Trump's behaviour and rhetoric have fuelled suspicions that only Special Counsel Robert Mueller's investigation of Trump's Russia ties, along with John Bolton, the wholly dispensable national security advisor, are constraining Trump's urge to cut a deal with Russian President Vladimir Putin, possibly at Europe's expense.

Finally, and importantly in the post-Brexit context, Trump clearly prefers transactional one-on-one relations at the expense of multilateral frameworks such as NATO. The possibility of Britain becoming an Atlantic version of Australia, which I hinted at in 2016, could become a default option if the US ceases to take NATO's role seriously. In this scenario, the UK would build on its special relationship with the US. The problem with this is that, without a robust NATO, any US–UK partnership would be one, like the US–Australia relationship, in which intelligence would be exchanged and à la carte coalition operations conducted at the United States' behest rather than as part of a multilateral alliance incorporating full-blown defence links, integrated command structures and shared strategic planning.[11] A Britain semi-detached from continental Europe would be a minus for Europe, but a deterioration of the continent's security would also hurt the UK's safety, as history has demonstrated.

The nuclear question

One of the consequences of Brexit has been the dampening of the Scottish quest for independence in the short run. This may seem counterintuitive, since 62% of Scottish voters chose to remain in the EU. However, with more than 60% of Scotland's trade being conducted with the rest of the UK, independence would be an even more painful economic separation for Scotland than Brexit is proving to be for the UK as a whole, even if it were to subsequently join the EU, to which it currently sends less than a quarter of its exports.[12]

As a result, the risk of Britain's having to remove its strategic nuclear forces from Scotland has shrunk in comparison with a few years ago. Their redeployment to England would be a costly and demanding undertaking. At a time of uncertainty in Washington and assertiveness in Moscow, the existence of a British nuclear deterrent is a substantial asset for Europe as a whole, and for Franco-British relations in particular. Paris greatly values burden-sharing and cooperation in the nuclear arena. However, attitudes in Scotland may swing back to independence as a result of either a painful post-Brexit recession or a violent reopening of the Irish question – both possible consequences of a botched Brexit.

The challenge of European defence

The word 'challenge' is rarely associated with the hitherto limited efforts to build up some form of EU defence. It remains unlikely that EU-led or -organised military operations will grow substantially beyond the unimpressive high point of more than a decade ago.[13] Different strategic cultures, most notably a militarily reticent Germany, will continue to hamper building up a European defence outside or inside NATO, notwithstanding the establishment of the Permanent Structured Cooperation (PESCO) framework.[14] The fear of being seen as pushing the Americans towards the exit will also limit European endeavours unless it becomes clear that the Americans are ceasing to invest in NATO. In any case, the UK can remain active in the European defence arena through participation in EU-led or ad hoc coalitions. The European Intervention Initiative (EI2), launched in June 2018 at France's suggestion, will also provide a European, albeit a non-EU, framework in which Britain will be a full partner.

One EU defence venture may break with this evolving pattern of limited European frameworks. The European Defence Fund (EDF), established in 2017, is slated to spend up to €500 million a year from 2021 to 2027 on defence research.[15] More ambitiously, the EDF also aims to provide 'adult money' to support the European-scale acquisition of defence materiel on the basis of criteria such as the number of EU countries involved, the definition of common specifications, and the location in the EU of the corresponding research and production facilities. The sums involved from the EU budget could represent up to €6.5 billion from 2021–27 for direct military purposes via the so-called capabilities window. The European Commission expects to leverage this prospect at a five-to-one ratio, which would net close to €5bn a year. EU member states currently spend €25–30bn a year on defence acquisition, excluding the UK (which spends about €10bn annually) and Denmark, which has opted out of the EU's defence endeavours.[16]

The EDF's budget objectives will probably shrink in 2019–20 in the negotiation of the EU's seven-year budget. Even so, at the end of the day, there will be serious money available. The bad news for the UK is that its companies will only be eligible to bid on the same third-country basis as other non-EU members such as the United States or Canada. This has already led to tension between the UK and the EU Commission regarding future access to the *Galileo* constellation of positioning satellites. Given the strong cross-channel value chains in defence and aerospace, it would be in European and British interests for the EDF to be open more widely to UK participation. EU-associated countries such as Norway, Israel and Switzerland are already participants in the €80bn Horizon 2014–20 framework programme for research. Much goodwill and time has been lost, but it may be worth the effort to re-engage on this topic during the post-withdrawal transition period extending to December 2020 and possibly beyond.

*   *   *

The impact of Brexit on European defence and security is heavily influenced by the broader context of UK–EU relations. The treatment of Britain as an ordinary third country in EU-funded defence programmes owed much to the poor climate affecting the Brexit negotiations overall in 2017. On the UK side, the turmoil surrounding the political management of Brexit has had dire consequences, neutering an exceptionally competent civil service's ability to weigh in and costing precious time. The EU, for its part, took a belts-and-braces attitude towards the risk of being seen as rewarding Brexit Britain. In short, much of what could go wrong has already gone wrong.

The economic consequences of Brexit will directly affect the UK's future defence capabilities and foreign-policy ambitions. Britain will no longer be a member of the EU's single market, from which it will have removed itself by the end of the transition period, currently planned for the end of 2020. In itself, this will not have a crippling impact provided there actually is a transition period (which would not be the case without a ratified withdrawal agreement before the date of exit), and if, at the end of the transition period, a stable trading regime enters into force between the UK and the EU, which is by far the UK's single-largest trading partner.[17] Under such conditions, the UK's economy could presumably sustain defence capabilities similar to those it possesses today, in keeping with its responsibilities as a permanent member of the UN Security Council and as a key player in NATO. This would be made more difficult – but perhaps not critically so – if the UK ceased to enjoy the competitive advantage provided by participation in the EU's network of free-trade agreements with countries such as Canada, Japan, Mexico, South Africa and South Korea.[18]

A no-deal Brexit would have dire economic consequences for the UK, which would not only be bereft of a stable trading regime with the EU but would still have to negotiate a return to the World Trade Organisation (WTO) as a full participant at a time when the WTO was itself entering a period of Trump-induced uncertainty. Britain could nominally meet NATO's 2% of GDP defence-spending target by virtue of a shrinking GDP rather than through adequate military expenditure. More broadly, however, the choice between preserving the UK's National Health Service, a key element of social cohesion, and sustaining the UK's status as a military and diplomatic power would become stark.

In 2016, it was reasonable to expect that governments sharing the same basic defence and security interests would behave rationally and work together to limit the negative consequences of Brexit. Now, in the wake of post-referendum fecklessness on both sides, it would in fact be reckless to assume that good sense will prevail in the coming months or years. Nor can one count in the near future on a reversal of the Brexit referendum's outcome. Withdrawal of the UK from the EU under Article 50 is slated to happen before any vote for reversal could realistically be taken by the British body politic to stop the withdrawal process it has set in motion.[19] There's really no easy way out.

Notes

1   François Heisbourg, 'Brexit and European Security', *Survival*, vol. 58, no. 3, June–July 2016, pp. 13–22.
2   'Treaty Between the United Kingdom and the French Republic for Defence and Security Cooperation', 2 November 2010, http://www.gov.uk/ government/uploads/system/uploads/ attachment_data/file/238153/8174. pdf; and 'Treaty Between the United Kingdom and the French Republic Relating to Joint Radiographic/ Hydrodynamics Facilities', 2 November 2010, http://www.gov.uk/

government/uploads/system/uploads/
attachment_data/file/238226/8289.pdf.

3   Heisbourg, 'Brexit and European
Security'.

4   *Ibid.*

5   US Department of Defense News
Briefing, 12 February 2002, http://
www.archive.defense.gov/transcripts/
transcript.aspx?/transcriptID=2636.

6   'The Government's Negotiating
Objectives for Exiting the EU: PM
Speech', 17 January 2017, https://
www.gov.uk/government/speeches/
the-governments-negotiating-
objectives-for-exiting-the-eu-pm-
speech.

7   Bratislava Declaration and
Roadmap', 16 September 2016,
https://www.consilium.europa.eu/
en/policies/eu-future-reflection/
bratislava-declaration-and-roadmap/.

8   See Jonathan Stevenson, 'Does Brexit
Threaten Peace in Northern Ireland?',
Survival, vol. 59, no. 3, June–July 2017,
pp. 111–28.

9   Aditya Chakrabortty, 'Airbus Has
Delivered a Body Blow to Brexit
Britain. It Won't Be the Last', *Guardian*,
22 June 2018, https://theguardian.
com/commentisfree/2018/jun/22/
airbus-brexit-britain-commonwealth-
plane-wings-north-wales.

10 Of NATO's members, 22 out of 29
(including the UK) belong to the EU.
Of the 28 members of the EU (including the UK), 22 belong to NATO. Two
other members of the EU, Sweden and
Finland, are part of NATO's closest
circle of cooperation partners.

11 See Stephan Frühling, 'Is ANZUS
Really an Alliance? Aligning the US
and Australia', *Survival*, vol. 60, no. 5,
October–November 2018, pp. 199–218.

12 See Scottish Government, 'Export
Statistics Scotland 2016', 18 January
2018, https://gov.scot/Topics/
Statistics/Browse/Economy/Exports/
ESSPublication.

13 The EU's largest military operation has not exceeded 3,700 soldiers
on the ground. All of its 1,000-plus
operations were set up before 2010,
including its naval anti-piracy operation, *Atalanta*, in the Indian Ocean. See
'Complete Operations and Missions',
European Union External Action
Service, http://eeas.europa.eu/csdp/
missions-and-operations/completed/
index_en.htm.

14 This EU endeavour established in
2017 includes all members of the
EU on a voluntary basis. Denmark
has opted out, Malta has not joined
and the UK is obviously on its way
out. PESCO has launched 17 projects
aiming to improve Europe's defence
capabilities, potentially dovetailing
with the European Defence Fund. See
'Permanent Structured Cooperation
(PESCO) Factsheet', 28 June 2018,
https://eeas.europa.eu/headquarters/
headquarters-Homepage/34226/
permanent-structured-cooperation-
pesco-factsheet_en.

15 See 'The European Defence Fund:
Questions and Answers, European
Commission Fact Sheet', 7 June 2017,
http://europa.eu/rapid/press-release_
MEMO-17-1476_en.htm; 'Budget:
20 milliards d'euros pour l'Union
Européenne de la Défense', *La Tribune*,
29 April 2018, https://www.latribune.
fr/economie/union-europeenne/
budget-20-milliards-d-euros-
pour-l-union-europeenne-de-la-
defense-777038.html; and 'UK and

US Companies Shut Out of 13 Billion Euro European Defence Fund', *Defense Post*, 12 June 2018, https://thedefensepost.com/2018/06/12/european-defence-fund-shut-out-uk-us/.

16 My ballpark figure was derived from European Defence Agency data published on 7 September 2018 (which estimated €36.2bn of investment spending by the EU in 2017, including the UK and excluding Denmark, out of total defence spending of €214bn) and NATO estimates for the UK in pounds sterling (UK defence equipment spending of 22.03% of total 2017 defence expenditures estimated at £43bn, which comes to roughly €10bn).

17 In 2017, trade with the EU represented 44.5% of UK exports and 53.1% of its imports. The actual figure for imports may be somewhat lower due to the trans-shipment of non-EU imports via EU ports, notably Rotterdam. House of Commons Library, 'Statistics on UK–EU Trade', Briefing Paper, 31 July 2018, https://researchbriefings.files/documents/CBP-7851.pdf. The UK's largest non-EU trading partner is currently the United States, with some 11% of UK trade.

18 The EU does not have free-trade agreements in force with the United States or China, the UK's two largest non-European trading partners.

19 The EU can extend the Article 50 transition period beyond its normal two years by a unanimous decision of the member states. But an extension of more than a few weeks after 29 March 2019 would be unlikely since the EU will be holding its parliamentary elections in May 2019. In the United Kingdom, the time frame necessary for a referendum conducted as a result of an act of parliament would normally be more than six months.

Brexit and Security

Nigel Inkster

As the deadline for negotiating the United Kingdom's departure from the European Union draws near, it remains unclear whether a deal can be done, if so what kind of deal, and whether that deal will prove acceptable to the parliaments of the UK and Europe. The situation has been enormously complicated by divisions within the UK's ruling Conservative Party about the kind of relationship – or lack thereof – the UK should have with the EU post-Brexit. As a result, Prime Minister Theresa May is negotiating with Brussels while fighting a political counter-insurgency campaign at home.

Infecting the negotiation is the apparent irreconcilability of the UK's desire to engage in what EU leaders have called 'cherry-picking' – seeking continuing access to some aspects of EU membership while no longer recognising the free movement of goods, services, capital and labour (the Four Freedoms) – and the European Commission's view that the UK cannot expect, as leading Brexiteer Boris Johnson put it, to have its cake and eat it. To date, the commission has maintained that 'Brexit must have consequences' for fear that a more accommodating approach towards the UK might encourage other EU member states to demand a more à la carte approach to EU regulation. Efforts by the UK government to bypass the commission and appeal directly to EU leaders to adopt a less bureaucratic and more strategic approach to Brexit have not borne fruit, as evidenced by the adverse reaction of the September 2018 Salzburg summit to the May

Nigel Inkster is a senior adviser to the IISS. He previously served for 31 years in the British Secret Intelligence Service, retiring at the end of 2006 as Assistant Chief and Director of Operations and Intelligence.

Survival | vol. 60 no. 6 | December 2018–January 2019 | pp. 27–34   DOI 10.1080/00396338.2018.1542797

government's 'Chequers' plan.[1] The summit showed that EU leaders could not be peeled off from the formal negotiating process.

Unsurprisingly, the Brexit negotiation is focused on addressing the enormous complexities of unravelling a dense network of economic, commercial and regulatory arrangements developed over many years. Arrangements bearing on security were not expected to be a significant agenda item, a reflection of the fact that under Article 4(2) of the Lisbon Treaty, national security is designated a purely national competency. The prevailing assumption had always been that the UK – a major security, intelligence and military power – would see it as in its own interests to ensure the closest possible collaboration with the EU post-Brexit, and that something closely resembling business as usual would ensue. But, as with virtually everything else to do with Brexit, the devil has been in the details, and efforts to address those details have fallen victim to the general acrimony that has characterised the wider Brexit negotiation.

British and European equities

The problems began in March 2017 with May's letter to the European Council triggering Article 50, the formal UK declaration of its intent to exit the EU. May said: 'In security terms, a failure to reach agreement would mean our cooperation in the fight against crime and terrorism would be weakened.' The response of Guy Verhofstadt, the European Parliament's Brexit coordinator, was that this represented an unacceptable effort by the UK to use its military and intelligence capabilities as a bargaining chip in the Brexit negotiations.[2] The UK subsequently made clear its intention to maintain security cooperation unconditionally, but the issue resurfaced at the February 2018 Munich Security Conference when EU President Jean-Claude Juncker warned that in the Brexit talks security should not be 'conflated with other questions relating to Brexit'.[3] Nevertheless, the issue of the border between Northern Ireland and the Republic of Ireland, ostensibly a disagreement about customs arrangements, has substantial security implications because of the role EU membership played in making possible the Good Friday Agreement bringing 'the Troubles' to an end.[4] The fact that both the Republic of Ireland and Northern Ireland were part of the EU made the long-standing Provisional Irish Republican Army demand for a united Ireland something on which they could compromise. The Irish border has now become the single-biggest stumbling block in negotiating post-Brexit trading arrangements with the EU.

For Western European states, the threat of Islamist terrorism remains the most immediate security concern. Following the demise of the Islamic State (ISIS)'s caliphate in Syria and Iraq in 2017, levels of terrorist activity have declined compared with the period between 2014 and 2017. But the threats from foreign fighters returning from Syria, and from a generation of home-grown terrorists and their ideological mentors now coming to the end of their prison sentences, remain significant. Turmoil in the Levant and North Africa will continue to negatively affect European security due to both the threat of uncontrolled migration and the propensity of Islamist groups like ISIS to leverage regional unrest for their own ends. The recent disman-tling in the Netherlands of a seven-person terrorist cell planning to launch attacks with explosive devices and automatic weapons is a reminder that these threats have not gone away.[5] They are still arising and the numbers of Islamist terrorist suspects in major EU states remain unmanageably large.

Brexit's practical impact

The need for greater European counter-terrorism coordination has led to the establishment of the Counter Terrorism Group (CTG), which consists of 30 European intelligence and security services that have developed an effective framework for multilateral counter-terrorism cooperation separate from the EU. The CTG maintains a shared database of terrorist suspects and a joint investigative platform based in the Netherlands. The UK intelligence com-munity is a major contributor to these shared arrangements. It is one of the few intelligence communities in the world with the capability to undertake counter-terrorism operations globally, including in denied areas, rather than having to wait until terrorists show up in its immediate territory, and is therefore able to provide valuable proactive and sometimes pre-emptive threat intelligence that would otherwise be unavailable. Most European intelligence agencies have a much more limited capability to operate in this way, or none at all.

The UK also contributes significant intelligence to the EU both at a strategic level, to the EU Intelligence and Situation Centre (EU INTCEN) that provides assessed intelligence drawn from national inputs to the European External Action Service (the EU's foreign- and defence-policy arm); and at the operational level, to the European police agency Europol. In fact, until recently, both organisations were headed by UK nationals. Following Brexit, the UK's participation in both entities will be limited at the EU's insistence. Equally if not more importantly, the UK will on present showing be denied continued participation in the Schengen Information System II (SIS II) and EU Passenger Name Record (PNR) programme. The former system facilitates the identification and monitoring of terrorism suspects travelling to the Schengen area and the UK. The latter, the establishment of which owed much to the UK's urging, enables participating states to identify terrorist and other criminal suspects in advance of travel. The PNR has shown its value in, for instance, identifying terrorist suspects travelling under aliases by tracing those aliases to telephone numbers associated with real identities that were used to book flights.

The UK has been a major contributor to and beneficiary of these data-bases. Losing access to them will have adverse implications for both UK and EU security, as the following hypothetical example illustrates. Imagine that UK agencies identify and begin investigating an ISIS terrorist suspect in Syria. Unbeknownst to the UK agencies, this suspect has been ordered to travel to Europe, including the UK, to meet ISIS sleeper cells and give them instructions to undertake terrorist attacks. He travels overland from Turkey to Bulgaria, then takes a flight to Spain, then Germany, France and the UK. If the suspect's details are entered in SIS II, the UK and Bulgarian services are in a position to register that he is travelling and can take action – either by arresting him in Bulgaria, or by monitoring his onward travel in conjunction with the other EU countries at risk, with the prospect in either case that the other ISIS sleeper cells can be identified and dismantled. If the UK is not part of SIS II, neither the UK nor Bulgaria will be alerted to his travel, and other EU states will similarly be in the dark.

In law enforcement, the UK looks to be a net loser if a comprehensive post-Brexit security package cannot be agreed. A particular concern is the European Arrest Warrant (EAW), which enables one EU member state to extradite suspects to another without lengthy legal or procedural preliminaries.[6] The UK has been a net contributor to this system insofar as eight suspects from other EU states are arrested in the UK for every one UK national arrested elsewhere in the EU. Other important databases to which the UK may be denied access are the European Criminal Records Information System (ECRIS) and the European Multidisciplinary Platform Against Criminal Threats (EMPACT), which collects information on serious organised crime and trafficking. Even under existing systems, it can take six days to determine whether EU nationals visiting the UK have criminal convictions in their home countries. Post-Brexit, the process could take up to ten times longer. Illustrating the EAW's value to the UK is the fact that the perpetrators of the Novichok nerve-agent attack on former Russian Main Intelligence Directorate (GRU) officer Sergei Skripal and his daughter are subject to an EAW, and currently risk being detained and extradited to the UK should they visit any other EU country.[7]

The other specific security issue Brexit is likely to affect is continued UK membership of the *Galileo* project, the EU's global satellite-navigation system and alternative to the Global Positioning System (GPS). In June 2018, the European Commission informed the UK that, following a vote by all 27 member states, it would not allow UK companies to bid for the next round of contracts for the project. UK companies had played a central role in the project's initial development, to which the UK government has contributed over US$1 billion. The commission's decision would not deny the UK military access to the system, including the Galileo Public Regulated Service, the encrypted signal designed to be used during national emergencies and military operations. But it would deny the UK proprietary knowledge of the relevant codes. The decision sparked anger on the part of London, which threatened not only to set up its own separate project, but also to revisit the terms of the financial commitments already agreed with the commission as part of the overall Brexit negotiations.[8]

Political–military consequences

One of the immediate results of Brexit has been the agreement by the UK to drop its long-standing objections to EU ambitions to develop military capabilities separate from NATO. Such plans reflect the EU's dawning recognition that soft power alone is insufficient and requires a hard-power complement to be effective, and that a hedge is needed in the face of US President Donald Trump's ambivalence towards NATO. But they fall far short of creating a European army. Instead, the EU has established a number of mechanisms to facilitate military research and development. These include the Permanent Structured Cooperation (PESCO) on defence, a Coordinated Annual Review on Defence (CARD) and a European Defence Fund (EDF). Without the UK's full-spectrum military and defence-industrial capabilities – which currently constitute 20% and 40% of the EU total, respectively – it seems likely that these initiatives will be slow to take off.[9] At the same time, the UK has been a significant beneficiary of EU research-and-development funding since 2007 and will feel the lack of it.

The inexorable logic of Brexit dictates that the EU and the UK will eventually go their separate ways militarily. In the meantime, the persistence of an acutely challenging and uncertain international environment suggests that they will engage in continuing but declining collaboration until EU capabilities are fully up and running. When that will be is impossible to determine.

*   *   *

Irrespective of what kind of Brexit comes into being, both the UK and the EU look set to be worse off in terms of overall security. How much worse off will depend on the extent of each party's flexibility and creativity in the final phases of the negotiation. No matter how fully these traits are mustered, however, negotiating efforts may founder on extreme Brexiteer parliamentarians' refusal to back any deal that does not involve a clean break with Europe.

At the tactical level of countering terrorism and organised crime, the adverse implications of diminished UK involvement with Europe's security institutions will be real but ultimately manageable. The main consequence will be some outcomes that are unnecessarily sub-optimal.

The strategic implications of a diminished involvement may take longer to become apparent, but may turn out to be more significant. At a time when major powers such as Russia and China are challenging the established global order, and the readiness of the United States to sustain that order is coming increasingly into question, Europe will need to address the resulting challenges through a combination of soft- and hard-power instruments. While the UK can be expected under most circumstances to sustain intelligence and security cooperation with European partners, the institutional expertise and experience of the UK will no longer play as strong a role in shaping EU policy in these areas as they did when the UK was a member state. In the worst case, in which the failure to reach a mutually satisfactory Brexit agreement leads to rancour and ill feeling between the UK and the EU, it is not difficult to imagine that security and intelligence cooperation would be adversely affected no matter how hard both parties tried to avoid it. Whichever way one looks at it, Brexit is likely to make the challenge of resisting undesirable change to the current world order that much harder.

Notes

1 Stephen Castle, 'Brexit Talks at "Impasse," Theresa May Says, After a Rancorous Summit', *New York Times*, 21 September 2018, https://www.nytimes.com/2018/09/21/world/europe/eu-theresa-may-brexit-salzburg.htm.

2 Anushka Asthana et al., 'Don't Blackmail Us Over Security, EU Warns May', *Guardian*, 30 March 2017, https://www.theguardian.com/politics/2017/mar/29/brexit-eu-condemns-mays-blackmail-over-security-cooperation.

3 Rob Merrick, 'Brexit: Security Cannot Be Bargained for a Trade Deal, Jean-Claude Juncker Warns Theresa May', *Independent*, 17 February 2018, https://222.independent.co.uk/news/uk/politics/theresa-may-brexit-munich-security-conference-defence-spending-trade-deal-bargaining-chip-jeanclaude-a8215621.html.

4 See Jonathan Stevenson, 'Does Brexit Threaten Peace in Northern Ireland?', *Survival*, vol. 59, no. 3, June–July 2017, pp. 111–28.

5 Mike Corder, 'Dutch Police Arrest Seven Men Suspected of Plotting Terror Attack', Associated Press, 27 September 2018, https://www.apnews.com/d263b4ecb7dc487c902a9875431d0835.

6 In a normal extradition, the judiciary of the state where the application is made must first make an affirmative finding that the offence is recognised as such in that state and that the evidence presented is convincing. An EAW is simply presumed to meet

these criteria.

7 'No-deal Brexit "Could Make Policing Harder"', BBC News, 11 September 2018, https://www.bbc.co.uk/news/uk-45561527.

8 Daniel Boffey, 'Security Row Over EU Galileo Satellite Project as Britain Is Shut Out', *Guardian*, 13 June 2018, https://www.theguardian.com/technology/2018/jun/13/eu-member-states-block-uks-access-to-galileo-satellite-programme-after-brexit.

9 Peter Round, Bastian Giegerich and Christian Moelling, 'European Strategic Autonomy and Brexit', IISS Military Balance Blog, June 2018, https://www.iiss.org/-/media/images/comment/military-balance-blog/2018/june/european-strategic-autonomy-and-brexit-iiss-dgap.ashx.

Four Things We Should Learn from Brexit

Erik Jones

The British referendum on membership in the European Union was a teach-able moment for anyone interested in democratic politics or European integration. Over the course of the past three years, the British have revealed the limitations of direct democracy, the importance of political rhetoric, the difference between integration and disintegration, and the meaning of 'rela-tionship' in the concept of international relations. None of these lessons is completely new or unexpected, yet each of them is nevertheless important. The British people are paying a high price to serve as a case study; the rest of the world would be wise to pay attention.

Power to the people

Of all the lessons to be drawn from the United Kingdom's Brexit experience, what the process has revealed about the limitations of direct democracy is probably the most important.[1] Fifty-two percent of the British population voted to leave the EU, while 48% voted to remain. This outcome did have the benefit of showing what the majority wanted to do. The vote also facili-tated an open conversation about Europe, something that David Cameron had promised in his Bloomberg speech in 2013, and that he stressed could not be avoided. By calling a referendum, he ensured that this conversation

Erik Jones is Albert O. Hirschman visitor at the Institut für die Wissenschaften vom Menschen (IWM) in Vienna; Professor of European Studies and Director of European and Eurasian Studies at the Paul H. Nitze School of Advanced International Studies (SAIS), Johns Hopkins University; Senior Research Associate at the Istituto per gli Studi di Politica Internazionale in Milan; and a contributing editor to *Survival*.

Survival | vol. 60 no. 6 | December 2018–January 2019 | pp. 35–44   DOI 10.1080/00396338.2018.1542799

took place. To be sure, the quality of debate was often very low. The Leave campaign touted erroneous facts about how much Europe costs and how much Britons could save; the Remain campaign presented exaggerated estimates of the short-term consequences of a decision to exit. But none of these errors went unchallenged. The people knew there were questions about the veracity of what both campaigns were saying, just as they knew the campaigners had a variety of motives for the positions they took. The important point is that the referendum allowed this debate to take place.

The limitations of the referendum are more obvious. At the same time, they are more complicated – not because the individual defects are difficult to identify, but because of how they interact with one another. To begin with, while the status quo defined the Remain option, there was no way for voters to know what the Leave option meant. Another limitation of the vote is that it has bound a population that inevitably changes: the 52% majority that voted to leave in June 2016 may no longer exist today. A third limitation is that the information available to British voters was incomplete due to a lack of experience. No country had ever left an organisation like the EU. By implication, no one could really anticipate what the true consequences of doing so would be. Add all this together and the underlying problem becomes clear. The British people have made a lasting decision to do something without knowing what that something is, and without building in any mechanism to modify that decision in light of new information about what is actually possible and how much it will cost them.

Although the British people needed to have a wide-ranging public debate about EU membership, an in-or-out referendum was a crude and costly way to achieve that objective. Moreover, the British Parliament is having a hard time overcoming the limitations of direct democracy as a decision-making process. The government can define more precisely what leaving the EU entails – moving from vague assertions that 'Brexit means Brexit' to more precise agreements on the terms of withdrawal, the structure of any transition period and the aspirations for a future relationship – but that is no guarantee that a majority of the British people will line up behind the arrangements. The government's plans may not even receive majority support in Parliament. If they don't, the resulting change will not be one that anyone actually chose; rather, it will be the default option. In that case, it would be hard to see any connection between the majority who voted to leave the EU and the outcome of that decision.

Holding another referendum on membership, or to approve whatever the government negotiates as the new UK–EU relationship, would only compound the problem. The original supporters of the Leave campaign would complain about the legitimacy of any outcome that reversed the original decision either directly, by a vote to remain in the EU, or indirectly, by rejecting the government's plans for leaving. By the same token, another majority in favour of leaving, or a new majority in support of the government's proposals, would still suffer from the limitations of direct democracy – the vote might be somewhat more precise in terms of the change on offer, but would provide no guarantees about the kind of relationship the British government could negotiate with the rest of Europe. It would also be binding on a population that continues to evolve, and lack any clear means of changing tack in light of new information about the implications of what everyone now knows to be an unprecedented experiment.

Representation and rhetoric

If direct democracy is such a bad procedure for making decisions on important issues like British membership in the EU, it is worth asking what the alternatives were, and why the Cameron government did not select them. The answer is obvious.[2] Cameron's alternative was to stake out a clear vision of Britain's relationship with Europe, and to campaign on that platform in the 2015 general election. Cameron did not choose that option because he knew that much of his party did not share his vision, and he worried that many Conservative supporters would defect to the UK Independence Party (UKIP) if he staked out a clear position. In other words, Cameron chose not to use Parliament to make important decisions about Britain's relationship with the EU because he worried about losing control over the decision-making process. Moreover, Cameron is hardly alone in having made that calculation. Jeremy Corbyn did much the same when Theresa May called for early elections in order to get a stronger mandate for her government to deliver Britain's exit from the EU. Corbyn refused to allow May to frame the campaign as a repeat of the referendum, and promised to use the decision-making machinery of Westminster to do something else instead. The Europe issue would have divided his Labour Party in 2017 almost as much as it would have divided Cameron's Conservatives in 2015. Corbyn hid behind the mandate of direct democracy in order to change the subject.

The willingness of the British people to talk about other matters is the second important lesson of the Brexit experience. This willingness reveals the power of political rhetoric.[3] Cameron breathed life into the debate about Europe; Corbyn switched to another topic. This switch revealed that there are any number of critical issues that can grab the attention of the public. The British people face a host of important problems, as do the people of other countries. The role of political leadership is to focus popular attention. Politicians do so by telling stories or building arguments to highlight where the public should look, and how they should interpret what they see.[4] This presents politicians with the challenge of diverting the public's gaze once it has an issue in focus. The only way to address that challenge is not to deny the importance of what the public sees, but rather to redirect attention to something even more important. Cameron used Europe to redirect the public away from the divisions within his Conservative Party. Corbyn used income inequality to redirect the public away from Europe.

This experience raises the question of whether Britain's relationship with Europe should ever have been a priority. The founders of European integration embarked on their project in order to tackle important issues that national governments could not manage as easily or effectively. In this sense, the story of integration can be told as the progressive expansion of Europe's policymaking machinery to include a larger number of governments and a wider array of problems. Somewhere along the way, however, the notion of Europe took on a life of its own. Politicians began to talk about integration as the objective and not the instrument. They began to focus public attention on the importance of Europe as a project. And, perhaps as a consequence, they drew attention away from other problems.

Political rhetoric matters not only because it highlights important issues, but also because it suggests priorities. The problem here is not that politicians exaggerated the significance of Europe; it is that each time they appealed to the people about Europe they implied that issues left unaddressed were less significant. When Cameron called his referendum, many of his constituents were left wondering who was focusing on matters closer to home. For people facing immediate concerns about income, housing or employment, appeals to focus on Europe were not just a distraction, they were an insult. By removing Europe from the national conversation, these voices have a better chance of being heard. Put another way, the alternative to EU membership is more domestic political attention. A vote to leave is a vote to put an end to a pointless conversation so that policymakers can focus on 'real' priorities. Politicians elsewhere in Europe should pay close attention to how their rhetoric frames political choices in this respect.

Integration and disintegration

Unfortunately, if the British who voted to leave the EU wanted more political attention, the experience of withdrawal suggests that they will not get it. Instead, the government will have to devote almost all of its resources to extricating Britain from Europe. This is the third lesson of Britain's recent experience: that disintegration is not only more complicated than integration, but also occurs at an accelerated pace.[5] This is because of the underlying nature of the process.

As noted, one way to view European integration is as a process for incrementally improving public policymaking by elaborating institutions and procedures for coordinating policies across national governments. 'Integration' is not the goal of this process, but rather a description of it. Instead, the goal is to improve policymaking. To achieve that goal, successive national governments in Europe chose how to work together in a series of discrete steps. The pace of those choices was very much a function of the challenges governments faced in adapting to the new relationship. Governments took the time to learn by doing; they often negotiated transition periods; and they occasionally requested or simply exercised opt-outs from those areas where they could not move forward as quickly as the rest. Of course, there were times when the process moved faster than governments anticipated, or the adjustment costs were higher than politicians expected. Integration was always a process of stops and starts. Sometimes that process imposed costs above and beyond what a society could manage without great hardship. Recent developments in Greece are a powerful (but not the only) illustration of this. Nevertheless, Europe's heads of state and government generally sought to calibrate the pace and scope of integration so that the benefits in terms of better policymaking outweighed the costs of participation.

The process of disintegration is different insofar as the goal is to 'leave'. This goal can be described in other ways – perhaps the most compelling characterisation would be the reassertion of domestic control over the public-policy process. But it would be difficult to describe this goal in terms of the step-by-step improvement in public policy through the elaboration of new instruments. For disintegration, leave and control are the objectives. These goals imply a much faster pace than does 'incremental improvement'.

It has become clear that many advocates of leaving the EU would accept less effective policymaking as a fair price for greater policy autonomy. As a result, it is unrealistic to expect that disintegration will restore the UK – or any other EU member – to the same state in which it found itself before joining the integration process. All the slow and painful adjustments that were required to participate in the EU cannot be undone at once. Moreover, the longer a country has participated in the European project, the more substantially those adjustments will have accumulated.

Conceiving of EU membership as a tangled mass of prior adjustments that would need to be unwound was always easily done in principle. What recent British experience reveals is the magnitude and the complexity of that mass. It is not enough to think about Brexit as a question of restoring control over discrete policy areas; all too often, those policy areas are interconnected in ways that do not suggest an obvious order of operations specifying what to do first, second or third. Moreover, doing everything at once is not an option. The state simply does not have that capacity. Worse, the state is not a unitary entity. National government and institutions play a leading role, but other levels of government are also implicated. Here too, the issues are interconnected, and the order of operations is not obvious. We might have expected this given what we know about the subtlety and complexity of 'Europeanisation'. Seeing how disintegration plays out in practice is nevertheless an instructive lesson in what other member states should expect if they choose to exit.

Beyond sovereignty

The fourth lesson that Britain is teaching (or re-teaching) the rest of Europe is that neither side actually controls the content of its relationships. Interdependence is not something that developed gradually in international relations; interdependence defines what an international relationship is. This seems obvious on one level. Britain has to agree with what Europe proposes, but Europe also has to agree with Britain. Even the default option is a matter of agreement. Somehow the aeroplanes have to keep flying and the goods have to keep moving; these things do not happen on their own. 'The market' is, first and foremost, a regulatory construct, even when market participants move from one country to the next.[6]

What Britain's Brexit experience reveals, however, is just how deeply this problem of interdependence extends across the borders of putatively sovereign entities. That is why the Northern Irish situation is so important. The fate of Northern Ireland does not rest solely in the hands of the British, the Northern Irish or the Irish who live in the southern part of the island. Somehow everyone is implicated at once. Moreover, Northern Ireland is only one, extreme example of this problem. Gibraltar is another example; so is Scotland. Less extreme, yet no less intractable, problems centre on distributed manufacturing, services provision and the goods trade. That is why international trade negotiations have become so complicated – again, not just for Britain, and not just in the context of Britain's exit from the EU. Economics does not merely cross borders, it permeates them and, in so doing, affects almost everything, from what we eat and wear, to what we watch, listen and read, not to mention how much it costs to do so – particularly in a digital age.

Here it is useful to go back to the Brexit debates, and particularly to the cost estimates released by the Remain camp. The short-term impact of the vote to leave was exaggerated at least in part because the forecasters did not anticipate the heroic efforts of the Bank of England to prevent the costs from reaching the predicted levels. They also did not expect the success of the European Central Bank's quantitative-easing programme in restarting the European economy, or the boom in American economic performance that somehow continued to gain momentum after Donald Trump was elected. In other words, policy responses and business cycles softened the immediate blow to the British economy. The reluctance of businesses to appreciate the full significance of Britain's departure from Europe also proved important. Many large multinational firms have hedged their bets and waited until the last minute to see if they can somehow minimise the costs of adjustment or, at a minimum, smooth the transition from one situation to the next.

But the fact that the immediate shock was not as dramatic as some feared does not mean the final cost will be similarly limited. On the contrary, economic activity will leak out of the British economy in a steady trickle of missed opportunities as supply chains adapt to the change in relative cost structures and as investors look to locate their assets where the returns from interdependence are more resilient. From a global perspective, the consequences will be limited; the UK is, after all, only one country – no matter how important that country is to those who live in it. But Brexit's consequences will also be cumulative insofar as other national economies will suffer from Britain's absence from Europe, and from the pattern of interdependence that the EU fosters. They will suffer even more if Brexit becomes the first of many departures from the European Union. So will the United Kingdom.

This fourth lesson is a harsh realisation for everyone, not just the British. The modern international system was built on two notions of sovereignty, one that points to the existence of national boundaries and another that respects the monopoly of decision-making authority within them. Both notions were always fictitious to a greater or lesser extent. What Britain's recent experience reveals is just how difficult and costly it is to insist on that fiction. The demonstration will not stop some politicians – one thinks of Donald Trump, Matteo Salvini, Viktor Orbán and Jaroslaw Kaczyński – from pretending.[7] But Britain's experience should shed some light on the consequences of such pretensions.

Notes

[1] This point about direct democracy was immediately apparent. See Erik Jones, 'Brexit's Lessons for European Democracy', *Survival*, vol. 58, no. 3, June–July 2016, pp. 41–9, and Erik Jones, 'The Meaning of Britain's Departure', *Survival*, vol. 58, no. 4, August–September 2016, pp. 211–24.

[2] See Matthias Matthijs, 'David Cameron's Dangerous Game: The Folly of Flirting with an EU Exit', *Foreign Affairs*, vol. 92, no. 5, September–October 2013, pp. 10–16.

[3] Another way to make the same argument would be to focus on the weakness and divisiveness of modern party politics. See, for example, Erik Jones, 'From the End of History to the Retreat of Liberalism', *Survival*, vol. 59, no. 6, December 2017–January 2018, pp. 165–74, and Erik Jones, 'Democracies Don't Die, They Are Killed', *Survival*, vol. 60, no. 2, April–May 2018, pp. 201–10.

[4] For the long view on this argument, see Matthias Matthijs, *Ideas and Economic Crises in Britain from Attlee to Blair* (London: Routledge, 2012).

[5] The difference between integration and disintegration was clear from the start. See Erik Jones, 'European Departures: British Process, Greek Event', *Survival*, vol. 57, no. 3, June–July 2015, pp. 79–85; and Erik Jones, 'Confronting Europe's Single Market', *Survival*, vol. 58, no. 1, February–March 2016, pp. 59–67.

[6] Matthias Matthijs, 'Europe After Brexit: A Less Perfect Union', *Foreign Affairs*, vol. 96, no. 1, January–February 2017, pp. 85–95.

[7] For the Italian case, see Erik Jones, 'Italy, Its Populists and the EU', *Survival*, vol. 60, no. 4, August–September 2018, pp. 113–22.

Hiding in Plain Sight: Political Effects of Cyber Operations

Travis Sharp

The ongoing drama caused by Russian-sponsored hacking during the 2016 US presidential election shows that cyber operations can produce profound political effects without physically breaking anything. Russia's operation employed rudimentary techniques that inflicted little permanent damage on US information systems. Yet by precipitating a crisis of legitimacy in which many Americans have questioned whether President Donald Trump won the election fairly, the Russian cyber operation weakened the United States' ability to act decisively on the world stage.[1]

This is not the first time a cyber operation has destabilised a country's internal politics.[2] The 2009 Stuxnet operation against Iran, reportedly conducted by the United States and Israel to sabotage Iran's uranium-enrichment programme, worsened an escalating feud between Supreme Leader Ayatollah Sayyid Ali Khamenei and former president Mahmoud Ahmadinejad, a political dispute that encouraged the supreme leader to change policy and restart nuclear negotiations with the West.[3] The 2014 North Korean cyber operation against Sony Pictures, launched to protest a film called *The Interview* featuring a satirical plot about assassinating North Korean leader Kim Jong-un, sparked heated disagreement among US policymakers about how much sensitive intelligence they should disclose

Travis Sharp is a research fellow at the Center for Strategic and Budgetary Assessments, a pre-doctoral fellow at George Washington University's Institute for Security and Conflict Studies, and a PhD candidate at Princeton University's Woodrow Wilson School of Public and International Affairs.

Survival | vol. 60 no. 6 | December 2018–January 2019 | pp. 45–53   DOI 10.1080/00396338.2018.1542800

to prove North Korea's culpability, and whether the attack represented an act of terrorism that demanded a forceful response by the US government.[4]

Given this pattern, one would expect cyber strategists to have focused on explaining why cyber operations succeed politically. Alas, that is not the case. Experts have instead expended enormous energy detailing why cyber operations fail technically, and gone to great lengths outlining cyber operations' limited capacity to wreak physical destruction or impose lasting harm.[5] Erik Gartzke, for example, has argued that issuing a cyber threat is 'like bringing a knife to a gun fight'.[6] If a country is serious in its intention to inflict harm, according to this logic, it will threaten to use *real* military power, such as ground forces or airstrikes. Yet expert scepticism does not match the real-world success of recent cyber operations. This mismatch exists because experts have conceptualised the strategic effects of cyber operations too narrowly, focusing disproportionately on the damage (or lack thereof) inflicted on an adversary's information-technology systems, data, connectivity and human capital.[7] I call this narrow conception 'techno-damage', a term denoting immediate technical consequences, not longer-term financial, operational or organisational results.[8] By emphasising techno-damage, experts have neglected the broader political consequences of cyber operations, even though techno-damage causes political effects. The two are analytically inseparable and should be studied together.

To be fair, strategists have had good reason to focus narrowly on techno-damage – they have sought to temper the alarmist scenarios floated by policymakers, such as a 'cyber-Pearl Harbor'.[9] They appear to have partially achieved their goal. While leaders still exaggerate cyber threats from time to time, the discourse has become more restrained over the past five years. Having contained one problem, strategists now must confront another: they must ask themselves why cyber operations have produced major political effects despite inflicting minimal techno-damage.

Money, leadership and secrecy

The answer lies in identifying those aspects of cyber operations which are uniquely suited to producing political effects in modern societies. Cyber operations may not impose much physical destruction, but they can squeeze at least three political pressure points: money, leadership and secrecy. These pressure points exist in governmental and non-governmental organisations, meaning both countries and companies will react to them.

Money

Few things generate political conflict faster than money lost or squandered. Cyber operations impose costs on their targets, inflicting cash losses that can foment political turmoil.[10] These costs encompass the direct monetary impact of any techno-damage plus any indirect effects on the target's economy, budget or finances. Even if the direct costs of techno-damage are small, the indirect costs can be quite large. The US government has spent $16.7 million (and counting) on the special counsel's investigation into the Russian government's 2016 election interference, an amount eight times larger than the $2m spent by Iran to repair damaged centrifuges following Stuxnet.[11] The interconnectedness of modern information technology enables a cyber operation to reach beyond the targeted system, including into the victim's economy. The private sector controls 85% of the World Wide Web's critical infrastructure, offering a vulnerable target for cost imposition.[12] A victim might have to take systems offline for repairs and stop other activities, including military operations. Resolving the vulnerability might entail a large repair bill if the technology or human capital is scarce. The target might suffer reputational costs too, if trade partners or consumers lose confidence. North Korea's 2014 operation against Sony Pictures illustrates the point. The company's stock price declined 11% during the attack's peak, nearly three times more than the S&P 500 Index did during the same period. The company's market share increased overall during 2014, so the losses were not part of any overall decline in its relative performance. After tallying the direct losses, investigation and remediation costs, and legal expenses, North Korea inflicted about $80m-worth of damage on Sony Pictures.[13] In comparison, the company's film profits during that quarter totalled only $51m.

Leadership

Political conflict will surely arise when powerful leaders become ensnared in public controversy. Cyber operations target leaders in remarkably personal ways by disclosing sensitive information.[14] Leaders of democracies may be especially vulnerable since embarrassing disclosures cause media and political frenzies that they cannot suppress. A case in point is Russia's 2016 release of hacked emails from the Democratic National Committee, a disclosure that raised questions about the integrity of the Democratic Party's presidential-nominating process.[15] Responsibility for managing information technology is diffused throughout most organisations and governments. Powerful leaders from the intelligence community, military and private sector will blame each other and jockey for position when things go wrong. In the United States, seven different Senate committees claim jurisdiction over cyber security, some of which undoubtedly include current or future presidential aspirants.[16] By destabilising these far-flung leadership circles, cyber operations can scramble governing coalitions, causing them to adopt new policies. These dynamics played out after Stuxnet, when Supreme Leader Khamenei, president Ahmadinejad and intelligence minister Heider Moslehi all manoeuvred to protect themselves from the political fallout associated with Stuxnet having exposed Iran's critical vulnerabilities.[17]

Secrecy

Secrecy intensifies political conflict by stoking uncertainty and heightening the risk that sensitive information will leak. Cyber operations entail layers of secrecy and complexity that prevent most policymakers from understanding them fully.[18] This lack of clarity increases the likelihood of vehement disagreements about how best to respond during emergencies. Some leaders may exhibit overconfidence. As scholar Robert Jervis has noted, 'in most organizations, uncertainties tend to get played down if not filtered out as things move up the hierarchy. In a crisis, the people at the top will feel unwarranted certainty about what the physical if not the political effects of cyber instruments would be.'[19] Other leaders may suffer crippling uncertainty. Former Estonian president Toomas Hendrik Ilves recalls that the 2007 operation against Estonia, perpetrated by attackers probably tied to Moscow in retaliation for the country's relocation of a controversial Soviet-era statue, 'was unheard of, and no one understood what was going on in the beginning'.[20] Under a fog of uncertainty, unscrupulous policymakers may resort to fear-mongering to win support for their preferred policy. Thwarting such behaviour is difficult because cyber operations are highly classified. The record cannot be set straight when it is Top Secret. Anyone attempting to do so risks being accused of improperly handling sensitive information, a charge carrying severe political ramifications. The politics of classified information have become exceedingly contentious as countries such as the United States have increased the number of people and organisations performing classified work.[21] In a digital age, governments are never more than one cyber attack away from suffering a full-blown political scandal.

*　　　*　　　*

We do not yet know how big the political effects of cyber operations will be in the future, because technologies and techniques are constantly evolving. However, the trends discussed in this article suggest a few plausible scenarios. A future cyber operation might topple a sitting democratic government by exposing inexcusable vulnerabilities or disclosing politically ruinous secrets. If Stuxnet had targeted a Western democracy rather than autocratic Iran, where the supreme leader never has to face the voters, the political fallout would presumably have resulted in investigations, votes of no confidence and resignations. A less sophisticated attack than Stuxnet might achieve similar effects if it inflamed existing animosities within a country's domestic politics, much as Russia has done through its meddling in the 2016 US election.

A less severe scenario involves a cyber operation spurring enough political dissension within the target state to limit its subsequent freedom of action on foreign policy. If decision-makers lack confidence about an attacker's identity, believe that an attack might have been easily prevented or worry that accusing an attacker will derail other priorities, they might refuse to support retaliation. The government would then find its hands tied politically as internal disagreement prevents decisive action. The United States has suffered this fate since the 2016 Russian operation, as some American policymakers and the public continue to debate whether Russia or President Trump bears more responsibility for the election controversy.

A third scenario involves a cyber operation triggering political infighting between allies that reduces their willingness to act together. NATO is vulnerable to such cleavages because the United States and its European allies possess differing conceptions of how best to balance internet privacy rights, free speech and government surveillance. The revelation by former National Security Agency contractor Edward Snowden that the United States and Germany attempted to intercept each other's high-level leadership communications demonstrates the political fissures that might be widened through a future cyber operation. If Western alliance leaders hope to prevail in the complex business of achieving security in the twenty-first century, they must remain attuned to the potential of cyber operations to create such political effects, both in the context of defending themselves from harm, and of harming those who threaten their interests and values.

Notes

1   See Director of National Intelligence, 'Background to "Assessing Russian Activities and Intentions in Recent US Elections": The Analytic Process and Cyber Incident Attribution', 6 January 2017, https://www.dni.gov/files/documents/ICA_2017_01.pdf.

2   Sometimes the political outcome does not neatly achieve the assailant's goal, but rather backfires. The 2007 cyber operation against Estonia caused an outpouring of public support for prime minister Andrus Ansip's government, an outcome that was presumably the opposite of what the attackers had intended. See Vello Pettai, 'Estonia', *European Journal of Political Research*, vol. 47, nos 7–8, December 2008, p. 966.

3   Semira N. Nikou, *Iran Splits over Intelligence Chief*, Parts I, II and III (Washington DC: United States Institute of Peace, 2011), available at http://iranprimer.usip.org/category/tags/intelligence-minister.

4   David E. Sanger, *The Perfect Weapon: War, Sabotage, and Fear in the Cyber Age* (New York: Crown, 2018), pp. 149–79.

5   Examples include, among many others, Thomas Rid, 'Cyber War Will Not Take Place', *Journal of Strategic Studies*, vol. 35, no. 1, February 2012, pp. 5–32; Jon R. Lindsay, 'Stuxnet and the Limits of Cyber Warfare', *Security Studies*, vol. 22, no. 3, August 2013, p. 389; Brandon Valeriano and Ryan C. Maness, *Cyber War Versus Cyber Realities: Cyber Conflict in the International System* (Oxford: Oxford University Press, 2015), p. 79; and David C. Gompert and Martin Libicki, 'Waging Cyber War the American Way', *Survival*, vol. 57, no. 4, August–September 2015, pp. 7–28.

6   Erik Gartzke, 'Fear and War in Cyberspace', *Lawfare*, 1 December

2013, https://www.lawfareblog.com/foreign-policy-essay-erik-gartzke-fear-and-war-cyberspace.

7 An effect is strategic if it shapes an adversary's capacity and willingness to conduct security operations in cyberspace and other domains. See Herbert Lin and Amy Zegart, 'Introduction to the Special Issue on Strategic Dimensions of Offensive Cyber Operations', *Journal of Cybersecurity*, vol. 3, no. 1, March 2017, p. 2.

8 Inflicting techno-damage does not mean wreaking irreversible physical destruction. Techno-damage might be temporary and involve little more than hacking an adversary's network to steal information. As used here, techno-damage implies losing value or usefulness, akin to 'damages' in the legal sense.

9 Elisabeth Bumiller and Thom Shanker, 'Panetta Warns of Dire Threat of Cyberattack on US', *New York Times*, 11 October 2012, http://www.nytimes.com/2012/10/12/world/panetta-warns-of-dire-threat-of-cyberattack.html.

10 While cyber operations can impose costs on a defender, planning such operations requires investment by the attacker. Relatively unsophisticated cyber operations cost the attacker little, but more elaborate operations demand surprisingly large sums for research, testing, and command and control. If a cyber operation triggers a digital arms race with an adversary, an attacker might end up spending much more than originally intended. See Rebecca Slayton, 'What Is the Cyber Offense–Defense Balance? Conceptions, Causes, and

Assessment', *International Security*, vol. 41, no. 3, Winter 2016/17, pp. 72–109.

11 Matt Zapotosky, 'Mueller's Investigation Cost $16.7 Million in Just Under a Year, New Documents Show', *Washington Post*, 31 May 2018, https://www.washingtonpost.com/news/post-nation/wp/2018/05/31/muellers-investigation-cost-16-7-million-in-just-under-a-year-new-documents-show/.

12 John O. Brennan, 'Remarks at the Center for Strategic & International Studies Global Security Forum', Washington DC, 16 November 2015, https://www.cia.gov/news-information/speeches-testimony/2015-speeches-testimony/brennan-remarks-at-csis-global-security-forum-2015.html.

13 Travis Sharp, 'Theorizing Cyber Coercion: The 2014 North Korean Operation Against Sony', *Journal of Strategic Studies*, vol. 40, no. 7, December 2017, p. 915.

14 While cyber operations can destabilise an adversary's politics, launching them incurs political risk for the attacker. Allies and domestic political critics may oppose using a cyber operation for political destabilisation. If decision-makers ignore these concerns and launch an attack anyway, their credibility may suffer if the operation is later attributed to them.

15 Nigel Inkster, 'Information Warfare and the US Presidential Election', *Survival*, vol. 58, no. 5, October–November 2016, pp. 23–32.

16 Kristin M. Lord and Travis Sharp, *America's Cyber Future: Security and Prosperity in the Information Age*, Volume I (Washington DC: Center for a New American Security, 2011), p. 36.

17 William Yong, 'Iranian Leader Asserts Power over President', *New York Times*, 23 April 2011, https://www.nytimes.com/2011/04/24/world/middleeast/24iran.html.

18 Cyber operations usually entail secrecy because the attacker seeks to achieve surprise and the defender seeks to limit wider knowledge of its vulnerability. In some cases, however, actors may abandon secrecy for strategic purposes. The attacker may issue a public threat to coerce its opponent, for example, while the defender may disclose its vulnerability to attract sympathetic third-party support.

19 Robert Jervis, 'Some Thoughts on Deterrence in the Cyber Era', *Journal of Information Warfare*, vol. 15, no. 2, Spring 2016, p. 71.

20 See Emily Tamkin, '10 Years After the Landmark Attack on Estonia, Is the World Better Prepared for Cyber Threats?', *Foreign Policy*, 27 April 2017, https://foreignpolicy.com/2017/04/27/10-years-after-the-landmark-attack-on-estonia-is-the-world-better-prepared-for-cyber-threats/; and Andreas Schmidt, 'The Estonian Cyberattacks', in Jason Healey (ed.), *A Fierce Domain: Conflict in Cyberspace, 1986 to 2012* (Washington DC: Cyber Conflict Studies Association, 2013), pp. 188–91.

21 Beverly Gage, 'The Strange Politics of "Classified Information"', *New York Times Magazine*, 22 August 2017, https://www.nytimes.com/2017/08/22/magazine/the-strange-politics-of-classified-information.html.

Noteworthy

Death in Istanbul

'Wish me luck.'
Jamal Khashoggi's last words to his fiancée, Hatice Cengiz, before entering the Saudi consulate in Istanbul on 2 October 2018.[1]

'Arab governments have been given free rein to continue silencing the media at an increasing rate.'
Khashoggi calls for press freedom in the Arab world in a column submitted by his assistant to the Washington Post the day after he was reported missing.[2]

'They confirmed two things: he was killed and his body was dismembered.'
Turan Kislakci, the head of Turkish Arab Media Association, comments on a phone call he received from Turkish officials on 6 October 2018.[3]

'The king firmly denied any knowledge of it … It sounded to me like maybe these could have been rogue killers.'
US President Donald Trump speaks to reporters following a phone call with Saudi Arabia's King Salman bin Abdulaziz Al Saud on 15 October 2018.[4]

'The preliminary investigations … revealed that the discussions that took place with the citizen Jamal Khashoggi during his presence in the consulate of the Kingdom in Istanbul … led to a fight and a quarrel between [the suspects] and the citizen Jamal Khashoggi … [T]he brawl aggravated to lead to his death.'
From a statement released by the Saudi government on 20 October 2018.[5]

'This was an operation that was a rogue operation. This was an operation where individuals ended up exceeding the authorities and responsibilities they had. They made the mistake when they killed Jamal Khashoggi in the consulate and they tried to cover up for it.'
Saudi Foreign Minister Adel Al Jubeir admits on 21 October 2018 that Khashoggi was killed in the Saudi consulate in Istanbul, but denies that Crown Prince Muhammad bin Salman had any knowledge of a plan to kill him.[6]

'It is clear that this savage murder did not happen instantly but was planned.'
Turkish President Recep Tayyip Erdogan comments on the Khashoggi case during a speech in Istanbul on 23 October 2018.[7]

'The US does not tolerate this kind of ruthless action to silence Mr Khashoggi, a journalist, through violence. Failure of any one nation to adhere to international norms and the rule of law undermines regional stability at a time when it is needed most.'
US Secretary of Defense James Mattis speaks at the IISS Manama Dialogue on 27 October 2018, quoting US Secretary of State Mike Pompeo.[8]

'This issue has become fairly hysterical. I think people have assigned blame on Saudi Arabia with such certainty before the investigation is complete.'
Adel Al Jubeir responds to a question during a session of the IISS Manama Dialogue on 27 October 2018.[9]

Survival | vol. 60 no. 6 | December 2018–January 2019 | pp. 54–56   DOI 10.1080/00396338.2018.1542801

Graceless exit

'This then, is a very British establishment sort of revolution. No plan and little planning, oodles of PPE tutorial level plausible bullshit, supreme self confidence that we understand others' real interests better than they do, a complete inability to fathom the nature and incentives of the ancien regime.'

Ivan Rogers, former UK permanent representative to the EU, delivers a lecture on 'Brexit as a Revolution' at the University of Cambridge on 10 October 2018.[10]

£2,310

Average annual net contribution made by adult migrants from the EEA to the UK to the country's public finances, relative to the average adult resident in the UK for 2016 17

−£70

Average contribution of British-born adults[11]

Amnesia?

'First of all, we're not angry. Now, if it's going to lead to resolution, you need to be able to build on what you already have, because, I mean, you remember the movie "50 First Dates," when you start all over again the following day. We can't. This is impossible. You need to be able to have a relationship that is based on some foundations. And we have a document that is a hundred and fifty pages long. It's not a two-page document.'

Iranian Foreign Minister Mohammed Javad Zarif discusses the fate of the Joint Comprehensive Plan of Action (JCPOA), from which the United States has withdrawn, with reference to the US agreement with North Korean leader Kim Jong-un.[12]

Brutally honest

'I told the military, what is my fault? Did I steal even one peso? My only sin is the extrajudicial killings.'

Filipino President Rodrigo Duterte speaks at Malacañang Palace on 27 September 2018.[13]

68

Percentage of Americans who believe their country's 'openness to people from all over the world is essential to who we are as a nation'

26

Percentage who believe 'if America is too open to people from around the world, we risk losing our identity as a nation'[14]

Expended deterrence

'Two American administrations, Democrat and Republican, have worked for nearly five years to bring Russia back into compliance … Eventually, we have to look reality in the eye.'

US Secretary of Defense James Mattis, speaking at the IISS Manama Dialogue on 27 October 2018, defends US plans to withdraw from the Intermediate-range Nuclear Forces (INF) Treaty.[15]

'This is a colossal mistake. Russia gets to violate the treaty and Trump takes the blame. I doubt very much that the US will deploy much that would have been prohibited by the treaty. Russia, though, will go gangbusters.'

Jeffrey Lewis, director of the East Asia Nonproliferation Program at the Middlebury Institute of International Studies at Monterey and a contributing editor to Survival.[16]

Sources

1 Martin Chulov, 'Jamal Khashoggi: Murder in the Consulate', *Guardian*, 21 October 2018, https://www.theguardian.com/world/2018/oct/21/death-of-dissident-jamal-khashoggi-mohammed-bin-salman.

2 Jamal Khashoggi, 'Jamal Khashoggi: What the Arab World Needs Most Is Free Expression', *Washington Post*, 17 October 2018, https://www.washingtonpost.com/opinions/global-opinions/jamal-khashoggi-what-the-arab-world-needs-most-is-free-expression/2018/10/17/adfc8c44-d21d-11e8-8c22-fa2ef74bd6d6_story.html?utm_term=.ff86e262fd93.

3 Carlotta Gall, Ben Hubbard and David D. Kirkpatrick, 'Turkey Believes Prominent Saudi Critic Was Killed in Saudi Consulate in Istanbul', *New York Times*, 6 October 2018, https://www.nytimes.com/2018/10/06/world/turkey-believes-prominent-saudi-critic-was-killed-in-saudi-consulate-in-istanbul.html.

4 Jill Colvin, Matthew Pennington and Fay Abuelgasim, 'President Trump Suggests "Rogue Killers" Are Responsible for Missing Saudi Journalist', *Time*, 16 October 2018, http://time.com/5425520/trump-saudi-arabia-jamal-khashoggi-turkey/.

5 Hamdi Alkhshali, 'Saudi Arabia's Full Statement on the Death of Journalist Jamal Khashoggi', CNN, 20 October 2018, https://edition.cnn.com/2018/10/19/middleeast/saudi-arabia-khashoggi-statement/index.html.

6 Bethan McKernan, Patrick Wintour and Jon Swaine, 'Jamal Khashoggi Death: Give Us the Facts, Western Countries Tell Saudis', *Guardian*, 22 October 2018, https://www.theguardian.com/world/2018/oct/21/jamal-khashoggi-germany-and-eu-condemn-saudi-explanation-of-death.

7 Carlotta Gall and Richard Pérez-Peña, 'Erdogan Says Saudis Planned Khashoggi's Killing in Turkey', *New York Times*, 23 October 2018, https://www.nytimes.com/2018/10/23/world/europe/turkey-saudi-arabia-erdogan.html?action=click&module=Top%20Stories&pgtype=Homepage.

8 James Mattis, 'US Policy in a Changing Middle East', IISS Manama Dialogue, Bahrain, 27 October 2018, https://www.iiss.org/-/media/images/dialogues/md/md-2018/documents/final/first-plenary-session--james-mattis-iiss-2018.ashx?la=en&hash=BF52087E24AEC4350040BB7CB5E004D50BBD532D.

9 Adel Al Jubeir, 'Shifting Relationships and the Emerging Middle Eastern Order: Question & Answer Session', IISS Manama Dialogue, Bahrain, 27 October 2018, https://www.iiss.org/-/media/images/dialogues/md/md-2018/documents/final/second-plenary-session--qa-iiss-2018.ashx?la=en&hash=E460408B83012E6CA225D79084F4BA6774DEBA28.

10 Ivan Rogers, 'Brexit as a Revolution', lecture delivered at the University of Cambridge, 10 October 2018, https://share.trin.cam.ac.uk/sites/public/Comms/Rogers_brexit_as_revolution.pdf.

11 Migration Advisory Committee, 'EEA Migration in the UK: Final Report', September 2018, p. 73, https://assets.publishing.service.gov.uk/government/uploads/system/uploads/attachment_data/file/740991/Final_EEA_report_to_go_to_WEB.PDF.

12 Robin Wright, 'The United States and Iran: It's Like "50 First Dates"', *New Yorker*, 1 October 2018, https://www.newyorker.com/news/news-desk/the-united-states-and-iran-its-like-50-first-dates.

13 Hannah Ellis-Petersen, 'Duterte Confesses: "My Only Sin Is the Extrajudicial Killings"', *Guardian*, 28 September 2018, https://www.theguardian.com/world/2018/sep/28/duterte-confesses-my-only-sin-is-the-extrajudicial-killings.

14 Hannah Hartig, 'Most Americans View Openness to Foreigners as "Essential to Who We Are as a Nation"', Pew Research Center, 9 October 2018, http://www.pewresearch.org/fact-tank/2018/10/09/most-americans-view-openness-to-foreigners-as-essential-to-who-we-are-as-a-nation/?utm_source=Pew+Research+Center&utm_campaign=8e2c48043c-Global_2018_10_15&utm_medium=email&utm_term=0_3e953b9b70-8e2c48043c-400005773.

15 James Mattis, 'US Policy in a Changing Middle East: Question & Answer Session', IISS Manama Dialogue, Bahrain, 27 October 2018, https://www.iiss.org/-/media/images/dialogues/md/md-2018/documents/final/first-plenary-session--qa-iiss-2018.ashx?la=en&hash=FC018A17743EF555DD3A73724806CDCEC8BE6019.

16 Julian Borger and Martin Pengelly, 'Trump Says US Will Withdraw from Nuclear Arms Treaty with Russia', *Guardian*, 21 October 2018, https://www.theguardian.com/world/2018/oct/20/trump-us-nuclear-arms-treaty-russia.

A Gardener's Vision: UAVs and the Dehumanisation of Violence

Neil C. Renic

The use of robotic technologies such as uninhabited aerial vehicles (UAVs) has changed the way we conduct and think about warfare.[1] The deeper significance of this change, however, is disputed. In terms of permissibility, many dismiss the revolutionary nature of these weapons, arguing instead that, just as with all other military force, UAVs are problematic only when they violate the explicit rules and standards of war. This line of reasoning, while understandable, too often serves to obscure a deeper challenge exposed by the growing dependence on robotic technology in war. UAVs, particularly when used in the absence of a significant ground presence, undermine the shared recognition of humanity between enemies that has historically functioned as a prerequisite for battlefield restraint. Within conditions of UAV-exclusive violence,[2] the distinction between war and judicial sanction has eroded to a degree that encourages the dehumanisation of those targeted.

Humanity at war, humanity in war

Despite humanity's long-term transition towards peace, and for all its noble qualities, humans continue to bear what Charles Darwin referred to as 'the indelible stamp of our lowly origin'.[3] Of these less desirable traits, perhaps the most harmful is our enduring capacity for cruel and destructive conduct. Central to the pacification of our species has been the steady taming of

Neil C. Renic is Lecturer in Peace and Conflict Analysis and International Security in the School of Political Science and International Studies at the University of Queensland.

Survival | vol. 60 no. 6 | December 2018–January 2019 | pp. 57–72   DOI 10.1080/00396338.2018.1542794

these baser qualities through morality, law, community and culture.[4] Yet, as any observer of war could attest, civilisation has merely restrained these impulses, not eradicated them. This is why war is such a terrible thing. In war, these chains, which have taken the full span of human history to craft, are broken. War upends the rules and standards of normal society, replacing them with an escalatory dynamic of bloodshed – man *in extremis*. For Carl von Clausewitz, this dynamic meant that war, as an act of force, was a phenomenon upon which no logical limits could be placed. Carl Schmitt echoed this idea in his own work, writing of the 'vicious circle of reprisals and anti-reprisals' that characterised warfare.[5]

Understood in this context, the warrior ethos, just-war tradition and laws of war are all attempts to 're-chain' fighters to a fixed set of rules. Even at their most effective, however, they do so imperfectly. The all-too-frequent descent of war into atrocity and massacre is historical testament to the ruinous consequences of this spiralling effect. If we are to follow this logic, more binding chains are needed in the form of more restrictive and enforceable battlefield regulations. In short, war must be more intensely civilised.

Complicating this, however, are numerous cases of battlefield conduct that fail to conform as neatly to the binary construct of civilisation and barbarism – that is, episodes in which the violence in question cannot be understood as merely a failure 'to contain the morbid natural predilections of whatever has been left of nature in man'.[6] History is replete with examples of a kind of administrative, routinised, purposive and dispassionate violence orchestrated by the very individuals and states that so proudly claim the mantle of civilisation. Here the work of Zygmunt Bauman is instructive, particularly his analysis of the intimate link between modernity and genocide. In his work *Modernity and the Holocaust*, Bauman writes:

> *Modern genocide is genocide with a purpose.* Getting rid of the adversary is not an end in itself. It is a means to an end: a necessity that stems from the ultimate objective … *of a better, and radically different, society* … This is a gardener's vision, projected upon a world-size screen … [W]eeds must die not so much because of what they are, as because of what the beautiful, orderly garden ought to be.[7]

Bauman describes a type of violence underpinned not by hatred and bloodlust, or a retreat to atavism, but rather by a modern and progressive determination to clear away all obstacles to a better future. This logic is central to understanding the link between UAV violence and the dehumanisation of those targeted.

The obvious should first be acknowledged. UAV violence, as it is currently exercised, is in no way genocidal, neither in intent nor in practice. The argument here is a more modest one. It is certainly correct that the mutual violence of the traditional battlefield can exacerbate feelings of hatred between enemies and lead to less restricted warfare. Crucially, though, problematic battlefield conduct can also result from the increasingly unidirectional and impersonal violence of robotic warfare. As Tony Erskine has argued, the preservation of essential limits on war 'is inextricably linked to the enemy's inclusion within … the sphere of equal moral standing'. Robotic violence divorces the stronger party from the physical experience and consequences of battle to a degree that imperils this inclusion, pushing an increasingly dehumanised enemy further outside the moral 'zone of application'.[8] What remains is a gardener's vision of war; a war of pest control.

Framed in these terms, UAV violence becomes not a destructive act, but rather a creative process of disinfection.[9] Terrorists are mere hindrances to be got rid of, cleared away. Hence the now common counter-terrorism expression, 'mowing the grass'. Adversaries are dehumanised. And central to this process of dehumanisation is the intensity of the military imbalance that characterises their status on the battlefield. Schmitt outlined these dangers in the concluding chapter of *The* Nomos *of the Earth*:

> If the weapons are conspicuously unequal, then the mutual concept of war conceived in terms of an equal plane is lacking. To war on both sides belongs a certain chance, a minimum of possibility for victory. Once that ceases to be the case, the opponent becomes nothing more than an *object of violent measures*.[10]

One of the surest safeguards against the imposition of this gardener's vision of war is the preservation of bonds of humanity between those that seek to kill one another. There is great worth in the basic recognition that those we fight are fellow moral agents – or, put more simply by Erich Maria Remarque, 'poor devils like us'. Observers of war have long maintained the importance of this standard. Emmerich de Vattel counselled military leaders to 'never forget that our enemies are men'. Thomas Nagel agreed, citing the importance of 'interpersonal' relationships in wartime. For Geoffrey Best, battlefield restraint was contingent on the refusal to 'believe in the total, unrecognisable alienness, the non-humanity of the enemy'.[11] A belief in the shared servitude – or victimhood – of enemies in war also rests at the heart of Michael Walzer's ongoing advocacy for the 'moral equality' of combatants. This concept establishes the realm of responsibility for all fighters as equally limited to that of *jus in bello* – the moral rules that govern battlefield conduct once hostilities have commenced.[12]

When this bond of shared humanity, victimhood and moral equality is sundered, an erosion of behavioural restraint often follows. Problematically, it is precisely this bond that is imperilled by the use of UAV-exclusive violence. The asymmetry of risk imposed between enemies has allowed for a monopolisation by the stronger party of both moral authority and violence.

Like most changes in war, this is not entirely without historical precedent. Technology has long had an important role in shaping the way in which states recognise and interact with those they wage war against. In a 1991 article titled 'Exterminating Angels', authors Asu Aksoy and Kevin Robins illustrated the extent to which technological proficiency during the Gulf War reinforced American claims of moral legitimacy, as well as a broader narrative of Western cultural and moral superiority.[13] This same impulse could be witnessed with the 1999 Kosovo bombing campaign by NATO forces. Kahn described the logic of the United States thusly: 'if our end is virtuous, there can be no justification for suffering "unnecessarily" in its pursuit'.[14] Robotic weaponry mitigates the reciprocal risk of battle for one side to such a degree that the inverse of this maxim applies: a given actor's end is virtuous *on account* of its lack of suffering. Operators of this technology are able to transcend the battlefield, not only physically, but also morally, directing a 'cleaner' mode of violence against barbaric wrongdoers on the ground.

To be clear, this article does not posit UAVs, or any other robotic technology, as the sole driver of this erosion of enemy status. There are a range of factors that explain the increasing tendency of the United States and other Western powers to criminalise and dehumanise those they conduct warfare against.[15] From the 1990s onwards, there has been a concerted effort among Western states to outlaw and pathologise war, while at the same time legitimising its use in the name of humanity. This general trend intensified following the attacks of 11 September 2001. The 'war on terror' has been the catalyst for the realisation of many of Schmitt's fears – most notably, that war as a symmetrical confrontation between 'just and equal enemies' would be replaced by punitive judicial measures against enemies reconceived as 'delinquents, troublemakers, pirates, and gangsters'.[16] What is argued here is that the profound disparity in capability, threat and risk between those currently empowered by this technology and those targeted, coupled with the physical dislocation of one set of combatants from the battlefield, has amplified and accelerated this trend. This is emphatically the case in the current context of American UAV violence.

Robotic violence and dehumanisation

The replacement of a human fighting force with machine proxies, as has occurred at times in theatres such as Somalia, Pakistan and Yemen, has terminated the long-standing configuration of the battlefield as a realm of mutual risk. What is imposed in its place is the closest approximation yet achieved to perfect military asymmetry – a unilateral projection of violence by weaponised aerial robots. In many cases, targeted enemies are not only defenceless at the precise moment of their death, but have been dispossessed of their very *capability* to apply lethal force against the military forces of the opposing side. This pushes the understanding of such violence beyond any conceivable notion of 'fighting', a term that presupposes some degree of mutual contestation. Rather, what prevails is a form of technological predation. Grégoire Chamayou, in his book *Manhunts: A Philosophical History*, defined war-as-hunting, or 'cynegetic war', as follows:

(1) It does not take the form of a direct confrontation, but a process of tracking down; (2) the power relationship is marked by a radical dissymmetry in weapons; (3) its structure is not that of a duel: a third term is mobilized as a mediation; (4) the enemy is not recognized as such, that is, as an equal – he is only a prey; (5) use is made of nonnoble means related to policing or hunting rather than to the classic military register.[17]

Juxtapose this description with an account provided by the *New York Times* detailing the process by which the Obama administration determined UAV targets:

It is the strangest of bureaucratic rituals … Every week or so, more than 100 members of the government's sprawling national security apparatus gather, by secure video teleconference, to pore over terrorist suspects' biographies and recommend to the president who should be the next to die.[18]

Barack Obama himself acknowledged that the UAV 'looks like a pretty anti-septic way of disposing of enemies'.[19] Importantly, though, the concern here goes beyond a question of aesthetics. The unilateral and physically discon-nected nature of this predation has eroded the moral relationship between the United States and those it targets. It has delivered to us a version of war in which dehumanisation has increasingly replaced moral equality as the defining feature of inter-belligerent relations.

One obvious counter to this argument is the enormity of the moral crimes perpetrated by many of those targeted by UAV violence. How, one could fairly ask, can any approximation of moral equality be maintained against adversaries for whom the deliberate targeting of civilians is a principal tactic? This objection is compelling, particularly when weighed alongside the ability of UAVs to minimise collateral damage to a greater extent than alternative modes of violence. Even if the objection is valid, however, the moderation of inter-combatant violence remains a worthwhile goal. For those committed to this task, the dehumanising potential of UAV violence must be recognised. According to one American intelligence source, the internal view of the special-operations community towards those hunted by UAVs is that:

'they have no rights. They have no dignity. They have no humanity to themselves. They're just a "selector" to an analyst. You eventually get to a point in the target's life cycle that you are following them, you don't even refer to them by their actual name.' This practice, he said, contributes to 'dehumanising the people before you've even encountered the moral question of "is this a legitimate kill or not?"'[20]

Evidence of this dehumanising effect can also be found among UAV operators themselves. Michael Hass, a former senior airman with the US Air Force, flew UAVs for six years. He recounts that during this time phrases such as 'cutting the grass before it grows out of control' and 'pulling the weeds before they overrun the lawn' were used to describe the use of UAVs against enemy insurgents.[21] Hass went on to say, 'ever step on ants and never give it another thought? That's what you are made to think of the targets – as just black blobs on a screen.' Some have seized upon these admissions as evidence that the physical disjointedness of the UAV creates a 'PlayStation mentality' – a psychological disconnectedness among operators that makes violence easier.[22] This claim, however, has received considerable pushback from those who stress the intimacy and psychological strain inherent to the use of UAVs.[23]

The most troubling implications of this dehumanisation lie not at the level of individual combatants, but rather within the broader UAV policy of the US government itself. The ease with which such violence can be administered has incentivised the adoption of targeting practices that skirt the line between morally questionable and outright violation. According to some reports, UAV targeting 'signatures' have at times included being a military-age male in an area of known terrorist activity, and 'consorting with known militants'.[24] Even if we accept that UAVs are more technically precise than military alternatives, the problem here is the targeting criteria themselves – specifically, the expansion of violence, at least potentially, to innocent targets. Evidence also exists of the US military retroactively classifying victims of collateral damage as 'enemies killed in action'.[25] Perhaps the most troubling of these allegations relates to the practice of 'double tap' strikes – using those injured in initial strikes as bait, and then targeting a second strike on those who arrive to offer assistance.[26]

Evidence of this behavioural decline can also be found in the growing influence of politics on targeting selection. According to a number of sources, in the wake of the 'enhanced interrogation' scandal of the Bush years, US officials have favoured UAV strikes as a more politically palatable alternative to capture.[27] In one illustrative instance, recounted by an International Security Assistance Force (ISAF) officer to journalist Chris Woods, it was determined that while there was insufficient evidence to further detain a suspected insurgent, there was enough to kill him:

> There followed a conversation. 'Ok, so how long do we need to wait [after] he's been released from custody before it would be appropriate to kill him?' Obviously, the easiest place to kill him was as soon as we've let him out of the front gate, but that would have been a bit unsporting.[28]

For UAVs, the grounds of acceptable force can drift more easily from a morally justifiable standard of 'defensive' and 'necessary' to merely 'preferential'. This is borne out by the available evidence which suggests that an overwhelming percentage of UAV strikes conducted during the years of the Obama administration were directed against low-level al-Qaeda, Taliban and other militant fighters.[29] This dispensation points to a worrying trend. Among those carrying out the United States' UAV programme, the perception of the weaker party has increasingly shifted from a gravely threatening opponent to be fought and overcome, to one that must simply be hunted and *done away with*.

To fully appreciate the problematic implications of this model of war, consider the domestic political context within which the United States' UAV programme now operates. Over eight years, the morally troubling aspects of this violence evolved under the guidance and overall supervision of Obama, a constitutional-law professor and determined critic of the military adventurism and overreach of the Bush years. Obama's successor, President Donald Trump, during his campaign openly advocated a return to torture,[30] as well as the deliberate violation of non-combatant immunity by American forces.[31]

Less than two years into his new administration, President Trump had already relaxed a number of rules established by Obama to curb the excesses of UAV violence. This includes the requirement that beyond the 'hot' battlefield, strikes be undertaken only against those who pose a 'continuing, imminent threat to U.S. persons'. Strikes are now formally permissible against 'foot-soldier jihadists with no special skills or leadership roles'.[32] More broadly, he has derided Obama-era measures for minimising civilian casualties as 'micromanagement', delegating increased operational authority to the military and decreasing the transparency of targeting decisions. Under Trump, the CIA has also regained its lead operational role on UAV strikes from the Pentagon and increased drone operations, particularly in Africa. The available evidence thus suggests that the dehumanisation of America's enemies will continue, and potentially worsen, especially as the technology that enables such conditions becomes more sophisticated.

Killing in the post-human age

With respect to emerging robotic technology, Christopher Coker has written that 'our ethical imagination is still failing to catch up with the fast expanding realm of our ethical responsibilities'.[33] This gulf between our martial capabilities and our moral comprehension of their impact seems set to widen as the technology itself gains autonomy. The US Department of Defense defines 'autonomous weapons' as systems that 'once activated, can select and engage targets without further interventions by the human operator'.[34]

Debate continues regarding the exact degree to which robotic autonomy will be realised on the battlefield. What is undeniable, though, is the strength of the motivations to advance such a goal. Proponents of autonomous warfare make frequent reference to the 'kill-chain' – the time required to 'find, fix, track, target, engage, and assess' potential enemies in battle. Specifically, they suggest that 'as the loop gets shorter and shorter there [eventually] won't be any time in it for humans'. At least one US Air Force research scientist has suggested that 'cultural resistance', rather than technological impediment, best explains current limits on autonomy.[35] If true, such opposition is unlikely to prove a sufficient bulwark. Heather Roff and Peter Singer report that as of 2016, the United States was working on at least 21 different projects that enhanced the autonomous capacity of military weapons systems.[36] In March 2018, the US Army announced plans to develop small UAVs capable of lethal force without human oversight.[37] Based on current evidence, it would seem to be a matter of when, rather than if, modern militaries cross the technological Rubicon and employ fully autonomous weaponised robots in battle.

The critical question remains: what impact, if any, will the emergence of robotic autonomy have on the relationship between enemies in war? A concern expressed throughout this article is that the extreme risk asymmetry and physical disconnectedness of UAV violence encourages the moral devaluation of the weaker party. Within these conditions, killing is more likely to be undertaken in the absence of the required recognition of the enemy's humanity. In some cases, this loss of recognition has contributed to an erosion of moral restraints on American violence. This is likely to worsen as war fighting shifts from military robots under the control of combatants to military robots *as* combatants. Scholars such as Ronald Arkin welcome the emergence of autonomous weapons, on account of their ability to more rigidly comply with the laws of war.[38] This disposition leaves unexamined, however, the potential of autonomous violence to further minimise the vital connection of a shared humanity between enemies.

*   *   *

Robotic military violence, specifically by way of UAVs, has the potential to fundamentally alter the basic logic of war from adversarial contestation to something approximating judicial sanction; from a battle between enemies of roughly equal standing to an administrative liquidation of obstacles. In the context of UAV-exclusive violence, this transformation in the dynamic between the United States and its enemies has contributed to the dehumanisation of the latter.

The potential for future autonomous technologies to further dislocate those empowered from the battlefield, both physically and morally, highlights the need for a more comprehensive assessment of their impact. To ignore this need and simply trust that our technological and moral landscapes will self-align is too great a gamble to take.

Acknowledgements

I would like to thank Sebastian Kaempf, Megan Price and Chris Reus-Smit for their insightful comments.

Notes

[1] The US Department of Defense defines UAVs as follows: 'A powered, aerial vehicle that does not carry a human operator, uses aerodynamic forces to provide vehicle lift, can fly autonomously or be piloted remotely, can be expendable or recoverable, and can carry a lethal or nonlethal payload.' Cited in Elizabeth Bone and Christopher Bolkcom, 'Unmanned Aerial Vehicles: Background and Issues for Congress', Congressional Research Service, 25 April 2003, https://fas.org/irp/crs/RL31872.pdf. This article focuses exclusively on the lethal variants of this technology.

[2] The term 'UAV-exclusive' refers to the ongoing use, most notably by the United States, of UAVs in the near-total absence of military alternatives, including ground-based forces – in short, UAVs as war, rather than in war.

[3] For an in-depth examination of the trend towards peace, see Steven Pinker, *The Better Angels of Our Nature: Why Violence Has Declined* (London: Viking Penguin, 2011). See also Charles Darwin, *The Descent of Man and Selection in Relation to Sex* (New York: Appleton and Co., 1883), pp. 618–19.

[4] Norbert Elias explored this in his influential work *The Civilizing Process*. Elias wrote of the taming of impulses, such as 'cruelty and joy in the destruc-

tion and torment of others', through 'increasingly strong social control anchored in the state organization'. The fragility of this control is exposed 'only at times of social upheaval [war] or where social control is looser [the frontier]'. Norbert Elias, *The Civilizing Process: The History of Manner and State Formation and Civilization* (Oxford: Blackwell, 1994), p. 192.

[5] Carl von Clausewitz, *On War*, ed. and trans. Michael Howard and Peter Paret (Oxford: Oxford University Press, 2008), p. 15; Carl Schmitt, *Theory of the Partisan: Intermediate Commentary on the Concept of the Political* (New York: Telos Press Publishing, 2007), p. 28.

[6] Zygmunt Bauman, *Modernity and the Holocaust* (Cambridge: Polity Press, 1989), p. 13.

[7] *Ibid.*, pp. 91–2. Emphasis in original.

[8] Tony Erskine, *Embedded Cosmopolitanism: Duties to Strangers and Enemies in a World of 'Dislocated Communities'* (Oxford: Oxford University Press, 2008), p. 195. See also Alex Honneth, *The Struggle for Recognition: The Moral Grammar of Social Conflicts* (Cambridge: Polity Press, 1995), p. 113.

[9] See Bauman, *Modernity and the Holocaust*, p. 92.

[10] Carl Schmitt, *The* Nomos *of the Earth: In the International Law of the* Jus Publicum Europaeum, trans.

G.L. Ulmen (New York: Telos Press Publishing, 2006), p. 320. Emphasis added.

11 Erich Maria Remarque, *All Quiet on the Western Front* (New York: Fawcett Crest, 1929), p. 223; Emer de Vattel, *The Law of Nations, or Principles of the Law of Nature, Applied to the Conduct and Affairs of Nations and Sovereigns* (London: G.G. and J. Robinson, 1797), p. 296; Thomas Nagel, 'War and Massacre', *Philosophy & Public Affairs*, vol. 1, no. 2, 1972, p. 136; Geoffrey Best, *War and Law Since 1945* (Oxford: Clarendon Press, 1994), p. 291.

12 Michael Walzer, *Just Unjust Wars: A Moral Argument with Historical Illustrations* (New York: Basic Books, 2006), pp. 34–7.

13 Asu Aksoy and Kevin Robins, 'Exterminating Angels: Morality, Violence and Technology in the Gulf War', *Science as Culture*, vol. 2, no. 3, 1991. For earlier examples of this same logic, see Michael Adas, *Machines as the Measure of Men: Science, Technology, and Ideologies of Western Dominance* (Ithaca, NY: Cornell University Press, 2014); and John Ellis, *The Social History of the Machine Gun* (Baltimore, MD: Johns Hopkins University Press, 1986).

14 Paul Kahn, 'War and Sacrifice in Kosovo', *Philosophy and Public Policy Quarterly*, vol. 20, no. 3, 1999, pp. 1–6.

15 'There is the danger', wrote Andrew Linklater, 'that [the liberal peace] will be grounded in a sense of superiority to the non-liberal world, in a lack of interest in the suffering of non-liberal peoples and in the belief that the principles that apply in the liberal world do not apply in wars with illiberal states.' Andrew Linklater, 'The Problem of Harm in World Politics: Implications for the Sociology of State-Systems', *International Affairs*, vol. 78, no. 2, 2002, p. 333. See also Michael Doyle, 'Kant, Liberal Legacies and Foreign Affairs', *Philosophy & Public Affairs*, vol. 12, no. 3, 1983, pp. 205–35; James M. Goldgeier and Michael McFaul, 'A Tale of Two Worlds: Core and Periphery in the Post-Cold War Era', *International Organisation*, vol. 46, no. 2, 1992, pp. 467–91; Michael Howard, *War and the Liberal Conscience* (Oxford: Oxford University Press, 1989); Yahya M. Sadowski, *The Myth of Global Chaos* (Washington DC: Brookings Institution Press, 1998); and Wouter G. Werner, 'From Justus Hostis to Rogue State: The Concept of the Enemy in International Legal Thinking', *International Journal for the Semiotics of Law*, vol. 17, no. 2, June 2004, pp. 155–68.

16 Carl Schmitt, 'Die Wendung zum Diskriminierenden Kriegsbegriff', in C. Mouffe (ed.), *The Challenge of Carl Schmitt* (London: Verso, 1999), pp. 60–1.

17 Grégoire Chamayou, *Manhunts: A Philosophical History* (Princeton, NJ: Princeton University Press, 2012), p. 73.

18 Joe Becker and Scott Shane, 'Secret "Kill List" Proves a Test of Obama's Principles and Will', *New York Times*, 29 May 2012, p. A1.

19 Quoted in Jonathan Chait, 'Barack Obama on 5 Days that Shaped a Presidency', *New York Magazine*, 2 October 2016, http://nymag.com/daily/intelligencer/2016/10/barack-obama-on-5-days-that-shaped-his-presidency.html.

20 Jeremy Scahill, 'The Assassination Complex', *Intercept*, 15 October 2015, https://theintercept.com/drone-papers/the-assassination-complex/.

21 Quoted in Ed Pilkington, 'Life as a Drone Operator: "Ever Step on Ants and Never Give it Another Thought?"', *Guardian*, 19 November 2015, http://www.theguardian.com/world/2015/nov/18/life-as-a-drone-pilot-creech-air-force-base-nevada.

22 For further reference to the 'PlayStation mentality' argument, see Philip Alston, 'Report of the Special Rapporteur on Extrajudicial, Summary or Arbitrary Executions', 2015, http://www2.ohchr.org/english/bodies/hrcouncil/docs/14session/A.HRC.14.24.Add6.pdf; C. Cole, M. Dobbing and A. Hailwood, *Convenient Killing: Armed Drones and the 'PlayStation Mentality'* (Oxford: Fellowship of Reconciliation, 2010), pp. 1–20; Claire Finkelstein, 'Targeted Killing as Pre-emptive Action', in J.D. Ohlin, A. Altman and C. Finkelstein (eds), *Targeted Killings: Law and Morality in an Asymmetrical World* (Oxford: Oxford University Press, 2011), p. 174; and Peter Olsthoorn, *Military Ethics and Virtues: An Interdisciplinary Approach for the 21st Century* (New York: Routledge, 2011), p. 126.

23 See Daniel Klaidman, *Kill or Capture: The War on Terror and the Soul of the Obama Presidency* (Boston, MA: Houghton Mifflin, 2012), p. 217; Chris Cole, '"It Was Incessant." Former RAF Reaper Pilot Speaks to Drone Wars', Drone Wars UK, 30 May 2017, https://dronewars.net/2017/05/30/justin-thompson-interview/; M.J. Boyle, 'The Legal and Ethical Implications of Drone Warfare', *International Journal of Human Rights*, vol. 19, no. 2, 2015, p. 106; Megan McCloskey, 'The War Room: Daily Transition Between Battle, Home Takes Toll on Drone Operators', *Stars & Stripes*, 27 October 2009, http://www.stripes.com/news/the-war-room-daily-transition-between-battle-home-takes-a-toll-on-drone-operators-1.95949; Peter Lee, 'Remoteness, Risk and Aircrew Ethos', *Air Power Review*, vol. 15, no. 1, 2012, p. 15; and Chris Woods, *Sudden Justice: America's Secret Drone Wars* (New York: Oxford University Press, 2015), p. 174.

24 See Becker and Shane, 'Secret "Kill List"'; 'Living Under Drones: Death, Injury and Trauma to Civilians from US Drone Practices in Pakistan', Stanford Law School International Human Rights and Conflict Resolution Clinic and NYU School of Law Global Justice Clinic, 2017, https://law.stanford.edu/wp-content/ ... /Stanford-NYU-LIVING-UNDER-DRONES.pdf; and Dexter Filkins, 'The Journalist and the Spies', *New Yorker*, 19 September 2011, http://www.newyorker.com/reporting/2011/09/19/110919fa_fact_filkins?currentPage=1. A number of counter-terrorism officials have argued that this approach 'is one of simple logic: people in an area of known terrorist activity ... are probably up to no good'. Becker and Shane, 'Secret "Kill List"'.

25 Scahill, 'The Assassination Complex'.

26 Stuart Casey-Maslen, 'The Use of Armed Drones', in S. Casey-Maslen (ed.), *Weapons Under International Human Rights Law* (Cambridge:

Cambridge University Press, 2014), p. 397; Sassan Gholiagha, 'Individualized and Yet Dehumanized? Targeted Killing via Drones', *Behemoth: A Journal on Civilization*, vol. 8, no. 2, 2015, p. 140; John Kaag and Sarah Kreps, *Drone Warfare* (Cambridge: Polity, 2014), pp. 32–3.

27 See Kenneth Anderson, 'Targeted Killing in U.S. Counterterrorism Strategy and Law', Working Paper of the Series on Counterterrorism and American Statutory Law, a joint project of the Brookings Institution, the Georgetown University Law Center and the Hoover Institution, 11 May 2009, http://papers.ssrn.com/sol3/papers.cfm?abstract_id=1415070; Becker and Shane, 'Secret "Kill List"'; Michael Hirsh, 'Slow Dance: Obama's Romance with the C.I.A.', *Atlantic*, 13 May 2011, http://www.theatlantic.com/politics/archive/2011/05/slow-dance-obamas-romance-with-the-cia/238849/; and Mark Mazzetti, *The Way of the Knife; The CIA, a Secret Army, and a War at the Ends of the Earth* (New York: Penguin, 2013), p. 247.

28 Woods, *Sudden Justice*, p. 220.

29 See Adam Entous, 'Special Report: How the White House Learned to Love the Drone', Reuters, 18 May 2010, http://www.reuters.com/article/us-pakistan-drones-idUS-TRE64H5SL20100518; Andre Barrinha and Luis da Vinha, 'Dealing with Risk: Precision Strikes and Interventionism in the Obama Administration', in W. Aslam et al. (eds), *Precision Strike Warfare and International Intervention: Strategic, Ethico-Legal, and Decisional Implications* (Abingdon: Routledge, 2015), p. 23; Rosa Brooks, 'Drones and Cognitive Dissonance', in Peter Bergen and Daniel Rothenberg (eds), *Drones, Remote Targeting and the Promise of Law* (Cambridge: Cambridge University Press, 2013), http://scholarship.law.georgetown.edu/facpub/1256; Rosa Brooks, 'Duck-Rabbits and Drones: Legal Indeterminacy in the War on Terror', *Stanford Law and Policy Review*, vol. 25, no. 2, 2014, pp. 301–16; 'The Civilian Impact of Drones: Unexamined Costs, Unanswered Questions', Report of the Columbia Law School Human Rights Clinic, 11 September 2012, p. 8, https://www.propublica.org/documents/item/553588-the-civilian-impact-of-drones; Jonathan S. Landay, 'Obama's Drone War Kills "Others", Not Just Al-Qaida Leaders', *McClatchy*, 9 April 2013, http://www.mcclatchydc.com/news/nation-world/world/middle-east/article24747826.html; Harry van der Linden, 'Drone Warfare and Just War Theory', in M. Cohn (ed.), *Drones and Targeted Killing: Legal, Moral, and Geopolitical Issues* (Northampton, MA: Olive Branch Press, 2015), p. 173; Shibley Telhami, *The Stakes: America in the Middle East: The Consequences of Power and the Choice of Peace* (Boulder, CO: Westview Press, 2004), p. 16; Peter Bergen and Jennifer Rowland, 'CIA Drone War in Pakistan in Sharp Decline', CNN, 28 March 2012, http://edition.cnn.com/2012/03/27/opinion/bergen-drone-decline/index.html; Bureau of Investigative Journalism, 'Drone Wars: The Full Data', 1 January 2017, https://www.thebureauinvesti-gates.com/category/projects/drones/drones-graphs/; Woods, *Sudden Justice*, p. 205; and Ryan Devereaux,

'Manhunting in the Hindu Kush:
Civilian Casualties and Strategic
Failures in America's Longest War',
Intercept, 15 October 2015, https://
theintercept.com/drone-papers/
manhunting-in-the-hindu-kush/.

30 Jenna Johnson, 'Donald Trump on
Waterboarding: "Torture Works"',
Washington Post, 17 February 2016,
https://www.washingtonpost.com/
news/post-politics/wp/2016/02/17/
donald-trump-on-waterboarding-
torture-works/.

31 See Tom LoBianco, 'Donald Trump on
Terrorists: "Take Out Their Families"',
CNN, 3 December 2015, http://
edition.cnn.com/2015/12/02/politics/
donald-trump-terrorists-families/.

32 Luke Hartig, 'Trump's New Drone
Strike Policy: What's Any Different?
Why It Matters', *Just Security*, 22
September 2017, https://www.
justsecurity.org/45227/trumps-drone-
strike-policy-different-matters/;
Charlie Savage and Eric Schmitt,
'Trump Poised to Drop Some Limits
on Drone Strikes and Commando
Raids', *New York Times*, 21 September
2017, https://www.nytimes.
com/2017/09/21/us/politics/trump-
drone-strikes-commando-raids-rules.
html.

33 Christopher Coker, *Ethics and War in
the 21st Century* (London: Routledge,
2008), p. 152.

34 US Department of Defense Directive
no. 3000.09, 'Autonomy in Weapon
Systems', 21 November 2012, https://
cryptome.org/dodi/dodd-3000-09.pdf.

35 Julian C. Cheater, 'Accelerating the
Kill Chain via Future Unmanned
Aircraft', Blue Horizons Paper, Center
for Strategy and Technology, Air War
College, April 2007, http://www.au.af.
mil/au/awc/awcgate/cst/bh_cheater.
pdf; Michael Mayer, 'The New Killer
Drones: Understanding the Strategic
Implications of Next-Generation
Unmanned Combat Aerial Vehicles',
International Affairs, vol. 91, no. 4,
2015, p. 775; Mary O'Connell, 'What's
Wrong with Drones? The Battlefield
in International Humanitarian Law',
in M. Evangelista and H. Shue (eds),
*The American Way of Bombing: Changing
Ethical and Legal Norms, From Flying
Fortresses to Drones* (Ithaca, NY:
Cornell University Press, 2014), p. 227.

36 Heather M. Roff and Peter Singer, 'The
Next President Will Decide the Fate of
Killer Robots – and the Future of War',
Wired, 6 September 2016.

37 US Department of Defense Small
Business Innovation Research solici-
tation A18-006, 'Automatic Target
Recognition of Personnel and Vehicles
from an Unmanned Aerial System
Using Learning Algorithms', 29
November 2017, https://www.sbir.
gov/sbirsearch/detail/1413823.

38 Ronald Arkin, 'The Case for Ethical
Autonomy in Unmanned Systems',
Journal of Military Ethics, vol. 9, no. 4,
2010, pp. 332–41.

The Demilitarisation of Cyber Conflict

Sergei Boeke and Dennis Broeders

Speculation over cyber war has moved beyond its initial poles of doomsday and dismissal.[1] Some argued that 'cybergeddon' or a digital Pearl Harbor was looming, others that cyber war had never occurred and probably never would.[2] The front line of the debate has since shifted to whether or not cyberspace has become militarised,[3] if deterrence is possible in cyberspace,[4] and, if the security dilemma applies, how it can be mitigated.[5] In strategic studies, the debate focuses on whether cyber conflict reaches Clausewitzean thresholds of violence and damage.[6] Legal scholars – for example through the Tallinn process – are attempting to define when cyber operations reach the level of an 'armed attack' and 'the use of force', triggering conventional legal reasoning under the framework of the Law of Armed Conflict.[7] While states have agreed – some with regret – that international law applies in the digital world as it does in the offline one, there is no agreement on how.[8] The last round of the United Nations Group of Governmental Experts failed to provide a consensus report in 2017, stalling the process to establish norms of responsible state behaviour in cyberspace.[9] Both the academic debate on cyber conflict and the international policy process to agree to 'rules of the road' are nonetheless built on the same premise: that cyber operations fall under the normative and legal frameworks regulating military conduct during war and peace.

Sergei Boeke is a researcher at the Institute of Security and Global Affairs (ISGA) at Leiden University. **Dennis Broeders** is an associate professor and senior fellow in The Hague Program for Cyber Norms at the ISGA.

Survival | vol. 60 no. 6 | December 2018–January 2019 | pp. 73–90   DOI 10.1080/00396338.2018.1542804

There are, however, good reasons to believe that the frameworks presumed applicable to cyber conflict are actually a bad fit. Two developments support the thesis that the militarisation of cyberspace may actually be the result of a *demilitarisation* of cyber conflict, as the main actors in cyber conflict are not actually military actors. Both the dominant role of foreign-intelligence and security agencies (as opposed to military actors) in cyber operations, and the use of proxies (either private contractors or other non-state actors) in cyber conflict, illustrate that, in practice, cyber conflict largely takes place outside the parameters of international humanitarian law. Other principles of international law still apply to interventions by intelligence services and proxies below the threshold of armed conflict. International law writ large is silent on espionage, but not on covert paramilitary actions or clandestine intelligence activities with disruptive effects. Many states use proxies precisely to render their potentially illegal actions deniable.[10] Nevertheless, if state practice, both directly and indirectly, indicates that there are non-military actors and legal gaps in the cyber domain, the international debate about state behaviour in cyberspace may at least partially be set in the wrong legal key.

Demilitarising cyber conflict?

In the security domain, traditional boundaries between military and civilian, and internal and external security, have long been blurring. The process has been especially intense in the cyber dimension. Lene Hansen and Helen Nissenbaum note that the internet has a tendency to blur classical distinctions deemed crucial to international relations and security studies: those 'between individual and collective security, between public authorities and private institutions, and between economic and political–military security'.[11] Some boundaries fade through technological developments or deliberate policy choices. The latter range from mitigating the problem of scarce resources, such as a shortage of cyber-security professionals, to the desire of state actors to operate with a degree of deniability. Two fundamental boundaries in particular determine under which normative and legal framework cyber operations should fall: the boundary between military operations and foreign-intelligence – that is, espionage – activities, and that between state and private actors in cyber operations.

Intelligence and security agencies vs the military

'Cyberspace operations, because of their nature, may be harder to pigeonhole within the range of military operations', write Gary D. Brown and Andrew O. Metcalf.[12] This may turn out to be an understatement, especially when foreign-intelligence operations are contrasted with regular military operations. Foreign-intelligence actors are primarily concerned with extracting information, and building and maintaining an information position within the enemy's networks (the long game). They face only national constraints on what is considered a legitimate and legal target. The dominant mode of operations is clandestine, such that the activities as well as the perpetrator must remain secret. By contrast, military operations are ultimately overt and are meant to display and use force against an enemy. These two models may meet in the middle in the form of covert action, in which the effects of the operation are visible to the adversary (and potentially the rest of the world), but the hand behind it is not. This creates room for plausible deniability, implausible deniability or at least confusion.[13] To be sure, international law applies regardless of whether intentional interference in the internal affairs of another sovereign state is conducted by military or intelligence services. State action is state action; it is simply tougher to prove in certain non-military cases. In such cases, however, the law is much harder to enforce. In effect, therefore, the legal regime for clandestine and covert operations is murky at best and most firmly grounded in national rather than international law.[14] This indeterminacy is intentional: states are reluctant to specify precisely how they instruct their intelligence officers to break other countries' laws.

Many of the most significant cyber attacks discovered so far are the suspected work of foreign-intelligence and security agencies rather than military actors. Thomas Rid surmised in 2012 that all the then-known politically motivated cyber attacks were merely versions of sabotage, espionage and subversion – and therefore did not amount to cyber war.[15] His observation can be taken one step further: in times of peace, these activities are conducted by intelligence agencies. The fact that some of these agencies, like the US National Security Agency (NSA), have some form of military signature or embedding does not mean that they necessarily operate under the legal regime for military operations. Even those that are an integral part of the military operate under the legal regime for foreign intelligence. Other countries, like the United Kingdom and Germany, have chosen to embed their foreign-espionage and cyber capacity in purely civilian agencies – Government Communications Headquarters (GCHQ) and the Federal Intelligence Service (BND), respectively.

There is a long and growing list of cyber operations, some labelled as specific Advanced Persistent Threats (APTs) by various cyber-security companies, that can be attributed to different intelligence services.[16] Stuxnet, sometimes heralded as the one cyber attack that reached the level of war,[17] has convincingly been ascribed to the US and Israel by cyber-security companies and investigative journalists (most notably, David Sanger of the *New York Times*).[18] The code was written by the NSA in cooperation with Israel's Unit 8200, but was unleashed – at least on behalf of the US – through the Central Intelligence Agency (CIA). In 2014, the UK's GCHQ was found responsible for a targeted attack on the Belgian telecommunications provider Belgacom, a rare documented case of one NATO ally running a sophisticated cyber-espionage operation on another.[19] In 2017 the virus NotPetya struck several targets in Ukraine, but the collateral damage to other companies worldwide amounted to $10 billion.[20] A coalition of countries attributed the attack to the Russian Federation, and more specifically to the GRU, Russia's military-intelligence agency.[21] In short, foreign-intelligence agencies, and not the regular military, are leading the charge in what is frequently mislabelled cyber war.

For both offence and defence there is a fundamental tension between intelligence collection and military (or policy) action. By their very nature, intelligence agencies lean towards keeping, expanding and deepening the information they possess, avoiding the temptation to use the intelligence and thereby lose the source. The classic example is the extreme secrecy surrounding the Allies' breaking of the Enigma cipher during the Second World War, precluding the operational use of the acquired intelligence in several instances. From a defensive perspective, the intelligence agency's reflex to protect sources inhibits the process of attribution, especially the release of evidence to support a public accusation. In attributing the Sony Pictures hack to North Korea in 2014 – the first public attribution of a cyber attack to another state – US officials omitted any evidence to back up the claim. Subsequently, officials acknowledged that the NSA had assets present in North Korean networks, and that they could not have provided evidence without compromising sources and methods.[22] Nearly four years later, the FBI indicted a North Korean hacker who was working for North Korea's main intelligence agency on the Sony hack and several subsequent cyber attacks, such as the WannaCry virus.[23] For offence, the same forces are at play. In describing the military effort against the Islamic State (ISIS), Ash Carter, the former US secretary of defense, has expressed his disappointment with US Cyber Command, stating that they never really produced effective cyber weapons or techniques. When they did produce something useful, he added, 'the intelligence community tended to delay or try to prevent its use, claiming cyber operations would hinder intelligence collection'.[24] In cyber operations, then, having your cake and eating it is generally not an option.[25]

'Don't get caught' is the rule

Most importantly, military operations and foreign-intelligence activities operate on the basis of different legal paradigms. Warfare has been subject to international law since Hugo Grotius published his seminal work on the laws of war and peace in 1625. Now International Human Rights Law, the UN Charter and the legal texts grouped under the Law of Armed Conflict regulate state behaviour during armed conflict, building on principles such as proportionality and distinction. By contrast, foreign-intelligence collection has not been regulated by international law, with limits provided by an undefined 'gentlemen's agreement'.[26] The international norm allowing peacetime espionage is partially built on the 1927 SS *Lotus* case by the Permanent Court of International Justice, which articulated an oft-cited principle in international law, essentially permitting everything that is not explicitly prohibited.[27] This leaves 'don't get caught' as the prime informal rule and 'everybody does it' as the first line of defence when one does get caught.

Most liberal democracies have legislated restrictions on how their foreign intelligence can operate abroad, but other regimes are less legalistic and give their agencies free rein. The use of force by intelligence agencies is a more complicated, and under-discussed, legal field. In essence, the nature of the targeted network already partly indicates whether the attacker's motive is espionage or sabotage. The networks of political parties and government departments are considered legitimate targets for foreign espionage; this generates political and strategic intelligence. Breaching the networks of critical infrastructure such as the electric grid, however, generates no political intelligence. It does, however, provide crucial intelligence for sabotage in times of conflict – but also in peace. During armed conflict, critical infrastructure can be a legitimate target according to the laws of war, but this does not legitimise 'preparation of the battlefield' in an intrusive way. Passive reconnaissance using signals intelligence (SIGINT), human intelligence (HUMINT) or imagery intelligence is accepted as part of the game. But actively hacking targets and leaving implants in the adversary's networks seem as illegitimate as laying remotely controlled sea-mines inside a port in peacetime. In doing so, the agencies step outside their own legal paradigm. Given the nature of cyber operations, more of these transgressions can be expected in the future. The use of covert action is not explicitly covered by international law, though constraints against it are implied in state-to-state rules such as the prohibition against the violation of sovereignty and territorial integrity, and the principle of non-intervention.[28] Any physical destruction rising to the level of an armed attack, however, would be subject to the Law of Armed Conflict.

How to apply recognised international laws in a new domain like cyberspace is subject to much debate. Most cyber operations fall well below the threshold of an 'armed attack' – which would trigger the Law of Armed Conflict – and are executed by foreign-intelligence agencies. Does that mean they are all espionage operations, and thus not explicitly regulated by international law? This question will become increasingly problematic as cyber operations proliferate. Strategic ambiguity may benefit the powerful, but this advantage diminishes in relative value as others join the playing field. Furthermore, the debate about the nature of cyber weapons – including whether that is even an appropriate and useful term – has important legal dimensions. Both the procurement and the use of a weapon are tied to legal rules and restrictions under domestic (military) law, so labelling something as a weapon has far-reaching legal, policy and political implications.[29]

It may make more sense to describe cyber weapons simply as operations, characterised by what Max Smeets calls their 'transitory nature'.[30] Cyber operations are tailor-made combinations of intelligence, intrusion and attack, and it is seldom clear where one phase ends and another begins. Moreover, the substance of the weapon is software code. This must be adapted and customised to evolving and unforeseen circumstances in the target's network and the overall development of the operation. A cyber weapon is therefore very different from, say, a tank, and it is an open question whether it should be subject to the same military rules with regard to procurement and operational use. Applying the rules – which would include reviewing all changes to the 'weapon' – might grind cyber operations to a halt. Not applying them would effectively keep all cyber operations under the label of foreign-intelligence operations.[31] Neither appears an attractive option in the long run.

Proxies vs state actors

Foreign-intelligence services and military actors may operate under different legal regimes, but they are at least recognised state actors. The Westphalian state system legitimises sovereign states as the security actors in the international domain, formally excluding non-state actors. Even though the monopoly on the legitimate use of force – for both Weberian internal sovereignty as well as Westphalian external sovereignty – is still a relatively new element of modern state formation, its symbolic power cannot be underestimated.[32] While developments such as failed states, international terrorism and private military companies have put cracks in this ideal vision of international security, this monopoly remains a fundamental basis of modern state power and legitimacy. As such, it underpins the international legal order. But actual malicious activities in cyberspace do challenge that standard. Across the board, non-state actors are involved in cyber operations, often in some formal or informal relationship with state actors. Such actors also vary in terms of political legitimacy.

Tim Maurer presents different models of the relationship between states and the proxies they use for cyber operations, based on the degree to which the state actually controls the actors conducting cyber operations on its behalf.[33] He identifies three main proxy relationships: delegation, orchestration and sanctioning.[34] In the first model, the state exerts the most direct control over the proxy; the last consists of only passive support, or even just the turning of a blind eye to their activities. As to legitimacy, there are various political models of the legitimate soldier that at the edges transgress into models that cover illegitimate combatants, such as vigilante forces and mercenaries. (These concepts are captured in Table 1.) Elke Krahmann identifies three types of legitimate combatants: the citizen soldier, embedded in political republicanism; the professional soldier, embedded in republicanism and liberalism; and the private military contractor. The latter is legitimate up to the point where he or she does not engage in actual combat, the preserve of states.[35] The citizen soldier runs the risk of turning into a vigilante, the private military contractor into a mercenary; both are considered unlawful combatants under international law.

Typology of legitimate and illegitimate combatants

The potential blurring of the various models of legitimacy and effective state control is obvious in the case of kinetic operations undertaken by non-uniformed combatants. In cyberspace, where operations are as a rule covert, the provenance of the actor, the nature of the activity and the guiding intent can all remain unclear. Unlike the capabilities of tanks, frigates and combat aircraft, a state's cyber capability is difficult to assess, and not easy to quantify or compare. It is clear, however, that the United States, Israel, China and Russia are the 'top tier' cyber powers. But each sports a different model. The United States combines the professional-soldier model with a heavy reliance on private contractors and private military companies. Israel combines

Table 1. **Types of combatants**

Vigilante	Citizen soldier	Professional soldier	Private military company	Mercenary
Illegal	Legal	Legal	Legal	Illegal
No democratic legitimacy	Republican democratic legitimacy	Mixed republican and liberal democratic legitimacy	Neoliberal legitimacy (contractual and private law)	No democratic legitimacy

the model of the citizen soldier with a heavy reliance on its cyber-security industry, as well as a revolving door between its military and that industry. China employs a hybrid model of the professional soldier and citizen soldier with elements of vigilantism. And Russia combines a model of the professional soldier with vigilante proxies.

In the United States, relations between the military and the defence contractors that cater to its needs have been close since the Second World War. This military–industrial complex has, in turn, given rise to an emerging cyber–military complex.[36] It consists of traditional defence contractors, now possessing cyber-security divisions, and a growing market of start-ups and boutique firms that conduct work substantially but not exclusively for the military.[37] Both the procurement of weapons from private industry and the outsourcing of certain non-combatant tasks to private military companies are considered legal and legitimate. In cyberspace, however, state security agencies are increasingly *contracting in* private cyber-security services and expertise instead of *sourcing out* tasks and product development. This modality results in public–private hybrids that operate behind the closed doors of security and intelligence agencies and the military. In cyber operations, especially where physical effects are generated, it has become increasingly difficult to define the 'tip of the spear'. In the traditional framework of the Law of Armed Conflict, this has implications for the combatants' rights and obligations.[38]

Some legal scholars have argued that the nature of cyber weapons challenges the idea that one can separate the triggermen from others involved in the process. The complex nature of cyber weapons leads 'states to use contractors with technical expertise to constantly modify the features of a weapon in order to overcome the defence of the target, thus blurring the line between the traditional civilian task of weapons development and the traditional combatant task of weapons use'.[39] The *Tallinn Manual*, a non-binding but influential document, argues that 'any civilian fighting in a cyberwar loses legal protections as a civilian'.[40] From an international-law perspective, this suggests that private contractors may shift into the category of mercenary when the effect of an operation transcends a certain level of force and damage. The large number of contractors working for, and in many cases in, the US intelligence community in cyber-espionage operations are even more difficult to place in an international legal framework.[41] The *Tallinn Manual 2.0*, extending the potential coverage of international law governing cyber operations to peacetime legal regimes, avoids identifying the elephant in the room, stating that peacetime cyber espionage is not per se regulated by international law.[42]

In Israel, the defence of the nation relies heavily on both society and business. Universal conscription underlines the citizen-soldier character of the Israel Defense Forces (IDF). Civil–military dependence also extends to the relationship between the military and industry. If anything, cyber security intensifies these civil–military ties as the country aims to be a central player in the international cyber-security industry.[43] The famous 'revolving door' that is symptomatic of relations between government and the defence industry in the US defines the cyber-security 'industrial complex' of Israel as well. According to the *Financial Times*, there are 'few other countries where the military establishment mingle so closely with academia and business, to all three sectors' profit', and the IDF's Unit 8200 – the SIGINT service that also conducts cyber operations – is at the centre of it all.[44] The intimate relationship between its veterans and the booming Israeli high-end security start-up community – combined with the strong tradition of reserve forces – provides a potentially powerful mixture of private contracting and a 'whole of nation' approach to cyber security and cyber operations.[45] As Maurer indicates, such a high level of integration raises questions about the long-term viability of norms that are built on the public–private distinction.[46]

In China, the People's Liberation Army (PLA) has always been emblematic of the citizen-soldier model, even though the organisation answers to the Communist Party rather than the state or the people.[47] Three developments characterise the Chinese model of operating in cyberspace. Firstly, the activity and importance of 'patriotic hackers' have declined relative to the operations of state agencies. Prolific in the early and mid-2000s, vigilante hacker groups have been reined in by the government, while the PLA has vastly expanded its operations. Secondly, a marked shift has occurred from what GCHQ director Iain Lobban described as 'industrial espionage on an industrial scale' to more targeted and subtle operations, and on a much more limited political and economic scale.[48] The massive theft of Western intellectual property was temporarily stemmed by Mandiant's APT 1 report in 2013, the FBI's indictment of five PLA officers the following year, and the summit between US president Barack Obama and Chinese President Xi Jinping in 2015. For Xi, the public shame of the US indictment coincided with his own effort to reassert his control of the PLA by culling its business interests and ensuring its loyalty.[49] These reforms prepared the ground for the third development: a new realignment between the PLA units conducting cyber operations and the civilian Ministry of State Security responsible for foreign intelligence. China did not have a long tradition of investing in foreign espionage, having focused predominantly on internal security, but has professionalised its intelligence acquisition in the last two decades. The PLA's cyber operations have been consolidated and centralised in the Strategic Support Force to ensure better support for military operations, while the Ministry of State Security has been running more sophisticated APTs. As the role of the citizen-soldier

Political and economic espionage has been outsourced

hackers has diminished, the importance of the business sector, including high-tech companies such as Huawei and ZTE, has grown.[50] As with the US and Israel, the public sector in China seems unable to function without the private sector's cyber capacity.[51] The difference is that in China, the private sector remains subservient to the state.

Russia has a long history of using proxies in cyberspace. The 2007 Distributed Denial of Service (DDOS) attacks on Estonian websites involved patriotic hackers coalescing with criminal elements to conduct operations that were at the very least condoned by the Russian state.[52] Many links between cyber crime and the state have since surfaced. Firstly, Russian criminal malware has been discovered that incorporates espionage functionalities (Gameover Zeus), or was adapted for sabotage purposes (BlackEnergy).[53] Secondly, there are several examples of criminal hackers being recruited as employees of the security services. Thirdly, as shown by the Yahoo hack in 2013–14 and the subsequent FBI indictment, political and economic espionage has been outsourced to criminal hackers.[54] This fits into the broader picture whereby, according to Mark Galeotti, the Russian state has subsumed the underworld, ruling by decree when it can, and criminal violence when it must.[55] At the heart of the intersection between the state and the underworld lie the nation's security services, and it is no coincidence that those that hail from these units – the *siloviki* – hold the reins of power in contemporary Russia. Although patriotic hackers and criminal networks are harnessed to serve the interests of the state, the Russian Federal Security Service (FSB) is deeply involved in hacking operations, and entities it has enlisted have been heavily sanctioned by the United States. The main APTs appear to be run from the intelligence and security services. The civilian foreign-intelligence service (SVR) is known for its refined espionage operations (APT 29). The military-intelligence agency (GRU) runs the aggressive APT 28, its espionage operations frequently mutating into sabotage and subversion. The hack of the Democratic National Committee is a good example. APT 29 had been spying on the organisation months before APT 28 intruded and transferred the stolen data to WikiLeaks, manipulating the US electoral processes.[56]

The wrong track?

In view of state practices in cyberspace, leading non-governmental organisations, scholars and analysts may be on the wrong track in attempting to regulate behaviour. The key actors are foreign-intelligence agencies and private proxies. The United Nations Group of Governmental Experts did at least mention proxies in its 2013 report, stating that 'states must not use proxies to commit internationally wrongful acts. States should seek to ensure that their territories are not used by non-State actors for unlawful use of ICTs [information and communication technologies].'[57] Foreign-intelligence agencies and espionage activities, however, were barely mentioned, and certainly were not made subject to proposed norms. A legal and normative process that fails to address the primary actors in a given field is not a viable approach in the long run.

On the issue of proxies, two measures are crucial. Firstly, states must themselves review and specify the relationship between their military and intelligence agencies, on the one hand, and the cyber–industrial complex, on the other. If distinctions between procurement and consulting, and between weapons and operations, are fading, new rules are required to delineate civil and military responsibilities. Secondly, the cost–benefit equation needs to be altered for states using illegal proxies to conduct malicious activities in cyberspace. Given that deniability, as opposed to the projection of power, is the main advantage gained from the use of these proxies, logic dictates that removing that advantage could alter the calculus of political utility. The trend in both Russia and China points to less reliance on criminal proxies and patriotic hackers, the countries' intelligence services being primarily responsible for quantitative and qualitative increases in cyber activities. For both illegal proxies and espionage activities that deviate from 'acceptable practice', naming and shaming through attribution can change the calculus for the attacker. The idea of imposing costs to deter malicious actors from blatant transgressions of acceptable state behaviour, such as attacking critical infrastructure or manipulating elections, is acquiring mainstream traction. By increasing the cost of cyber attacks, the calculus for the defender may change too. If a well-founded and credible case of public attribution risks the loss of an intelligence source, that loss might be a lesser evil than the continued impunity of the aggressor.

Finally, states need to address the issue of espionage. Intelligence agencies have not only been responsible for a host of cyber attacks, but in many countries have also become the hub of expertise in cyber defence. The UK and Canada, for example, are making their SIGINT agencies the one-stop shop for all national cyber-defence activities, and many countries have embedded government computer-emergency response teams in the intelligence community.[58] Cyberspace has thus facilitated the diversification of spying activities beyond traditional espionage, with responsibilities ranging from the protection of government networks to executing offensive cyber operations abroad. States have traditionally been reluctant to address espionage in international forums, privileging the freedom of manoeuvre that silence afforded. Over time, however, the widening gap between state practice and the putative legal framework is not tenable. States are increasingly regulating intelligence activities at the national level. Solving the conundrum of cyber conflict and intelligence would require them to restrict their foreign-intelligence agencies purely to espionage. This is as unrealistic in cyberspace as it is in international relations. States, in general, are reluctant to unilaterally limit their own capabilities.[59]

An international framework therefore needs to be considered. For the past 100 years, an evolving body of international law and custom has shaped and restricted military activities. It is now time to start the process for espionage.

Notes

1   Isabelle Duyvesteyn, 'Between Doomsday and Dismissal: Collective Defence, Cyber War and the Parameters of War', *Atlantisch Perspectief*, 20 October 2014.

2   Compare Richard Clarke and Robert Knake, *Cyber War: The Next Threat to National Security and What to Do About It* (New York: Harper Collins, 2010) with Thomas Rid, *Cyber War Will Not Take Place* (London: C. Hurst and Company, 2013).

3   See Myriam Dunn Cavelty, 'The Militarisation of Cyberspace: Why Less May Be Better', in C. Czossceck, R. Ottis and K. Ziolkowski (eds), *4th International Conference on Cyber Conflict* (Tallinn: NATO CCD COE Publications, 2012); and Ronald J. Deibert, 'Black Code: Censorship, Surveillance, and the Militarisation of Cyberspace', *Millennium: Journal of International Studies*, vol. 32, no. 3, 2003, pp. 501–30.

4   Joseph Nye, Jr, 'Deterrence and Dissuasion in Cyberspace', *International Security*, vol. 41, no. 3, 2017, p. 50.

5   See Ben Buchanan, *The Cybersecurity Dilemma: Hacking, Trust and Fear Between Nations* (Oxford: Oxford University Press, 2017).

6   See Lucas Kello, 'The Meaning of the Cyber Revolution: Perils to Theory and Statecraft', *International Security*, vol. 38, no. 2, 2013, pp. 7–40; Thomas Rid, 'Cyber War Will Not Take Place', *Journal of Strategic Studies*, vol. 35, no. 1, February 2012, p. 5; and John Stone, 'Cyber War Will Take Place!', *Journal of Strategic Studies*, vol. 36, no.1, February 2013.

7   Michael Schmitt (ed.), *Tallinn Manual on the International Law Applicable to Cyber Warfare* (Cambridge: Cambridge University Press, 2013); Michael Schmitt (ed.), *Tallinn Manual 2.0 on the International Law Applicable to Cyber Operations* (Cambridge: Cambridge University Press, 2017).

8   'Report of the Group of Governmental Experts on Developments in the Field of Information and Telecommunications in the Context of International Security', UN General Assembly, Doc. A/70/174, 22 July 2015.

9   See Alex Grigsby, 'The End of Cyber Norms', *Survival*, vol. 59, no. 6, December 2017–January 2018, pp. 109–22.

10 Rory Corman and Richard Aldrich, 'Grey Is the New Black: Covert

Action and Implausible Deniability',
International Affairs, vol. 94, no. 3, May
2018, pp. 477–94.

11 Lene Hansen and Helen Nissenbaum,
'Digital Disaster, Cyber Security and
the Copenhagen School', *International
Studies Quarterly*, vol. 53, 2009, pp.
1,155–75.

12 Gary D. Brown and Andrew O.
Metcalf, 'Easier Said than Done: Legal
Reviews of Cyber Weapons', *Journal of
National Security Law & Policy*, vol. 7,
2014, pp. 115–38.

13 See Corman and Aldrich, 'Grey Is
the New Black: Covert Action and
Implausible Deniability'.

14 See, for example, Ashley S. Deeks,
'Confronting and Adapting:
Intelligence Agencies and
International Law', *Virginia Law
Review*, vol. 102, no. 3, 2016, pp.
599–685; Craig Forcese, 'Pragmatism
and Principle: Intelligence Agencies
and International Law', *Virginia Law
Review*, vol. 102, no. 1, 2016, pp. 67–84;
and Alexandra H. Perina, 'Black Holes
and Open Secrets: The Impact of
Covert Action on International Law',
Columbia Journal of Transnational Law,
vol. 53, no. 3, 2015, pp. 507–83.

15 Rid, 'Cyber War Will Not Take Place'.

16 See, for example, the cyber-operations
tracker maintained by the Council on
Foreign Relations, https://www.cfr.
org/interactive/cyber-operations. The
most convincing forensic evidence is
often made public by private security
firms. Most of these firms are Western,
and focus on APTs from China and
Russia. Some non-Western firms, such
as Kaspersky, are considered untrust-
worthy. See Thomas Rid and Ben
Buchanan, 'Attributing Cyber Attacks',
Journal of Strategic Studies, vol. 38, nos
1–2, 2014, pp. 4–37.

17 See James P. Farwell and Rafal
Rohozinski, 'Stuxnet and the Future
of Cyber War', *Survival*, vol. 53, no. 1,
February 2011, pp. 23–40.

18 David E. Sanger, *Confront and Conceal:
Obama's Secret Wars and Surprising Use
of American Power* (New York: Crown,
2012).

19 See Ryan Gallagher, 'Operation
Socialist', *Intercept*, 13 December 2014,
https://theintercept.com/2014/12/13/
belgacom-hack-gchq-inside-story/.

20 Andy Greenberg, 'The Code that
Crashed the World', *Wired*, September
2018, pp. 52–63.

21 Stilgherian, 'Blaming Russia
for NotPetya Was Coordinated
Diplomatic Action', *ZDNet*, 12 April
2018, https://www.zdnet.com/article/
blaming-russia-for-notpetya-was-
coordinated-diplomatic-action/.

22 See, for example, Jack Goldsmith, 'The
Sony Hack: Attribution Problems,
and the Connection to Domestic
Surveillance', *Lawfare*, 19 December
2014, https://www.lawfareblog.com/
sony-hack-attribution-problems-and-
connection-domestic-surveillance.

23 See David E. Sanger and Katie
Benner, 'U.S. Accuses North Korea
of Plot to Hurt Economy as Spy Is
Charged in Sony Hack', *New York
Times*, 6 September 2018, https://www.
nytimes.com/2018/09/06/us/politics/
north-korea-sony-hack-wannacry-
indictment.html.

24 Ash Carter, 'A Lasting Defeat: The
Campaign to Destroy ISIS', Harvard
Belfer Center Special Report, October
2017, p. 33, https://www.belfer-
center.org/sites/default/files/2017-10/

Lasting%20Defeat%20-%20final_0.pdf.

25 See, for example, Chris Bing, 'Command and Control: A Fight for the Future of Government Hacking', *Cyberscoop*, 11 April 2018, https://www.cyberscoop.com/us-cyber-command-nsa-government-hacking-operations-fight/.

26 Brown and Metcalf, 'Easier Said than Done'.

27 See Darien Pun, 'Rethinking Espionage in the Modern Era', *Chicago Journal of International Law*, vol. 18, no. 1, Summer 2017, pp. 361–2.

28 See Perina, 'Black Holes and Open Secrets'; and Forcese, 'Pragmatism and Principle'.

29 See Brown and Metcalf, 'Easier Said than Done', p. 128.

30 Max Smeets, 'A Matter of Time: On the Transitory Nature of Cyberweapons', *Journal of Strategic Studies*, vol. 41, nos 1–2, February 2017, pp. 6–32.

31 Brown and Metcalf, 'Easier Said than Done'.

32 See Janice E. Thompson, *Mercenaries, Pirates and Sovereigns* (Princeton, NJ: Princeton University Press, 1994).

33 Tim Maurer, *Cyber Mercenaries: The State, Hackers, and Power* (Cambridge: Cambridge University Press, 2018).

34 *Ibid.*, p. 20.

35 See Elke Krahmann, *States, Citizens and the Privatization of Security* (Cambridge: Cambridge University Press, 2010), pp. 21–50.

36 See Shane Harris, *@War: The Rise of the Military–Internet Complex* (Boston, MA: Houghton Mifflin Harcourt, 2014); and Lillian Ablon, Martin C. Libicki and Andrea Golay, *Markets for Cybercrime Tools and Stolen Data: Hackers' Bazaar* (Santa Monica, CA:

RAND Corporation, 2014).

37 See Maurer, *Cyber Mercenaries*, pp. 73–6.

38 *Ibid.*, pp. 14–16.

39 Vijah M. Padmanabhan, 'Cyber Warriors and the Jus in Bello', *International Law Studies*, vol. 89, 2013, pp. 288–308. See also Sean Watts, 'Combatant Status and Computer Network Attack', *Virginia Journal of International Law*, vol. 50, no. 2, 2010, pp. 391–447.

40 Schmitt (ed.), *Tallinn Manual*, Rule 35.

41 See, for example, Tim Shorrock, *Spies for Hire: The Secret World of Intelligence Outsourcing* (New York: Simon & Schuster, 2008).

42 Schmitt (ed.), *Tallinn Manual 2.0*, Section 5, Rule 32. See also Asaf Lubin, 'Cyber Law and Espionage as Communicating Vessels', in T. Minárik, R. Jakschis and L. Lindström (eds), *10th International Conference on Cyber Conflict – CyCon X: Maximising Effects* (Tallinn: CCD COE Publications, 2018), pp. 203–25.

43 See Dmitry Adamsky, 'The Israeli Odyssey Toward its National Cyber Security Strategy', *Washington Quarterly*, vol. 40, no. 2, 2014, pp. 113–27.

44 John Reed, 'Unit 8200: Israel's Cyber Spy Agency', *Financial Times*, 10 July 2015, https://www.ft.com/content/69f150da-25b8-11e5-bd83-71cb60e8f08c.

45 Alexander Klimburg, 'The Whole of Nation in Cyberpower', *Georgetown Journal of International Affairs*, vol. 11, 2010, pp. 171–9.

46 Maurer, *Cyber Mercenaries*, p. 154.

47 Nigel Inkster, *China's Cyber Power*, Adelphi 456 (Abingdon: Routledge for the IISS, 2016), pp. 88–93.

48 Gordon Corera, *Intercept: The Secret History of Computers and Spies* (London: Weidenfeld & Nicholson, 2015), p. 235.

49 See Mara Hvistendahl, 'The Decline in Chinese Cyberattacks: The Story Behind the Numbers', *MIT Technology Review*, 25 October 2016.

50 See Ana Swanson and Cecilia Kang, 'White House Considers Barring Chinese Telecom Sales as Tensions Mount', *New York Times*, 3 May 2018.

51 See Inkster, *China's Cyber Power*, p. 104; Maurer, *Cyber Mercenaries*, p. 108.

52 See Sheera Frenkel, 'Inside The Hunt for Russia's Hackers', *BuzzFeed*, 21 April 2017, https://www.buzzfeed.com/sheerafrenkel/inside-the-hunt-for-russias-hackers.

53 See Michael Schwirtz and Joseph Goldstein, 'Russian Espionage Piggybacks on a Cybercriminal's Hacking', *New York Times*, 12 March 2017.

54 Indictment, *United States vs. Dokuchaev*, US District Court for the Northern District of California, filed 28 February 2017, https://www.justice.gov/opa/press-release/file/948201/download.

55 Mark Galeotti, *The Vory: Russia's Super Mafia* (New Haven, CT: Yale University Press, 2018), pp. 257–8.

56 See Eric Lipton, David E. Sanger and Scott Shane, 'The Perfect Weapon: How Russian Cyberpower Invaded the U.S.', *New York Times*, 13 December 2016.

57 'Report of the Group of Governmental Experts on Developments in the Field of Information and Telecommunications in the Context of International Security', UN General Assembly, Doc. A/68/98, 24 June 2013.

58 Sergei Boeke, 'National Cyber Crisis Management: Different European Approaches', *Governance*, vol. 31, no. 3, July 2018, pp. 449–64.

59 See Dennis Broeders, 'Aligning the International Protection of "The Public Core of the Internet" with State Sovereignty and National Security', *Journal of Cyber Policy*, vol. 2, no. 3, November 2017, pp. 366–76.

The Strategic Challenge of Society-centric Warfare

Ariel E. Levite and Jonathan (Yoni) Shimshoni

Some 40 years ago, Michael Howard reminded us that strategy should comprise four dimensions – operations, technology, logistics and society.[1] In his 1979 article for *Foreign Affairs*, 'The Forgotten Dimensions of Strategy', he chastised strategists who failed to consider all four in an integrated fashion and to identify which is dominant in a particular situation, warning that doing so could result in poorly formulated and even dangerous strategies.[2] Howard argued that the social dimension was mostly forgotten in the twentieth century, even though Carl von Clausewitz, writing more than 200 years earlier, had underscored the importance of popular passions ('the people') as one of the three elements of war that together formed his 'remarkable trinity'.[3] The oversight is all the more noteworthy given the decisive role played by societies in shaping the outcomes of a number of strategic encounters, the war in Vietnam being a prominent twentieth-century example.

Howard's admonition came in the midst of the Cold War, at the heart of which lay strategies that threatened to annihilate all of humankind. That conflict provides a dramatic example of how technological advances (in this case, nuclear weapons) can blind the West from seriously considering the social dimension when formulating strategy.[4] Howard's observation is no less relevant today, in a conflict environment characterised by a new set

Ariel E. Levite is a Senior Fellow at the Carnegie Endowment for International Peace Nuclear Policy and Technology and International Affairs programmes. **Jonathan (Yoni) Shimshoni** is a Wilson Fellow at the Woodrow Wilson International Center for Scholars and a Research Affiliate at the MIT Security Studies Program.

Survival | vol. 60 no. 6 | December 2018–January 2019 | pp. 91–118   DOI 10.1080/00396338.2018.1542806

of technologies, including high-accuracy and autonomous conventional weapons, sensors, communications, computing and artificial intelligence.

While the social dimension has long been deeply ingrained in warfare and strategy, its centrality to twenty-first-century conflict has become extreme. Virtually all the actors now challenging the West – large and small, state and non-state, from al-Qaeda and Hamas to China and Russia – have adopted multifaceted strategies with society at their core. Indeed, these could be called society-centric strategies.[5]

Those Western powers most directly engaged in military confrontation – especially the United States and Israel, but also France, the United Kingdom and other NATO members, as well as Australia – have made important adaptations to address these challenges.[6] Yet none of them has fully come to terms with the rise of society-centric conflict. This shortfall, while understandable, can have serious unintended consequences, among them the preparation of misguided strategic assessments and the pursuit of impractical goals, resulting in unmet expectations, frustration, and civil–military and political friction. This essay explores the evolution, manifestations and logic of society-centric warfare, and reflects on its implications for apposite Western strategy formulation.

The social dimension

Regardless of the particular form it assumes, warfare is essentially a confrontation between societies; hence, the social dimension of strategy is always pertinent. Indeed, it could be seen as *primus inter pares* with respect to the other dimensions. Societies on all sides of a confrontation are typically tested in terms of their willingness to support (or otherwise influence) their leaders and warriors, to make sacrifices and demonstrate resilience, and to provide fighters and other resources for the fight. Unsurprisingly, leaders and strategists throughout history, when faced with or contemplating conflict, have been preoccupied with the future, behaviour and role both of their own societies and those of their adversaries.

Typically, strategists' first task in dealing with a society-oriented challenge is to buffer their own societies from the vagaries of war while mobilising their support, or at least their acquiescence. In some cases, strategists endeavour to 'de-societise', or detach, their own society from a conflict (for example, through the use of mercenaries and proxies) as a means either of enabling the state to pursue the conflict without engendering internal resistance, or, conversely, to avoid any build-up of social pressure to pursue or escalate a conflict. In other cases, leaders, perhaps perversely, do the opposite by putting their own citizens in harm's way, either as a deterrence strategy (as in the case of mutually assured destruction) or as a means of mobilising the population's support and garnering solidarity from other communities. In addition, leaders and strategists have often had to confront the corresponding challenge of undermining or otherwise shaping the adversary society's support for its own leadership and warriors, while either mobilising or keeping at bay any third-party societies which may have an interest in, or could potentially influence, the conflict.

Despite the perennial relevance of the social dimension, history has witnessed significant fluctuations in its centrality and role in strategy. In pre-modern contests of champions (as between David and Goliath) it was nearly absent from strategic consideration, a characterisation that also applies to medieval contests between knights and, later, to wars of mercenaries. This exclusion was possible largely because strategists on both sides could safely assume that their respective societies would accept (perhaps involuntarily) the outcomes of any contest in which they played no direct role, even when such confrontation had real bearings on their fortunes.

In other instances, the social dimension has been much more important, if not decisive. In these cases, it has been a critical enabler of leaders' strategies by facilitating the leveraging of the technological, operational or logistical dimensions. Howard, for example, saw Union strategy in the US Civil War in this light. Per his reading, the North enjoyed a logistical advantage, made possible by its social and economic wherewithal, that allowed it to circumvent the Confederacy's superiority in operations. In the Second World War, American wealth and social mobilisation combined with the exceptional sacrifices made by Soviet society to enable the technological and logistical superiority needed to overwhelm German operational excellence. Israel's strategy in the run-up to the Six-Day War is yet another example. Socio-economic constraints – the vulnerability of the Israeli population, the country's heavy dependence on a reserve army, and the expected toll of this army's mobilisation on the economy and society – dictated particular strategic principles. These included intolerance for protracted inactive mobilisation and the initiation of actual hostilities to break a fully mobilised and armed standstill, as well as a rapid offensive and conclusive blitzkrieg into enemy territory. These, in turn, leveraged Israel's superior human and social capital, and its small geography (in military parlance, its 'interior lines'), to create an operational advantage that offset the logistical and numerical edge enjoyed by the country's enemies.

In some situations, the social dimension is so central (Howard would say 'dominant'[7]) that it could be described as the principal foundation of a strategy. Where this has been the case, action on other dimensions is intended to endow strategic advantage through the social realm. Examples abound: early in the Peloponnesian War, for instance, the Athenian strategist Pericles, facing a technologically and operationally superior Sparta and a wary Athenian society, elected to evacuate the rural battlefields, an intense strategic move applied to his own society. It was designed to deprive Sparta of the opportunity to exploit its absolute advantage in land-based battles of annihilation, while allowing Athens to apply its own force with a societal logic, aiming to induce helot slaves to rise up against Spartan society to drive internal weakening.[8] Any number of historic sieges, blockades, sanctions, episodes of indiscriminate killing and forced migrations could also be considered instances of society-centric strategies. The often brutal conquest and subjugation of local societies by the European colonial enterprise represents an obvious application against militarily inferior foes, while Mao Zedong's guerrilla-warfare doctrine demonstrates a society-centric theory of victory, one that was dramatically and effectively implemented by the North Vietnamese against the otherwise superior US during the Vietnam War. At a sophisticated extreme, strategists have leveraged their opponents' actions on, say, the technological or operational dimensions to create a decisive advantage on the social front. A case in point is Mahatma Gandhi's Judo-like employment of passive resistance in the face of British brutality, which was intended to help Indians prevail over their militarily superior opponents by manipulating British and international opinion.[9]

Although this analysis has presented strategy formulation as a series of discrete choices, it is important to note, firstly, that the interplay between the various dimensions of strategy is often dynamic as strategists make adjustments in response to changing conditions. For example, Germany began the Second World War with an operations-dominant strategy. When victory proved elusive, however, it reverted to attacking British society directly with the intention of knocking the country out of the war through demoralisation. Correspondingly, as patience waned and frustration grew among the Allies, their strategy evolved from a rather classical approach centred on military-to-military operations to one centred on the massive conventional firebombing of cities in Europe and Japan, which ultimately escalated to the devastating nuclear attacks on Hiroshima and Nagasaki.

It is also important to understand how the assessment of the social dimension informs strategy development. The formulation of strategy is typically preceded by an assessment of both sides' critical vulnerabilities and relative strengths, and of any risks and opportunities across the four strategic dimensions. Importantly, even when such an assessment identifies the social dimension as critical, the resultant strategy may not necessarily be society-centric. The strategy developed by Israel's David Ben-Gurion in the late 1940s and 1950s is a case in point. His analysis concluded that Israeli society, which was then economically poor, had a high proportion of immigrants and was situated on a rather tiny piece of real estate, could not possibly withstand an extended conflict on Israeli territory. This judgement led him to formulate the operations-centric strategy described earlier, which was designed to offset these critical social vulnerabilities.

Societal challenge in the twenty-first century

Although the relative importance of the various dimensions of strategy has fluctuated over time, the social dimension appears to have appropriated centre stage in the twenty-first century, both in general terms and in the specific context of the challenges currently faced by the West. Some scholars and practitioners have begun to explore this development and to analyse its relevance to particular types of challengers, for the most part smaller, non-state entities.[10] Nevertheless, we believe that society-oriented or -centric challenges are today even more prevalent and comprehensive in nature than has been understood (or at least acknowledged) by scholars and strategists, and that this has profound implications for strategy formulation in the West. While we cannot exclude the possibility of a 'classical' technology- or operations-driven direct military clash between the US and China, such as over Taiwan or the East or South China seas, or with Russia, perhaps over the Baltic republics, these types of scenarios have become increasingly rare. Instead, strategies in which the West's challengers position social impact as the driving logic of actions on the technological and operational dimensions have become far more prevalent. This trend is apparent not only among smaller, non-state actors, but also applies to the West's peer rivals – Russia and China. In short, society-centric strategies have become mainstream.

Contemporary society-centric strategies are not only more prevalent, but have also become all-encompassing. They increasingly manifest a choice by strategists to influence, engage and penetrate, at an early stage, *all* of the societies relevant to a conflict, so as to achieve a variety of aims: offensive, defensive, deterrent and compellent. In addition, these strategies have become comprehensive in terms of the wide array of tools they employ. They apply military technology and operations to achieve direct and indirect societal impacts, while at the same time 'weaponising' and employing toward the same aim a plethora of social tools, dual-use technologies, the law, social networks, cyber, demographics and economics. Figure 1 depicts how people, organisations and civilian technologies and processes have themselves often become, separately and at times in concert, the direct goals (or ends) of conflict, the venue or battlespace chosen for operations, the weapons (means) and the methods (ways) applied.[11] One might term this phenomenon 'societal warfare', that is, warfare conducted by, within, through and against people and societies.

The choice by the West's adversaries to engage in this kind of warfare is usually motivated by their societies' relative weakness on the traditional, military-to-military operational and technological dimensions – and in some cases by their own social vulnerabilities – and is enabled by changes in technology, global society and economics. Other inducements include

Figure 1: **Twenty-first-century societal warfare**

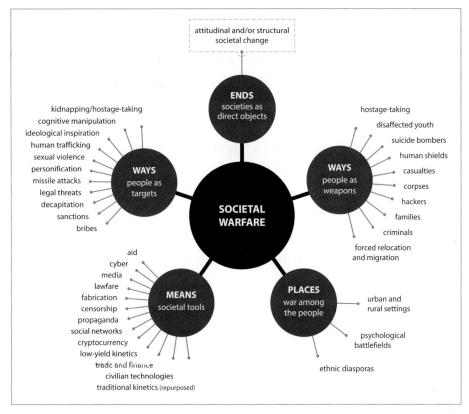

Western states' social penetrability, as well as a belief that the West is both structurally vulnerable and ill-prepared to confront such challenges.

Such all-encompassing, society-centric strategies are evident among the non-state challengers of Western nations, such as the Islamic State (ISIS). The group is well known for its brutal physical violence against civilians, images of which it has distributed through social and mainstream media in order to create certain psychological effects, pacify conquered areas and peoples, and penetrate and influence Western societies, not least to recruit and mobilise warriors to conduct operations on their own. In a different theatre, Hamas has been purposeful and effective in employing unarmed civilians, especially women and children, to conceal its warriors and to induce Israel to apply tremendous kinetic force in Gaza both to accord its own fighters immunity, and to leverage the resulting civilian casualties and physical destruction to influence all the societies relevant to the group's conflict with Israel – in Europe, the US, Israel, the wider Middle East and Gaza itself. Hizbullah, similarly, has focused its strategy vis-à-vis Israel on the social dimension and, like Hamas, has put civilians in harm's way by concentrating key military assets within heavily populated areas (as well as in schools, mosques and hospitals), and even by using ambulances for military operations. The key difference is that Hizbullah, which enjoys significant assistance from Iran, does so on a larger and more sophisticated scale. In pursuit of a deterrent threat that circumvents Israeli technology and offensive manoeuvre and fire operations, it has been systematically building up a diverse arsenal of some 150,000 rockets and missiles to target the entire Israeli population, while engaging in a massive propaganda and intimidation effort, much of it aimed directly at Israeli society.

Russian strategy blurs classical distinctions

Moving on to the competition between the West and its peer challengers, Russia's contemporary non-linear-warfare doctrine, in keeping with the tsarist and, even more so, Soviet–Leninist strategic tradition, reflects a society-centric paradigm. It is a multidimensional and multidisciplinary strategy that consciously blurs the classical distinctions between warriors and non-combatants, front and rear, peace and war, state and proxies, and fact and fiction; and which employs a variety of tools – military technology and operations, information and cyber, economic pressure, ethnic bridgeheads and sensitivities – in order to manipulate both rival societies and its own. By engaging in extensive deceit, deception and subterfuge, 'dispersing' confrontations to a number of different 'fronts', and 'diluting' the stark and unmistakable elements of military technological and operational action, the Russians have been challenging Western interests while remaining under the traditional *casus belli* threshold – a kind of twenty-first-century 'salami strategy'. Russia has applied elements of this society-centric approach in Chechnya, Crimea, Ukraine (and Eastern Europe more generally), Syria and with extensive meddling in US and Western European society and politics, directly targeting pre-identified societal groups and individuals.[12]

Seeing itself as being in an existential confrontation with an aggressive and revisionist West that has both domestic and international dimensions, Russia's strategy devotes much attention to all relevant societies. Even when formulating and executing offensive strategy, Russia directs considerable energy inward, to buffer its own society from any independent (particularly Western) sources of information and other means of influence, while employing a massive domestic censorship and propaganda machine, as well as more aggressive and sinister acts of intimidation, such as the selective elimination of regime opponents both in Russia and abroad. Local society is fed heavy doses of government propaganda to mobilise support for the state, while the regime acts simultaneously to maintain its freedom of action by de-societising – that is, by keeping Russian society in the dark about the actual costs (in resources and casualties) endured in conflicts it chooses to pursue. Russian strategy also endeavours to influence Western societies directly through attempts to penetrate and manipulate domestic processes via highly targeted campaigns, enabled by the new world of cyber and social media. These methods are rendered effective by virtue of striking Western (that is, liberal-democratic) weak spots that Western societies have difficulty in defending. They are also methods that the West is loath to use in retaliation.

Like Russia, China sees its confrontation with the external world as being closely intertwined with its domestic politics. China treats the social dimension as critical in its competitive relationships both generally and in the particular case of a potential future conflict with the US. In China, this orientation draws on a long history of society-oriented strategic approaches, stretching from Sun Tzu to Mao, of whom the latter's strategic framework and philosophy continue to guide and underlie Chinese strategic culture. It is evident in both the offensive and defensive realms, with the defensive realm being of particular contemporary significance in light of repeated and brutal colonial incursions by Japan and the West. A symptom of China's basic contemporary orientation is the social–political nature of its threat perception, which, like Russia's, focuses to a large extent on foreign – especially Western – ideological and cultural penetration as a major strategic threat. Western economic clout also looms large, and any dependence on

Western economies is perceived to be an acute source of vulnerability, a kind of Trojan Horse.

China's strategic response is similar to Russia's, but also distinct.[13] As embodied in the country's own variant of multi-domain warfare, the Chinese pursue, both offensively and defensively, the logical integration of traditional military technologies and operations with a variety of societal tools and capabilities encompassing geo-economics and demographic manipulation (including forced migrations and resettlement); information, propaganda and cyber; and diverse mechanisms for strict and intensifying domestic control and mobilisation. In pursuing its strategy, China exploits two related advantages that Russia has not: conventional military power and economic wherewithal. Developing economic (and related technological) strength has enabled China to build a formidable, all-domain military machine in keeping with the slogan 'rich nation strong army', one that is powerful enough to give the US (and its allies) serious pause in considering a conflict over Chinese territorial claims and aggression on its periphery. This aspect of China's strategy is more operations- and technology-centric, and in recent years has greatly amplified societal mobilisation to drive the technological dimension. One could reasonably claim that China has a dual-mode strategy that is at once technology- and society-centric.

China applies its economic clout to moves aimed directly at the social dimension both at home and abroad. Some of the latter are intended to disrupt the Western alliance system in Asia. These include various Belt and Road initiatives, China-led alternatives to World Bank-like institutions (such as the Asian Infrastructure Investment Bank), and outright economic coercion (for example, of the Philippines). Direct attitudinal and cognitive operations include undertakings such as Confucius Institute activities on university campuses worldwide. On the domestic front, the state imposes extreme measures to both fan nationalist sentiments and ensure tight control of information flows within its own society. At the same time, Chinese economic development has created a wealthy elite with a loyalty stake in the system.

China also makes more direct strategic use of its economic clout as a deterrence tool. It has sent a clear message to the US that, in the event of hostilities, it will not afford Americans the luxury of limiting the exchange to the traditional technological and operational spheres (in which the West will likely possess an advantage for some years to come). Rather, if necessary it will exploit its position in the Western economic and financial systems to wreak sociopolitical havoc. Remarkably, China has made skilful use of these techniques to target not only foreign governments, but also prominent foreign private-sector players and broad swaths of foreign populations, with the goal of motivating them to act as a kind of 'fifth column' in their home countries that would act to moderate action in the event of hostilities, even if aimed to check Chinese expansionism.

The West

An environment in which adversaries confront Western powers with predominantly society-centric strategies poses acute challenges for the West, particularly those Western powers that find themselves at the cutting edge of such confrontations. Yet the difficulty does not emanate from a Western inability or ingrained aversion to engage on the social dimension. On the contrary, Western states have themselves long displayed a willingness to coerce or otherwise influence adversary societies directly. At times, this aim has been pursued with great brutality, as in the colonial enterprise, the American West, and the firebombing of London and Tokyo. In other cases, efforts have been covert and underhanded, such as the practice of bribing drug lords to buy freedom for military action in Southeast Asia; and sophisticated, such as Dwight Eisenhower's public Cold War diplomacy. Some attempts have involved the coercive application of economic instruments (such as the Iran sanctions), while others have employed constructive economic tools (such as the Marshall Plan). Western manipulative efforts have even been aimed at allied societies, such as the British campaign to sway American public opinion in favour of entering the Second World War; and domestically, as exemplified by the extensive disinformation-based manipulation of the American public by US administrations during the war in Vietnam.

There is ample evidence that Western strategists are slowly waking up to the sobering reality that the strategic environment has become rife with social-centric challenges. However, this understanding has been evident mainly with respect to smaller and non-state challengers. In that context, various conceptual formulations have been devised, such as 'fourth-generation war', 'asymmetric warfare', 'new war' and 'war among the people'. In the US, new operational approaches such as counter-insurgency and stability operations have emerged, buttressed by attempts to establish organisational 'infrastructure', such as the Human Terrain System.[14]

In pursuing these operational constructs, Western militaries have exhibited a remarkable degree of adaptation. Thus, traditional force formations, armed with super-high-tech weapons that were designed for more conventional wars, have been fundamentally refashioned for societal settings. This has been done, for example, by focusing on the stand-off capacity to engage in the discriminate targeting of warriors and materiel with highly accurate (and in some cases very low-yield) munitions, uninhabited aerial vehicles (UAVs) and even battle tanks, and thus to avoid the risks (and casualties) of ground-force incursions. Moreover, and in keeping with Western militaries' proclivity to meet operational challenges with technological solutions, a massive effort has recently been launched to leverage breakthroughs in artificial intelligence and telecommunications, with the aim of fielding autonomous fighting capabilities designed to enable Western forces to engage in messy societal conflicts without the use of ground troops (or 'boots on the ground'), thus sparing them the agony of physical friction with adversary societies. At a higher level of organisation, the US has attempted to approach such conflicts with 'all of government' or diplomatic, informational, military and economic (DIME) formulations, reflecting an understanding that addressing a society-centric challenge requires the application of multiple tools in a coordinated fashion.

Similarly, in its own 'long war' with Hamas and Hizbullah, Israel has made important strategic adjustments for what it terms 'campaigns between the wars'. In its approach to these extended periods between major flare-ups, Israel Defense Forces (IDF) command has adopted a 'crisis management' mindset. It employs a strategy aimed at preventing, or at least

> *The IDF has a 'crisis management' mindset*

postponing, major flare-ups rather than seeking elusive military solutions to these intractable conflicts. This approach is pursued through a thoughtful combination of various carefully crafted kinetic and intelligence operations on the one hand, and more directly population-oriented efforts on the other. Operations consist mainly of surgical airstrikes and special operations, but also encompass massive, technologically rich defensive deployments of missiles and anti-tunnel defences. These activities aim to enhance traditional deterrence and to prepare for war, but strive to steer clear of attacking or even indirectly targeting civilian populations. These operations are commonly accompanied by and integrated with large-scale communications campaigns aimed directly at adversary societies. They are designed to impress on them the perils of another round of military confrontation with Israel, their likely defeat in any such encounter and the pain their people will endure in the process.

The IDF's actions and words during its interwar campaigns are also combined to drive home the point that Israel is not keen for another round of fighting, and to dissuade adversary populations from supporting such adventures, a message repeatedly reinforced by conciliatory economic and humanitarian activity aimed directly at Palestinian, Syrian (especially in the Golan Heights) and Lebanese societies in general, and in Gaza in particular. This approach has found its most dramatic expression (given the visceral enmity between Israel and Hamas) in Israel's Gaza policy since 2014. The IDF (alongside the General Security Service) has been lobbying Israeli political leaders to encourage and facilitate significant improvements in Gazans' quality of life as a way to help avert wars of social desperation, and thus prevent another unwanted round of military confrontation. Indeed, the IDF and its related Ministry of Defense organs have recently gone so far as to actively solicit international help in providing humanitarian assistance and undertaking massive civilian reconstruction in Gaza.

In response to the targeting of their own homelands, Western states have become increasingly attentive to the strategic role of their own societies. This has mostly been reflected in a heightened emphasis on defensive measures. Western security responses, which have evolved gradually and often in a belated or ad hoc way, have aimed to protect domestic societies from physical or cyber-based attack, as well as manipulation and subversion. Responses have included aggressive intelligence and police efforts, ever tighter immigration controls and transportation-security measures, cyber defences, country-wide missile defence (most prominently in Israel), selective censorship of social media, and (in Israel and the US) physical walls and border fences. In addition, Western regimes have acted instinctively to diminish the domestic social footprint of often contentious foreign operations by exploiting stand-off systems, minimising ground-force operations, and using special-operations forces and professional soldiers, as well as subcontractors and proxies, instead of conscripts or reservists wherever possible.

Despite the growing awareness of, and adjustment to, society-centric challenges by key Western militaries and security establishments, it is fair to say that their strategic responses still fall short. Firstly, there is a reluctance to recognise the prevalence and mainstreaming of society-centric strategies among all of the West's major rivals, and to respond in kind to this development. Thus, the US has remained focused on operations- and technology-centred military confrontations with China and Russia, devoting only modest effort toward society-centric strategies for small wars. By the same token, Israel's paradigm of action for war (as distinguished from its campaigns between the wars) continues to reflect a traditional and heavy-handed technology- and operations-dominant strategy, as though a classical military-to-military logic applies.[15]

Secondly, Western militaries and defence establishments have had understandable difficulty in responding holistically to the truly comprehensive nature of twenty-first-century society-centric challenges. Even where adjustments *have* been made to address the social dimension in small confrontations, the entire social ecosystem of a given conflict is rarely taken into account, and integrated consideration of offence and defence, or of all the relevant societies, is lacking. Thus, American counter-insurgency and stability operations do (by definition) account for and incorporate rival or target societies, but do not consider or integrate any analysis of the impact on (and requirements of) US and third-party societies. On the flip side, while homeland-security efforts have been made to defend against physical, informational and cyber attacks on Western societies, these have largely been implemented without considering their impact on other relevant societies, and the strategic implications thereof. An extreme recent example of this is the hastily decreed and politically inspired US ban on immigration from several predominantly Muslim countries.

Israel, for its part, has been guilty of ignoring the broader societal ramifications of its actions. The IDF has devoted much innovative energy to the protection of its own society and to severing it from conflict. At the same time, it has invested extensive resources and much effort to diminish non-combatant casualties and minimise collateral damage in combat. Yet the IDF remains wedded to the application of immense kinetic pressure in operations, with only scant and superficial attention given to the impact of these military operations on adversary societies in Lebanon and Gaza, and relatively little consideration of their effect on Palestinian, Arab, Muslim and Western societies. Where the IDF does account and aim for societal impact, this is done more as an afterthought, peripheral to, or supportive of, the 'core' military effort.

'Winning' may not be an option

Perhaps the most severe shortcoming is conceptual. For the most part, Western military strategists are still largely fixated on quickly and efficiently inflicting maximal harm to armed adversaries to secure a military decision. With the exception of insurgency or stability challenges, they have not yet fully grasped that enduring success may only be achievable on the societal battlefield. Indeed, in cases where conflicts are driven by rival sociopolitical motivations – as in the cases of the Vietnam War and Israel's conflict with the Palestinians – 'winning' may not even be an option. And while fighting and killing may be inevitable, 'bombing (longer and more intensely) to win' often serves only to make matters worse.[16] Yet Western strategists have failed to fundamentally adjust the logic of their military operations in line with society-centric conflict or to drive the development of supporting holistic, integrated, behavioural-science-informed theory. In the absence of such theory, even when consideration of the social dimension does occur, this is mostly intuitive and misguided, and frequently leads to an ever stronger proclivity to further refine, upgrade and apply existing technological and operational solutions.

Western nations have been paying dearly for this mismatch between the nature and requirements of the society-centric battlefield and their own strategic responses. They have misread a range of contemporary challenges and opportunities, and pursued strategic objectives that are simply unachievable within established ethical standards and at acceptable prices. The result has often been frustratingly costly, agonisingly protracted and ultimately unwinnable external engagements. Recent cases in point include Western campaigns in Iraq and Afghanistan, Libya and even Mali. All of these conflicts illustrate the potential consequences of confronting smaller and otherwise inferior rivals on the wrong dimensions. Israel, for its part, has endured a series of sobering lessons in both Gaza and Lebanon, to say nothing of earlier Palestinian uprisings in the 1980s and 1990s. In all of these cases, Western forces have discovered that, while overwhelming military might and technological dominance can be leveraged effectively against classical combatants, they may ultimately fail against presumably inferior but very highly motivated adversaries that implement society-centric strategies.

Israel has endured sobering lessons

If this is true of confrontations with dramatically inferior military adversaries, imagine the likely consequences of a Western conflict with peer or near-peer competitors that are no less adept at, and willing to engage in, society-centric warfare. Looking to the future, Western nations risk a debacle with profound political and strategic consequences if they engage in a society-centric confrontation with Russia, China or Iran without having adequately prepared. Some might suggest that this kind of confrontation is inevitable, or indeed, already under way, yet there is little evidence that Western nations have absorbed and adjusted to what is fundamentally a societal challenge. Worse still, a form of cultural blindness among Westerners rooted in a failure to understand how their adversaries see the world can only serve to make a confrontation more likely. Western nations may be unwittingly motivating their rivals to pursue confrontation by failing to see how threatening the West's 'peaceful' activities to promote democracy, human rights and the rule of law appear to other countries – let alone less-than-peaceful interventions in the name of the Responsibility to Protect.

If the strategic mismatch is so obvious, and if the price of misdirection is so high, why haven't the US and Israel at least, as the Western states with the most to gain *and* lose, fully aligned their strategies to the society-centric environment? Three clusters of non-mutually exclusive reasons suggest themselves. The first encompasses organisational bias and bureaucratic conservatism. Mainstream Western militaries are fundamentally reluctant to conceive of their core mission as dealing with societies, whether their own society (which largely lies outside the legitimate constitutional scope of their activity) or those of its adversaries. Their deeply held self-identities, which in democracies are often constitutionally enshrined, compel them to regard their *raison d'être* as confronting adversaries' military might and achieving victory through conquest, destruction and killing. They live by crucial dichotomies such as war and peace, victory and defeat, combatants and non-combatants, front and rear, and legitimate battlefield and home front – distinctions that tend to lose their meaning in a social-centric environment. Western militaries recoil from any notion that their mainstay is high-intensity, open-ended commitments that embed them in politically fraught situations involving non-combatants and their own societies, that defy standard military metrics of effectiveness and success, and that detract from their focus on high-end confrontation with peer adversaries.

Secondly, there is strong political and cultural aversion among Western societies, and even more so among their governing elites, to acknowledge – and to educate their publics to accept and support – society-centric conflicts, which very often are open-ended engagements that are not aimed at achieving clear-cut victory in a relatively short period of time. This reluctance has immediate bearing on publics' willingness to provide the resources and make the necessary constitutional adjustments to come to grips with the challenges presented by society-centric warfare. This is a formidable problem, because the adoption of a society-centric strategic approach would have to be preceded by a truly painful choice to actually wage society-centric warfare, to confront its implications at home, and to accept that most Western states already engage in this kind of warfare, even if only inadvertently. These problems are further exacerbated by the objective difficulty of defining goals and missions in an amorphous society-centric environment – a daunting and high-risk task that leaders are happy to avoid, often by simply denying the social nature of the challenge and the required response, or by taking refuge in Western societies' unmatched capacity to devise and field technological solutions.

The third type of barrier lies in the enormity of the task of adjusting to society-centric warfare, which would require much more than aligning military organisation and force structure. Doing so would entail a fundamental reorientation of how the military and defence establishments think and prepare to engage adversaries. It would necessitate a holistic theory incorporating a new language, a different set of variables and a logic that revolves around societal influence, an adjusted framework for civil–military relations, and even new ethical constructs. Thus far, neither of the parties that would be needed to bring this about – defence and military establishments, and academics specialising in the behavioural sciences – has shown any sustained interest in this project, though there have been important focused forays that could serve as a starting point.[17]

To be fair, all this would be a very steep order, and the evident reluctance among Western governments to take these steps is understandable. Yet the relevant strategic challenges will not go away simply because Western states are disinclined to deal with them. The time has come for Western military and political leaders, regardless of whether they favour isolation, restraint or intervention, to formulate the required strategy for this environment.

Formulating strategy for a society-centric environment

The military and security principals of all Western states aim to devise strategies that achieve high-level goals within the constraints, guidelines and considerations defined by national political leaders.[18] Examples of high-level goals might be to 'conquer', 'expel', 'contain', 'stabilise' or 'defend against'. Examples of constraints or guidelines might include statements such as 'all-out war is acceptable'; 'hostilities, but without ground troops'; 'conciliation is out of the question'; 'in any case, keep us out of trouble with x'; 'do not target the adversary's leaders as we will need them in order to secure a settlement'; 'the time limit for execution is y weeks (note the lack of support at home for prolonged violent engagement)'; 'it is apparent that our rival is motivated by internal political strife'; and 'our two sides have irreconcilable nationalist and religious aims'. In explicitly providing such guidance, or at least implicitly revealing such preferences, national leaders would also naturally steer the military toward a basic posture, such as defence, deterrence, compellence, outright offence (including pre-emption) or attrition warfare.

Some of these examples underscore the importance, in a society-centric strategic environment, of infusing the deliberations regarding high-level goals with a competitive consideration of the social strengths, weaknesses, vulnerabilities, motivations and intents on all sides of the conflict, alongside a high-level assessment of the societal dynamics and impacts that could flow from different modes of confrontation. This analysis would also consider how to 'sell' policy choices to various relevant constituencies, how to protect one's own society from any undesirable consequences of the selected goals, and how to maximise the desirable effects both on the adversary's society and on international publics, all while minimising any counterproductive impact on both the adversary's society and international public opinion. An important aspect of this kind of analysis and decision-making should be a hard critical look at the extent of achievable goals, given that the society-centric strategic environment has a way of playing havoc with strategies that aim for clear, deep and far-reaching achievements.[19]

The natural expectation is for military leaders to translate this guidance and analysis into a coherent strategy – an ends–ways–means chain or theory of victory.[20] Such an exercise should help identify the respective social vulnerabilities that need to be offset and the opportunities that might be seized upon in the course of a confrontation, including opportunities to address an opponent's advantages on the social dimension, or to circumvent them by emphasising another dimension. Importantly, serious attention must be paid to the social dimension regardless of which dimension is deemed central, as that is where the rival will likely be focusing its efforts.

Proceeding on the assumption that strategic planners do choose society as the central pillar of their strategy, they would then turn to formulating and operationalising this strategy with its particular set of concepts and logic, weaving it into the classical ends–ways–means construct. Attention should first turn to ends (or objectives), which in this case would pertain to both the adversary's society and to the planners' own, in addition to any relevant third-party societies. Society-centric ends could include the restoration of societal support for an incumbent foreign regime, as in counter-insurgency strategies; hastening the establishment of a regime that enjoys popular support; encouraging social fragmentation and state disintegration; weakening or suppressing (temporarily or permanently) an adversary's social mobilisation and reorienting its problematic policies; and even mobilising (or demobilising) international society. As regards planners' own society, objectives might include protecting it from attack or subversion, creating support for the chosen strategy or, alternatively, de-societising the conflict with the goal, inter alia, of inducing public indifference.

Moving on, the socially oriented strategist would next need to concentrate on the ways to accomplish these goals. A first challenge would be to identify the social equivalent of the traditional military centres of gravity. Having done so, strategists would then need to determine how critical elements of the adversary society could be induced to perform particular actions or adopt desired attitudes, for example though coercion, persuasion, bribery, subversion, diversion or even positive inducements. Some portions of the society might need to be effectively pacified, say by decapitation, intimidation, detention, demographic control or relocation – threatened or actual. Strategic planners may also have to devise ways to interdict possible third-party interventions in support of the adversary, possibly by acting on global public opinion, allies, sympathisers and courts. And planners' own societies should not be overlooked: depending on the situation, physical or information-based protections may need to be devised, and informational and attitudinal 'engineering' (including calibration of expectations) may be necessary to mobilise society and secure its support. De-societising, for example by avoiding the use of ground troops, might also be necessary. Naturally, such analysis should be extended to relevant third-party societies as well. In any event, the choice of ways should not merely be guided by considerations of expediency, but ought to be governed by Western legal and ethical standards and constraints.

Finally, a coherent society-centric strategy must provide the means to enable these ways. These may include geo-economic tools, cyber operations, the use of social media and other information channels, physical walls and missile defence, the employment of large conscript or professional forces, military alliances, and the use of proxies and subcontractors. Naturally, traditional military technological and operational arsenals might also be relevant. However, in designing their application, careful consideration must be given to their potential societal impact, so that they work together in synergy with the other selected means in support of the overall strategy. Most importantly, this approach rejects outright prevailing schemes featuring two separate missions, one directed at cognition and attitudes by applying 'soft' or 'sharp' means, the other kinetic in nature and aimed at battlefield results. Full integration is imperative.[21]

Inducements warrant special attention in society-centric situations because these may be most effective in swaying peoples' motivations, certainly when applied – in harmony with Thomas Schelling's

Full integration is imperative

work on the strategic role of promises and threats[22] – in combination with coercive measures. In addition to humanitarian aid, these positive levers may include security assistance, reassurances and confidence-building measures with various factions in society, as well as geo-economic moves such as permitting economic development, promoting investment, or offering outright assistance to the targeted population as a whole or an especially important subset thereof. Such tools may be particularly effective when the desired end is to achieve long-term attitudinal change.

In a sense, the task facing the strategist can be seen as one of 'social engineering'. Hence, success in this endeavour hinges on developing operable theories of social influence and relating them to the employment of the more traditional technological, operational and logistical elements of war in concert with the newer – social – set of arrows. Digging deeper, this will require a profound and broad socio-psychological understanding of such elements as identity and affiliation, perceptions, emotions and motivations, religious beliefs and predilections, and attitudes to time – all of which are often infused with economic behaviour – both at the individual and the collective levels. In short, a bridge must be built between social theories of influence from the behavioural disciplines and traditional military science.

The aim should be to provide Western strategy a supporting model (or theory) of societal impact (and its limits) on which to draw for more apposite strategic analysis and formulation.[23]

To be actionable and effective, such an approach will require a new conceptual language, translating socially oriented ends, ways and means into terminology that is militarily comprehensible. Traditional terms, such as 'deterrence', 'compellence' and 'security dilemmas', might still be applicable when related to societies, but will assume new meanings and may also have to be used differently. This is also true for core military concepts such as centres of gravity (*schwerpunkts*), combatants and non-combatants, front and rear, and peacetime and wartime. Furthermore, non-military concepts, such as conciliation and inducement, might have to be admitted into the military–strategic lexicon. Finally, and most critically, it will be imperative to jettison, or at least loosen the hold of, the seductive victory–defeat dichotomy, and replace it with the admittedly less inspiring idea of 'success'. As one American general put it, 'perhaps we need to ask at every stage of a confrontation "who's winning", but without expecting or striving to get to "who won"'.[24]

It *can* be done

Lest this proposition seem too unwieldy, theoretical and ambitious, it is worth recalling that in 2007–08, the US did actually think through and formulate strategy along the lines envisioned here in mounting the surge in Iraq. The point of departure for this innovative strategy was the sobering realisation, late in the post-invasion period, of the dual challenge faced by Washington. The US was failing miserably in its efforts to arrest the accelerating violence in Iraq, to stabilise the country and even to effectively protect its own forces, having alienated critical parts of Iraqi society and destroyed sociopolitical infrastructure (such as local security forces) which could have assisted the regime in solidifying control. At the same time, these processes, with no end in sight, were quickly undermining political and public support in the US for this extended, bloody and unsuccessful engagement. There was also a growing realisation that the goal of building a Western-style democratic Iraq was 'a bridge too far', a mission that was not just unattainable but counterproductive.

Development of a more fitting strategy began with the attribution of failure to the 'disconnect' between the more classical military deployment and strategy employed theretofore, and the particular social dynamics prevalent in Iraq, along with the challenges that these presented. A critical first step in adjusting the US approach was to minimise and redefine mission goals, rolling them back from the earlier expansive and unrealistic idea of birthing a peaceful, democratic Iraq to the much lower benchmark of moderating the level of violence enough to allow the US to withdraw most of its forces. Another important redirection was to recognise and leverage the actual (as opposed to the wishfully imagined) dynamics of Iraqi society. This, in turn, dictated a shift in focus from the national leadership to local and tribal leaders to create alliances, muster support and gain control of the population in ways that were effective in Iraqi society, even though some of these methods sat uneasily with prevailing American military norms.

The surge in US force levels enabled the military to prop up local confidence, mostly by 'embedding' troops within local communities, physically compartmentalising rival groups in urban areas, and conducting numerous special operations intended to reduce insurgent fighting, limit the insurgency's financial capabilities and cripple its leadership. These activities were intended to promote confidence and catalyse local alliances, as a foundation for social–political moves such as expanding the Sunni Awakening, fostering economic and civil-infrastructure development, empowering the judicial system and encouraging reconciliation. They were reinforced by local public-relations and targeted-information campaigns in Iraq, as well as by efforts to maintain public and political support in the US. The success of this effort made it possible to fundamentally alter the situation on the ground, stabilising the country enough to rekindle support and patience back home and, ultimately, for the US to be able to dramatically decrease its military presence in Iraq.[25] The surge thus embodied an attempt to fashion a comprehensive and integrated strategy oriented around the social dimension, weaving together multiple elements – including traditional military technology and operations – but fundamentally subjecting their employment to a society-centred logic based on a deep understanding of the actual dynamics of Iraqi society.

It is true that the strategic reorientation of American strategy in Iraq occurred only after bitter setbacks, but this allows for a useful comparison of 'before and after'. In ways that echo and illustrate important insights gained from the long history of British and French counter-insurgency, the Iraqi experience demonstrates that, when facing a society-centric strategic challenge, even one that is military or coercive in nature, the key to strategic success does not rest exclusively, nor even primarily, with the leveraging of classical technology or operations. Nor does it lie with the pursuit of military victory or even influence, much as hands-on coercive means may remain an important part of the strategic mixture. Instead, a multidimensional, society-centric strategy is called for, one founded on a deep understanding of the social forces at play on all sides, and on an analysis of ways to leverage these forces through the integrated application of various tools of force, society and statecraft.

The approach to strategy formulation described here is not offered as a 'technical fix' that can guarantee success. In a world of society-centric warfare, the 'fog of war' is likely to be even murkier than in the case of traditional technology- and operations-centric conflicts, further amplifying the fortune-setting roles of the unforeseeable and the incomprehensible – and of plain good luck. However, adopting this approach should minimally ensure that Western nations and their forces approach the correct battlespace with the right mindset, suitably trained and armed with the relevant equipment, and with a good understanding of the conflict's guiding logic and rules of engagement. As Clausewitz himself put it: 'The first, the supreme, the most far-reaching act of judgment that the statesman and commander have to make is to establish … the kind of war on which they are embarking.'[26]

Acknowledgements

The authors wish to thank the MIT Security Studies Program for providing critical support in the early stages of our work, and the Carnegie Endowment for International Peace for its sustained encouragement and support of our research programme. In addition, we are grateful to the Office of Net Assessment at the US Department of Defense and its Associate Director Andrew May for sponsoring a workshop dedicated to the issue of society-centric warfare. The authors are further indebted to the workshop participants for their invaluable insights and suggestions: Eliot Cohen, Jacqueline Newmyer Deal, Etienne de Durand, Aaron Friedberg, Kelly Greenhill, Bruce Jentleson, Athanassios Platias and Katarzyna Zysk. We also thank Taylor Fravel, George Perkovich, Roger Petersen, Barry Posen, Stephen Van Evera and Robert Willig for their critical input, insight and feedback as our work progressed.

Notes

1 The authors are grateful to Eliot Cohen for drawing their attention to Michael Howard's conceptual contribution and its relevance to this study.

2 Michael Howard, 'The Forgotten Dimensions of Strategy', *Foreign Affairs*, vol. 57, no. 5, Summer 1979.

3 The other two elements are usually translated as 'the army' and 'the government'.

4 We refer to 'strategy' as the embodiment of an actor's 'theory of victory' for a possible or actual confrontation, while 'confrontation' refers to an exchange of blows as well as to coercive postures (moves), such as deterrence and compellence.

5 While we believe that society-centric conflict characterises both domestic and international conflict, this essay focuses on the international expression of war and strategy.

6 Western states (principally the US, the UK, France and Israel) may have much in common in terms of the general challenges they face, but their strategic approaches display some significant differences, partly because the immediacy of various threats changes from country to country, and partly because of their differing histories. This essay focuses primarily on the US and Israel as the countries at the forefront of society-centric confrontations, but its findings are broadly applicable to all Western states.

7 Whereas Michael Howard used the term 'dominant', we have chosen to use the term 'central', as in our view it better conveys the idea of a dimension as an axis or a hub, in systemic

and mutual interaction with the other three dimensions.

8 See Athanassios G. Platias and Constantinos Koliopolous, *Thucydides on Strategy* (Athens: Eurasia Publications, 2006).

9 Another illustration would be the strategy underpinning mutually assured destruction during the Cold War. While this might appear at first to be a purely technology-centric deterrent strategy, it may be more appropriately described as society-centric, for it rested on putting both one's opponents' and one's own societies at risk of annihilation, a strategy necessitated and then supported by advanced capabilities in the technological realm.

10 For a truly remarkable early foray into this territory, see Andrew Mack, 'Why Big Nations Lose Small Wars: The Politics of Asymmetric Conflict', *World Politics*, vol. 27, no. 2, January 1975, pp. 175–200. More recent studies include Roger W. Barnett, *Asymmetrical Warfare: Today's Challenge to US Military Power* (Washington DC: Brassey's Inc., 2003); Lawrence Freedman, *The Future of War: A History* (New York: Hachette, 2017); Efraim Inbar (ed.), *Democracies and Small Wars* (London: Frank Cass, 2003); Mary Kaldor, 'In Defence of New Wars', *Stability: International Journal of Security and Development*, vol. 2, no. 1, 2013, pp. 1–16; William S. Lind et al., 'The Changing Face of War: Into the Fourth Generation', *Marine Corps Gazette*, October 1989, pp. 22–6; Emile Simpson, *War from the Ground*

Up: Twenty-First-Century Combat as Politics (New York: Oxford University Press, 2013); Rupert Smith, *The Utility of Force: The Art of War in the Modern World* (New York: Alfred A. Knopf, 2005); and Martin Van Creveld, *The Transformation of War* (New York: The Free Press, 1991). For an ongoing discussion and exchange with respect to small wars, see *Small Wars Journal* at http://smallwarsjournal.com/.

11 Figure 1 also draws attention to the manner in which the application of traditional military technologies has been adapted to serve the logic of a society-centric environment.

12 While there is general agreement that such a direct societal attack is a very serious matter, whether it should be seen as equivalent to an armed attack is a matter of some contention.

13 For an interesting framing of Russian and Chinese strategies as 'comprehensive coercion', see Thomas G. Mahnken, Ross Babbage and Toshi Yoshihara, *Countering Comprehensive Coercion: Competitive Strategies Against Authoritarian Political Warfare* (Washington DC: Center for Strategy and Budgetary Assessments, 2018).

14 For the US approach with respect to insurgency, stability and special operations, see *US Government Counterinsurgency Guide* (Washington DC: US Department of State, 2009); US Joint Chiefs of Staff, 'Stability', Joint Publication 3-07, August 2016; US Army, *FM 3-24 Counterinsurgency* (Washington DC: US Army Headquarters, December 2006); and United States Special Operations Command, 'Doctrine for Special Operations', August 2011.

15 While the IDF's impressive effort to mitigate the risk of international opprobrium for illegal or unethical behaviour on the society-centric battlefield may reflect an understanding that 'things have changed', the IDF has *not* amended its basic strategic approach, nor the core principles of its campaign planning.

16 See Robert A. Pape, *Bombing to Win: Air Power and Coercion in War* (Ithaca, NY: Cornell University Press, 1996).

17 The integration of behavioural scientists in field combat units was actually attempted in the US Army Human Terrain System experiment in Afghanistan and Iraq. The difficulties of such bridging are illustrated by the experiment's demise. For an overview, see Christopher Sims, 'Academics in Foxholes: The Life and Death of the Human Terrain System', *Foreign Affairs*, 4 February 2016.

18 This section attempts to present and argue for a way of *thinking* about strategy, and therefore presents a stylised process. In reality, strategy-making does not proceed in a strictly linear fashion, but rather is determined to a large extent by a country's strategic culture and by the decisions of domestic actors with varying degrees of political power.

19 Of note in this regard is General Raymond Odierno's call in 2008 to come to terms with an 'irreducible minimum' level of violence in Iraq. See reference in Anthony H. Cordesman, Adam Mausner and Elena Derby, *Iraq and the United States: Creating a Strategic Partnership* (Washington DC: CSIS, 2010), p. 27. See also US Department of Defense,

'News Transcript Briefing with General Ray Odierno', 4 March 2008.

20 Although the formulation of ends–ways–means chains is presented here as a one-way, linear process, it is clear that military planners need to clear these with political leaders, a more circular process that may very well lead to the modification of high-level goals or guidelines and, of course, to amendments of strategic ends.

21 For an example of this kind of formulation in the Israeli context, see Gabi Siboni and Gal Perl Finkel, 'The IDF's Cognitive Effort: Supplementing the Kinetic Effort', *INSS Insight*, no. 1,028, 1 March 2018, http://www.inss.org.il/publication/the-idfs-cognitive-effort-supplementing-the-kinetic-effort/.

22 See Thomas Schelling, *The Strategy of Conflict* (Cambridge, MA: Harvard University Press, 1960)

23 As noted, important efforts have been made (mainly in the US) to come to grips with the new strategic reality through innovations such as 'all of government' thinking, and various operational and doctrinal adaptations such as *FM 3-24* (see endnote 14). Yet the former are scarcely implemented principles of organisation and process, while the latter, which sets out an approach that is limited mostly to situations of counter-insurgency, does provide a framework, but does not drill down to offer theory- or behavioural-science-informed direction for planning, action and societal impact.

24 Remark by US General David G. Perkins during a closed workshop/seminar on societal warfare at TRADOC Headquarters, Fort Eustis, VA, 11 April 2017.

25 We recognise that there is still significant disagreement as to the originality and impact of the surge. Our purpose is not to take a view on these debates, but simply to use the episode as an illustration of the way in which strategy should be assessed and developed when facing a society-centric challenge.

26 Michael Howard and Peter Paret (eds and trans), *Carl von Clausewitz: On War* (Princeton, NJ: Princeton University Press, 1976), p. 88.

Russian Strategy and the End of the INF Treaty

Michael Fitzsimmons

The embattled Intermediate-range Nuclear Forces (INF) Treaty appears to have finally met its demise. Originally adopted in 1987 by the United States and the Soviet Union, the treaty instituted a bilateral ban on ground-launched missiles with ranges from 500–5,500 kilometres, and has generally been viewed as a pillar of European security. But since 2014, the US has accused Russia of violating the treaty by developing and later deploying a new cruise missile with prohibited capabilities. In response, Russia has levelled its own counter-accusations of US violations.[1]

The Trump administration's policy, like the Obama administration's before it, had been to remain faithful to the treaty and to push Russia to return to compliance. At the same time, the most recent National Defense Authorization Act directed new research and development – which the treaty allows – to study options for US systems that would contravene the treaty.[2] This approach was buttressed by fairly broad bipartisan agreement among experts and policymakers that the United States should not yet withdraw from the treaty, but also that Russia's return to compliance was unlikely.[3]

On 20 October, however, President Donald Trump changed course. Citing years of Russian violations and China's freedom from INF Treaty constraints, he announced that the United States would soon withdraw from

Michael Fitzsimmons is Visiting Research Professor at the Strategic Studies Institute, US Army War College. The views expressed are those of the author and do not necessarily reflect the official policy or position of the US Department of the Army, the US Department of Defense or the US government.

Survival | vol. 60 no. 6 | December 2018–January 2019 | pp. 119–136   DOI 10.1080/00396338.2018.1542802

the treaty.[4] Trump's announcement immediately produced an avalanche of commentary around the globe, ranging from long-deferred satisfaction[5] to apocalyptic anxiety.[6] Criticism has heavily outweighed approval, including among many US allies in Europe.[7]

Riddle, mystery, enigma

Curiously absent from the current INF debates is a reckoning of why Russia has been violating the treaty in the first place. Indeed, no one in Washington seems to have had a firm grasp on Moscow's motivations on this front for some time now. In autumn 2017, the Center for Strategic and International Studies hosted a debate on the future of the INF Treaty.[8] Teams lined up on either side of the proposition: 'The United States should respond to Russia's INF violations by developing and deploying additional nuclear capabilities and refusing to negotiate any further arms control agreements until Russia complies with Treaty.' Arguing in favour was the veteran nuclear policy-maker and expert Frank Miller. When asked about Russia's motivations for its violation, Miller replied:

> What new capability do the Russians get out of this missile? I don't know. But the Russian general staff believes so strongly, and Putin believes so strongly, that they made a decision to violate one of the fundamental two treaties of the Cold War era. And they don't do things like that lightly … [T]hey therefore think it's very important.

A few months later, the moderator of a Brookings Institution discussion on the subject summed up the panel's speculations on Russia's motivations with a rueful, 'It is a bit of a mystery still'.[9] Think-tank experts are not the only ones scratching their heads. Senior national-security officials have been similarly perplexed. In December 2015, Rose Gottemoeller, then under-secretary of state for arms control and international security affairs, testified to Congress:

> To be honest with you … we're puzzled as to why [the Russians] think they need a ground-launched cruise missile that is in violation of this

important treaty, because we see they have, in our view, adequate capabilities to cover these threats with other systems at their disposal and that are entirely in accord with the INF Treaty.[10]

Nearly three years later, the Trump administration had not solved the riddle, with Pentagon official David Trachtenberg telling the Senate Foreign Relations Committee, 'I believe it's important that we consider why the Russians are violating the INF Treaty in the way they are. Because they must see some advantage to doing it, either militarily, politically, or otherwise.'[11]

So what is really going on here? Public statements from Russian officials are of little help. Most constitute categorical denials of Russian violations and insistence that the United States, instead, is violating the treaty through its deployment of *Aegis* Ashore missile-defence systems in Eastern Europe, its use of drones and its use of missiles as test-range targets.[12]

Ultimately, assessing the US withdrawal decision and the prospects for what will come next depends in substantial part on understanding Russia's goals for its new weapons. There are five alternative explanations for Russia's motivations. The fifth one illuminates how recent Russian strategy and military doctrine provide a framework for integrating most or all of Russia's plausible goals. Indeed, the likely capabilities of the new missiles fit so well with emergent Russian strategy that, notwithstanding the real disadvantages of immediate US withdrawal, Russia's return to treaty compliance is beyond reach.

The missile in question

In April 2018, the US State Department's annual report on arms-control-treaty compliance identified, for the first time, the INF-violating missile with its Russian designator, 9M729.[13] In NATO parlance, it is the SSC-8. Details on the capabilities of this ground-launched cruise missile (GLCM) remain shrouded in mystery, but analysts outside government believe it is probably similar to the *Kalibr* sea-launched cruise missile (SLCM). *Kalibr* missiles may have ranges as long as 2,500 km,[14] but are treaty-compliant because they are sea-launched. The SSC-8 may also be fired from the mobile *Iskander*-M launch platform, which is otherwise used for shorter-range ballistic and cruise missiles.[15] If either or both of these speculations are accurate, the missile could well be capable of carrying nuclear as well as conventional warheads, and its range could be much greater than the 500 km treaty limit.

Senior US officials have also alleged since early 2017 that the missile has moved beyond development and is now deployed in limited numbers. In March 2017, Vice Chairman of the Joint Chiefs of Staff General Paul Selva confirmed news stories of the deployment,[16] while other reports indicate that one operational missile battalion (comprising perhaps two dozen missiles) was deployed at a missile test site near Astrakhan, and a second near Ekaterinburg in the Ural Mountains.[17] Russian officials, for their part, have acknowledged the existence of the 9M729, but have denied that it has a treaty-busting range. The United States' claimed proof to the contrary remains classified. Assuming the US accusations are correct, a key question is what the Russians are trying to accomplish.

Explanations for Russian motivations

There appear to be five alternative but not necessarily exclusive explanations, based on both Western and Russian analysis and reporting about the missile in question.

Explanation 1: gain conventional military advantage in Europe

The most straightforward explanation is that the Russians seek simply to offset US and NATO advantages in conventional precision strike. US forces have long enjoyed unchallenged superiority in the capabilities and capacities of their SLCMs and air-launched cruise missiles (ALCMs). Improvements in these areas have been a priority for the Russian military's modernisation efforts over the past decade, and have borne fruit in the form of the *Kalibr* family of sea-launched systems and the Kh-101 and Kh-102 ALCMs.[18] Indeed, Russian President Vladimir Putin has dismissed US claims about treaty violations on the grounds that Russian ALCMs and SLCMs make new GLCMs unnecessary.[19]

Even so, Russia has several incentives that differ from those of the United States to prefer GLCMs to SLCMs and ALCMs.[20] As a continent-spanning land power with maritime approaches somewhat constrained by other states, Russia enjoys greater flexibility in deployment, mobility, concealment and targeting with land-based missiles than sea-based ones. Geographic depth also provides Russian land-based systems with better protection than air and naval forces. Moreover, even sophisticated mobile ground launchers are generally cheaper to produce and maintain than long-range aircraft and warships.

For these reasons, what might at first glance appear to be a duplicative capability – covering targets with GLCMs in addition to SLCMs and ALCMs – could be a reasonable investment to enhance flexibility and survivability. Such missiles would certainly expand Russia's options for holding at risk targets such as NATO missile defences and critical infrastructure throughout Europe, without necessarily having to depend on missiles based in the Kaliningrad *oblast* or in Belarus.[21]

Interestingly, the US Department of Defense's public comments on the threat the SSC-8 poses to Europe have been equivocal. In his March 2017 congressional testimony, Selva said the missiles pose a risk to most US facilities in Europe. That same month, General Curtis Scaparrotti, NATO Supreme Allied Commander Europe and US European Command chief, also expressed concern, telling Congress that Russia's fielding of the prohibited system 'creates a mismatch in escalatory options with the West'.[22] But in testimony a few months later, Selva indicated that the system does not give Russia any particular military advantage in Europe 'given the location of the specific missiles and deployment'.[23] In his responses to Senate questions for his confirmation as secretary of defense, James Mattis judged that Russia's violation of the treaty 'increases the risk to our allies and poses a threat to US forces and interests', but also that the violation would not provide Russia with a 'significant military advantage'.[24]

Some European analysts have also downplayed the importance of any new capabilities the missile would confer to Russia. Douglas Barrie has argued that 'the deployment of a single battalion of the road-mobile SSC-8s – conventionally armed – would not be of huge military significance … Even with reloads from resupply vehicles, the total number of missiles would almost certainly be well below 100.'[25] Ulrich Kühn and Anna Péczeli reached a similar conclusion, that 'even if Russia were to deploy a limited number of INF systems – say on the order of 50 to 100 missiles – such a deployment would not immediately alter the overall military balance between NATO and Russia, given the general conventional superiority of NATO'.[26] The consensus, then, is that while the SSC-8 clearly has some conventional military utility in Europe, the missile, at least if deployed in modest numbers, would not fundamentally alter deterrence and war-fighting conditions.

Explanation 2: decoupling redux – sow division within NATO

A second explanation posits that Moscow's focus is less on the operational military balance than on potential strategic and political advantages. The SSC-8 could serve these ends in at least two ways, both related to the vulnerable target of NATO cohesion. Firstly, the SSC-8 could reintroduce one of the core strategic problems that the INF Treaty was originally designed to solve – that of decoupling. The SS-20 intermediate-range ballistic missile, first deployed in 1976, provided the USSR with greatly expanded capabilities to conduct nuclear strikes on Western European NATO allies from the relative sanctuary of Soviet or Warsaw Pact territory, but could not reach the United States itself. Allied thinking at the time ran that if the Soviet Union attacked European NATO members with such an intermediate-range missile, the US, already significantly deterred by strategic parity, might then refrain from acting to defend its European allies. A nuclear-capable SSC-8 could, in principle, represent the same type of coercive threat today, thus undermining confidence in NATO's core Article V commitment to collective defence. NATO's eastward expansion since the Cold War could exacerbate the challenge insofar as the new missiles could discourage western NATO members from responding to Russian aggression against more eastern members, thus decoupling European allies from one another.

Secondly, Russia's violation could help drive a wedge between NATO members over the most appropriate response. Indeed, this is already happening.[27] Reflecting wide variations within the Alliance on the general assessment of the Russian threat, allies are – and likely will continue to be – divided on several INF issues. These include the nature of the Russian treaty violation itself; the validity of Russia's counter-allegations against the United States; the wisdom of US withdrawal; and the advisability of various potential countermeasures. Especially contentious would be any efforts to deploy new US missile systems in European territory in response to Russia's new capabilities. Such deployments in the 1980s generated political firestorms within several NATO countries, even in the context of wider agreement on the seriousness of the Russian military threat to eastern allies than exists today.

Some European analysts have concluded that these political effects may, in fact, be the most significant motivations for Russia's INF violations. Jacek Durcalek has argued that 'violation or circumvention of the INF Treaty has a primarily psychological impact. It demonstrates that Russia strives to acquire diverse and tested options for a missile strike against Europe.'[28] Kühn and Péczeli have called the INF crisis 'the perfect political tool to test NATO's cohesion', and conclude that 'the Kremlin's motivations stem more from political than from purely military considerations, even though it is hard to find incontrovertible evidence to support this conclusion'.[29]

Explanation 3: gain military advantage in Asia
Another logical Russian motivation for its INF violation is to respond to threats in Asia. China has dramatically expanded its short- and intermediate-range missile arsenal in the decades since the INF agreement. India, Iran, North Korea and Pakistan all possess intermediate-range missiles as well. As Russia's then-deputy minister of defence, Anatoly Antonov, put it to a reporter in 2014, 'nowadays almost 30 countries have such missiles in their arsenals. The majority of them are in close proximity to Russia.'[30] While most Russian commentators do not acknowledge any treaty violation, this point about Asian threats is the most commonly heard explanation of why the treaty is valued more by Washington than by Moscow.[31]

Russia's concerns about these threats are long-standing. According to former senior American officials, Moscow proposed a joint termination of the treaty in 2005[32] and again in 2007,[33] with the stated rationale of allowing Russia to deploy intermediate-range missiles outside of Europe to counter China, Pakistan, North Korea and others. At no point did the US government seriously consider agreeing to such a move, but US officials also did not seem to doubt the sincerity of the Russian concerns on this front.[34] Past Russian efforts to pursue a multilateral version of the INF Treaty could be seen as evidence in support of this Asia-focused explanation as well. In 2007, Russia and the United States actually issued a joint proposal in the United Nations General Assembly that floated the prospect of a multilateral ban on intermediate-range land-based missiles.[35] Its failure was perhaps inevitable, and certainly anticipated.[36] Together, these moves do not prove that Asian threats were foremost in Russian minds, but they do, at a minimum, indicate Asia's relevance to Moscow's thinking about the INF Treaty.

Explanation 4: accommodate bureaucratic or technological momentum

Another possible motivation for Russia's INF violation may be found outside the realm of strategy and geopolitics. Some analysts have suggested that the SSC-8 is best understood as a product of bureaucratic momentum. This explanation remains even more speculative than the others, since Russia has not acknowledged – and the United States has not yet disclosed – the most technical details of the violation. But there is at least some possibility that no one in the Kremlin explicitly decided to violate the treaty. Instead, Russian missile developers may have simply tested an intermediate-range *Kalibr* SLCM from a launcher that was otherwise employed for short-range land-based missiles.[37] While this scenario could still involve a treaty violation, it might have done so in only the most narrow technical sense, given that certain land-based launchers are permissible for use in testing sea-based intermediate-range missiles, while others are not.

This explanation would have little of the flavour of strategic gamesmanship and its associated implications for Russian intent that mark the other explanations. Instead, as analyst Pavel Podvig recently put it, perhaps 'Russia stumbled into this crisis largely through poor oversight of its defense industry and a bit of overconfidence in its ability to convincingly defend its case'.[38] This explanation also resonates with scholar Dima Adamsky's observations of 'chronic inconsistency between official nuclear policies, theoretical nuclear thinking and actual practice on the ground' in post-Cold War Russian planning.[39]

As unlikely as it may appear, the emergence of an important military capability initially unsanctioned by the Kremlin would not be unprecedented. According to Nikolai Sokov, it is 'the long-standing tradition of Russian defense industry to pay little attention to international agreements. In the past, that propensity created more than one head-ache for both the Foreign Ministry and the military.'[40] The most prominent example is the Soviets' construction of an early-warning radar installation near Krasnoyarsk during the 1980s. Because of its location, the radar violated the 1972 Anti-Ballistic Missile Treaty, but the senior decision-makers at the time evidently were not aware of this technicality.[41] The site became a sticking point in arms-control negotiations, and Mikhail Gorbachev, then Soviet head of state, eventually agreed to dismantle the facility. Even if this explanation were valid in the initial stages of the SSC-8's development, however, it could hardly still hold in light of the 2017 deployments of units equipped with the missile. Whether or not its creation was a strategic choice in the first instance, its integration into Russia's arsenal has apparently become one.

Explanation 5: strategic deterrence

The motivations discussed above are not, for the most part, mutually exclusive. Indeed, a single explanation is capable of integrating all of Russia's plausible goals for the SSC-8 under a coherent, overarching framework. Specifically, recent developments in Russian strategy and military doctrine provide an implicit but clear rationale for expanded capabilities of precisely the kind proscribed by the INF Treaty.

In the past few years, the Kremlin's security policies and official Russian written assessments of strategy and doctrine have been converging on a concept Western analysts have labelled 'strategic deterrence'[42] or 'cross-domain coercion'.[43] Melding Western concepts of deterrence, coercion and compellence, the concept envisions holistic, integrated employment of a diverse range of tools, spanning nuclear and conventional, overt and covert, military and non-military elements of power. Two key, related aspects of Russian strategic deterrence deserve highlighting with respect to the INF problem.

First is the imperative for integrating the roles of conventional and nuclear capabilities. Russian strategy increasingly values the flexibility afforded by coordinated employment of many diverse tools. Thanks to Russia's high-profile cyber attacks and operations in Ukraine, the informational and paramilitary dimensions of this strategic concept have received much attention in recent years. At the same time, analysts have charted a growing emphasis in writings by Russian military officers and defence intellectuals on 'pre-nuclear' deterrence, a concept paired with more traditional theories of nuclear deterrence. The concept suggests, as the prominent Russian strategist Andrei Kokoshin put it, 'improving credibility by increasing escalation levels, through a threat of launching long-range conventional precision-guided munitions strikes. Selective damage to the military and civilian infrastructure should signal the last warning before limited low-yield nuclear use.'[44]

In her review of Russian professional military literature, Kristin Ven Bruusgaard noted that 'emphasis on the interchangeability of conventional precision weapons and non-strategic nuclear weapons is habitual'.[45] NATO analyst Dave Johnson has called this pairing the 'regional deterrence dyad',[46] and concluded that

> Russia's political–military leaders appear to envision scenarios in which employment of conventional precision weapons, *coupled* with a nuclear deterrent threat, could be sufficient for 'accomplishment of global and regional deterrence aims, de-escalation and termination of regional and large-scale aggression.' Non-nuclear and nuclear deterrence are conceptually linked because strategic nuclear deterrence is viewed as creating the necessary preconditions for non-nuclear deterrence (by conventional precision weapons) to be effective.[47]

Thus, a precision-guided, intermediate-range missile, dual-capable for supporting both conventional and nuclear operations, would be precisely the sort of capability Russian planners would be apt to pursue in order to underwrite their stated vision of strategic deterrence. It should come as no surprise, then, that both existing systems associated with the SSC-8 – the *Kalibr* SLCM and the *Iskander* mobile launcher – are dual-capable.

The second aspect of Russian strategic deterrence that is essential for understanding the INF issue is a focus on precision strike as a potentially pre-emptive means for neutralising infrastructure targets.[48] Johnson has identified a specific Russian concept for these types of strikes known as 'strategic operations for the destruction of critically important targets', or SODCIT.[49] These operations may be diverse in nature, but their common focus, in the words of one Russian military analyst, is to target

> key military infrastructure facilities at the tactical or operational level, and economic infrastructure facilities or dual-purpose facilities, the timely destruction (neutralization) of which leads to the guaranteed reduction of the combat potential of a group of forces (military formation), denies control and mobility for an extended period and creates the threat of disruption or failure of fulfilment of the assigned military task.[50]

Both precision and range appear to be important elements of SODCIT, given the simultaneous needs to calibrate damage for purposes of escalation management and to reach enough 'critically important targets' to be effective. Here again, an intermediate-range GLCM, as the SSC-8 is reported to be, provides an excellent fit for the military mission envisioned in the concept.

One perennial question about written military doctrine and strategy is the extent to which they reflect the thinking or intentions of political leaders. Correlations between the two may be strong or weak. In this case, however, Putin himself has shown signs of his alignment with these concepts, writing in 2012, for example, that 'by the mass adoption of high-precision non-nuclear weapons of a large radius of action, the tendency to consolidate behind them the role of weapons of decisive victory over the enemy, including in global conflict, will become more and more evident'.[51]

It is also worth noting that the overall thrust of these fairly esoteric arguments about strategy – and their implications for Russia's compliance with the INF Treaty – has infiltrated more policy-oriented commentary in Russia. Notwithstanding the steady drumbeat of denials from the Kremlin and foreign ministry regarding INF violations, several Russian analysts and former officials in recent years have articulated why Russia should be fielding intermediate-range precision missiles, often reflecting principles of strategic deterrence that are increasingly evident in Russian doctrine.[52]

Furthermore, while evolving Russian strategy seems harder and harder to reconcile with the constraints of the INF Treaty, Moscow's disincentives to build a treaty-busting missile, of which there are two possibilities to consider, are unlikely to have decisive influence on Russian decision-making. Firstly, there is the political price of being caught cheating. Yet a pattern of barely disguised Kremlin mischief – from war in Ukraine to election interference in the United States to assassination attempts in England with chemical agents – suggests a clear readiness on Putin's part to accept international censure.

A second incentive for Moscow to show restraint in developing these capabilities is their potential to undercut strategic stability and crisis stability. These risks come not only from the potential 'decoupling' of NATO allies discussed earlier, but also from the shortened decision cycles that a nuclear strike with intermediate-range missiles would force on political leaders due to reduced missile flight times. Stability concerns have heavily shaped US nuclear strategy over the years, but such debates have not been nearly as prominent or important in Russian nuclear strategy. And many specialists on Russian strategy worry that Moscow consistently underestimates the propensity of other countries to attribute hostile intent to its military doctrine and force-planning choices.[53]

*   *   *

Russia's evolving concept of strategic deterrence offers a unifying framework for understanding most of the Kremlin's plausible motivations to move away from the INF Treaty. The demands of Russian strategic deterrence span Europe and Asia, conventional and nuclear forces, and operational and strategic levels of war. As such, this explanation is consistent with the first three explanations – namely, offsetting NATO precision-strike advantages, undermining NATO cohesion and countering Asian threats. It could also track with the last of the explanations – that is, that the treaty violations were originally driven more by bureaucratic momentum than strategic choice. Such an explanation is still speculative, but given the gradual and parallel evolution of Russia's doctrine and technological developments in Russia's defence industry, it remains plausible that the treaty violation occurred first without deliberate Kremlin approval, but was later sanctioned in line with an emerging strategy. In social-science terms, Russia's pursuit of capabilities banned by the treaty is 'overdetermined'. That is, the Kremlin has several good reasons to do it and not many reasons not to do it.[54]

Meanwhile, US treaty compliance has looked increasingly like unilateral restraint. The rationale for the manner and timing of the Trump administration's withdrawal announcement is unclear. Indeed, the global reaction has fulfilled fears that withdrawal would risk shifting blame and attention from Russia's violations to America's high-handed unilateralism. Nevertheless, the apparent capabilities of the relevant new missile fit so neatly with emerging Russian strategy that the decision to abandon hope of Russian compliance is both justified and unsurprising.

At the same time, the end of the INF Treaty need not be a disaster for NATO strategy or European security. In spite of some new advantages that future SSC-8 deployments would provide Russia, the capability does not fundamentally alter the operational military balance in Europe. Moreover, the incremental benefits Russia will enjoy can be partially offset through modest capability enhancements on the US–NATO side. These might include improved cruise-missile defences, bolstered infrastructure resilience and more diversified, forward-postured strike capabilities. A symmetrical US–NATO response in the form of new GLCMs in Europe is neither practical nor necessary to sustain effective deterrence and assurance.[55]

In addition, policymakers should strenuously avoid allowing the failure of the INF Treaty to prevent the five-year extension of the New Strategic Arms Limitation Treaty (START) from 2021 to 2026. Russian perfidy on the INF Treaty and other arms-control agreements[56] does not, by itself, invalidate the value of continued transparency on strategic nuclear systems provided by New START.

The opportunity cost to the United States of continuing to observe the treaty's limitations is most acute with respect to Asia, where China's land-based intermediate-range missile arsenal threatens a wide range of targets and poses a stark contrast to US missile capabilities.[57] Thus, debates over the end of the INF Treaty should now focus on how best to limit the risks that new weapons systems might pose to strategic stability in Asia, as well as in Europe. They should leave behind the vanishing prospects of Russia's return to compliance.

Notes

1 For an overview, see Ankit Panda, 'The Uncertain Future of the INF Treaty', Council on Foreign Relations Backgrounder, 21 December 2017; Amy F. Woolf, 'Russian Compliance with the Intermediate Range Nuclear Forces (INF) Treaty: Background and Issues for Congress', Congressional Research Service, 5 October 2018; and 'Russian Military Accuses US of "Destroying" Arms Control Pact', *Moscow Times*, 21 May 2018.

2 See US Department of Defense, 'Nuclear Posture Review', 2018, pp. 10, 74; and 'National Defense Authorization Act for Fiscal Year 2018 Conference Report', House of Representatives Report 115-404, Title XII, Subtitle E, 9 November 2017.

3 For representative views from former Obama officials, see 'After Deployment: What? Russian Violations of the INF Treaty', Transcript of Joint Hearing Before the House Armed Services Subcommittee on Strategic Forces and Committee on Foreign Affairs Subcommittee on Terrorism, Nonproliferation, and Trade, 30 March 2017. For the Trump administration's position prior to announcing its intention to withdraw, see 'Trump Administration INF Treaty Integrated Strategy', US Department of State Press Statement, 8 December 2017, https://www.state.gov/r/pa/prs/ps/2017/12/276363.htm.

4 Julian Borger and Martin Pengelly, 'Trump Says US Will Withdraw from Nuclear Arms Treaty with Russia', *Guardian,* 20 October 2018. As this article went to press, the United States had not issued formal notification of its intent to withdraw. Under the terms of the treaty's Article XV, withdrawal would be effective six months after such a formal notification.

5 See, for example, James Carafano, 'Trump's INF Treaty Termination Puts China on Notice – At Last', *National Interest,* 23 October 2018; and Elbridge Colby, 'The INF Treaty Hamstrings the U.S. Trump Is Right to Leave It', *Washington Post,* 24 October 2018.

6 'Humanity is threatened with absolute chaos in the realm of nuclear weapons', said senior Russian legislator Konstantin Kosachyov. Quoted in Annett Meiritz, 'Trump Provokes a New Conflict', *Handelsblatt,* 22 October 2018. More mainstream critiques include Daryl G. Kimbal, 'Trump's Counterproductive Decision to "Terminate" the INF Treaty', *Arms Control Today,* Issue Brief, vol. 10, no. 9, 21 October 2018; and Mikhail Gorbachev, 'A New Nuclear Arms Race Has Begun', *New York Times,* 25 October 2018.

7 See Robin Emmott, 'NATO Urges Trump Officials Not to Quit Nuclear Treaty – Diplomats', Reuters, 25 October 2018.

8 'Debate: Future of the INF Treaty', Center for Strategic and International Studies, 27 September 2017, https://www.csis.org/events/debate-future-inf-treaty. The cited comment begins at 1:18:45.

9 'The Intermediate-Range Nuclear Forces Treaty: Does It Have a Future?', Brookings Institution, 8 December 2017. Video available at https://www.

youtube.com/watch?v=8orssp7UZb4.
The cited comment begins at 43:07.

10   Joint Hearing on Russian Arms
Control Before the House Armed
Services Subcommittee on Strategic
Forces and House Foreign Affairs
Subcommittee on Terrorism,
Nonproliferation, and Trade,
Washington DC, 1 December 2015.

11   Senate Foreign Relations Committee
Hearing on the Status of U.S.–Russia
Arms Control Efforts, Washington
DC, 18 September 2018. Video available at https://www.foreign.senate.
gov/hearings/status-of-us_-russia-
arms-control-efforts-091818. The cited
comment begins at 1:05:37.

12   For an overview, see Sergey Ryzhkov,
'Who Is Gunning for the Treaty?
The US Intends to Withdraw the
Agreement on the Elimination of
Intermediate and Lesser Range
Missiles', *Krasnaya Zvezda Online*, 21
May 2018.

13   US Department of State, 'Adherence to
and Compliance with Arms Control,
Nonproliferation, and Disarmament
Agreements and Commitments', April
2018, p. 12. This confirmed an earlier
reference by Assistant Secretary of
State Christopher Ford. See Missile
Defense Project, 'US Official Identifies
Missile Believed to Violate INF
Treaty', Center for Strategic and
International Studies, 8 December
2017; and Kevin Ryan, 'After the INF
Treaty: An Objective Look at US and
Russian Compliance, Plus a New
Arms Control Regime', *Russia Matters*,
7 December 2017.

14   National Air and Space Intelligence
Center, 'Ballistic and Cruise Missile
Threat', June 2017, p. 37 (*Kalibr* is

identified as 3M-14).

15   See Pavel Podvig, 'The INF Treaty
Culprit Identified: Now What?',
Russian Strategic Forces blog, 5
December 2017; Dave Majumdar,
'Novator 9M729: The Russian Missile
that Broke INF Treaty's Back?',
National Interest, 7 December 2017;
and Nikolai Sokov, 'Bill Gertz, New
Russian SLCM, and the True Nature
of Challenge to US and NATO',
posted by Jeffrey Lewis under the title
'Sokov on Russian Cruise Missiles',
Arms Control Wonk, 25 August 2015.

16   Michael R. Gordon, 'Russia Has
Deployed Missile Barred by Treaty,
US General Tells Congress', *New
York Times*, 18 March 2017; Michael
R. Gordon, 'Russia Deploys Missile,
Violating Treaty and Challenging
Trump', *New York Times*, 14 February
2017.

17   Greg Thielmann, Oliver Meier and
Victor Mizin, 'INF Treaty Compliance:
Path to Renewal or the End of the
Road', Deep Cuts Issue Brief #8, May
2018, pp. 4–5.

18   See Roger N. McDermott and Tor
Bukkvoll, 'Tools of Future Wars –
Russia Is Entering the Precision Strike
Regime', *Journal of Slavic Military
Studies*, vol. 31, no. 2, 2018, pp.
191–213.

19   'Russia Isn't Tempted to Violate
INF Treaty, As It Has Air-launched,
Sea-launched Missiles', Interfax, 19
October 2017.

20   See Vladimir Frolov, 'Intermediate
and Less Harmful Missiles: Nuclear
Stability in Jeopardy', *Republic*,
21 November 2017; and Mikhail
Tsypkin and David Yost, 'Responding
to Russian Noncompliance with

Nuclear Arms Control Agreements', Naval Research Program Project Documents, 2015, p. 14.

21 See Ian Anthony, 'European Security After the INF Treaty', *Survival*, vol. 59, no. 6, December 2017–January 2018, p. 65; Woolf, 'Russian Compliance with the Intermediate Range Nuclear Forces (INF) Treaty', p. 24; and Jacek Durcalek, 'Russia's Violation of the INF Treaty: Challenges for NATO', *Polish Institute of International Affairs Bulletin,* no. 107, 13 August 2014, p. 2.

22 General Curtis M. Scaparrotti, 'Prepared Statement Before the House Armed Services Committee', 28 March 2017, p. 5.

23 General Paul Selva, Transcript of Hearing Before Senate Armed Services Committee, 18 July 2017.

24 Quoted in Woolf, 'Russian Compliance with the Intermediate Range Nuclear Forces (INF) Treaty', p. 3.

25 Douglas Barrie, 'Allegation, Counter-Allegation and the INF Treaty', *Survival*, vol. 59, no. 4, August–September 2017, p. 36.

26 Ulrich Kühn and Anna Péczeli, 'Russia, NATO, and the INF Treaty', *Strategic Studies Quarterly*, vol. 11, no. 1, Spring 2017, p. 87.

27 See Emmott, 'NATO Urges Trump Officials Not to Quit Nuclear Treaty – Diplomats'.

28 Durcalek, 'Russia's Violation of the INF Treaty: Challenges for NATO', p. 2.

29 Kühn and Péczeli, 'Russia, NATO, and the INF Treaty', pp. 75, 93–4.

30 Yuriy Gavrilov, 'Russian Deputy Defense Minister Says INF Allegations Part of US "Anti-Russian" Spin Campaign', *Rossiyskaya Gazeta*, 14 August 2014.

31 See, for example, Evgeny Buzhinsky and Alexander Khramchikhin, 'Russia Will Not Lose from the Denunciation of the INF Treaty', Valdai Discussion Club, 28 June 2017; and Anton Lavrov, 'Military Expert Believes INF Treaty Must Be Modernized Along with the Weapons', *Izvestiya Online,* 19 June 2018.

32 Frank Rose, 'After Deployment: What? Russian Violations of the INF Treaty', Prepared Testimony for Joint Hearing Before the House Armed Services Subcommittee on Strategic Forces and Committee on Foreign Affairs Subcommittee on Terrorism, Nonproliferation, and Trade, 30 March 2017, p. 2.

33 Robert M. Gates, *Duty: Memoirs of a Secretary at War* (New York: Alfred A. Knopf, 2014), p. 154.

34 See, for example, Jon Brook Wolfsthal, 'After Deployment: What? Russian Violations of the INF Treaty', Prepared Testimony for Joint Hearing Before the House Armed Services Subcommittee on Strategic Forces and Committee on Foreign Affairs Subcommittee on Terrorism, Nonproliferation, and Trade, 30 March 2017.

35 US Department of State, 'Joint US–Russian Statement on the Treaty on the Elimination of Intermediate-Range and Shorter-Range Missiles at the 62nd Session of the UN General Assembly', New York, 25 October 2007, http://2001-2009.state.gov/r/pa/prs/ps/2007/oct/94141.htm.

36 'Russia's Lavrov Says US Wants Multilateral Missile Treaty', RIA Novosti, 28 October 2018.

37 See Sokov, 'Bill Gertz, New Russian SLCM, and the True Nature of

Challenge to US and NATO'. At least one Russian source has also offered this explanation: see Russian International Affairs Council, 'Can the US and Russia Find a Path Forward on Arms Control?', 4 June 2018.

38 Pavel Podvig, 'Inspections Will Not Resolve the INF Treaty Dispute', Russian Strategic Forces blog, 1 July 2018.

39 Dmitry (Dima) Adamsky, 'If War Comes Tomorrow: Russian Thinking About "Regional Nuclear Deterrence"', *Journal of Slavic Military Studies*, vol. 27, no. 1, 2014, p. 165.

40 Sokov, 'Bill Gertz, New Russian SLCM, and the True Nature of Challenge to US and NATO'. Olga Oliker also raised the plausibility of this explanation during a panel event in Washington. See 'The Intermediate-Range Nuclear Forces Treaty: Does It Have a Future?', Brookings Institution, Washington DC, 8 December 2017.

41 Raymond L. Garthoff, 'Case of the Wandering Radar', *Bulletin of Atomic Scientists*, vol. 47, no. 6, July 1991, pp. 7–9.

42 See Kristin Ven Bruusgaard, 'Russian Strategic Deterrence', *Survival*, vol. 58, no. 4, August–September 2016, pp. 7–26; Anya Loukianova Fink, 'The Evolving Russian Concept of Strategic Deterrence: Risks and Responses', *Arms Control Today*, July/August 2017; Dave Johnson, 'Russia's Conventional Precision Strike Capabilities, Regional Crises, and Nuclear Thresholds', Livermore Papers on Global Security, No. 3, February 2018; and McDermott and Bukkvoll, 'Tools of Future Wars – Russia Is Entering the Precision Strike Regime'.

43 Dmitry (Dima) Adamsky, 'From Moscow With Coercion: Russian Deterrence Theory and Strategic Culture', *Journal of Strategic Studies*, vol. 41, nos 1–2, 2018, pp. 33–60.

44 Quoted in *ibid*.

45 Ven Bruusgaard, 'Russian Strategic Deterrence', p. 13.

46 Dave Johnson, 'Nuclear Weapons in Russia's Approach to Conflict', Fondation pour la Recherche Stratégique, November 2016, p. 35.

47 Johnson, 'Russia's Conventional Precision Strike Capabilities, Regional Crises, and Nuclear Thresholds', p. 26. Emphasis in original.

48 See Alexander Velez-Green, 'The Unsettling View from Moscow: Russia's Strategic Debate on a Doctrine of Pre-emption', Center for a New American Security, April 2017.

49 Johnson, 'Russia's Conventional Precision Strike Capabilities, Regional Crises, and Nuclear Thresholds', pp. 52–4.

50 Quoted in *ibid*., p. 53. Note that 'dual-purpose' here refers to civilian and military capability, not nuclear and conventional capability.

51 *Ibid*., p. 46.

52 See, for example, Mikhail Aleksandrov, 'INF Treaty Has Ceased to Meet Russia's Interests', *Regnum*, 18 January 2015; Sergey Ishchenko, 'United States Attacks Our Borders: They Are Trying to Blind Russia by a Long-Dead Treaty', *Svobodnaya Pressa*, 6 December 2014; Dmitriy Litovkin, 'By Intermediate Criteria: Key Treaty Concluded Over 20 Years Ago Is Once Again Becoming a Topic of Discussion for Russia and the United States', *Vzglyad Online*,

10 September 2014; 'Former Russian CGS Sets Out Reasons for Quitting INF Treaty', Interfax, 30 July 2014; and Vladimir Mukhin, 'Moscow Readying Medium-Range Missiles for Action', *Nezavisimaya Gazeta*, 19 July 2014.

53 See Alexey Arbatov, 'Understanding the US–Russia Nuclear Schism', *Survival*, vol. 59, no. 2, April–May 2017, pp. 33–66; Adamsky, 'From Moscow With Coercion', pp. 21–3; Ven Bruusgaard, 'Russian Strategic Deterrence', p. 20; and Johnson, 'Nuclear Weapons in Russia's Approach to Conflict', p. 36.

54 For a similar argument, see Alexander Velez-Green, 'Moscow Has Little Reason to Return to the INF Treaty', *Defense One*, 4 May 2018.

55 See, for example, Steven Pifer and Oliver Meier, 'Are We Nearing the End of the INF Treaty?', *Arms Control Today*, January/February 2018; Wolfsthal, 'After Deployment: What?';

Kühn and Péczeli, 'Russia, NATO, and the INF Treaty', pp. 87–9.

56 See Keith B. Payne and John S. Foster, 'Russian Strategy: Expansion, Crisis, and Conflict', *Comparative Strategy*, vol. 36, no. 1, 2017, chapter 5.

57 See Scott A. Cuomo, 'It's Time to Make a New Deal: Solving the INF's Strategic Liabilities to Achieve U.S. Security Goals in Asia', *Texas National Security Review*, October 2018; and Eric Sayers, 'The Intermediate Range Nuclear Forces Treaty and the Future of the Indo-Pacific Military Balance', *War on the Rocks*, 13 February 2018. See also Jacob L. Heim, 'Missiles for Asia?', RAND Corporation, 2016; Matthew Hallex, 'China's Mighty Missile Threat: What Should America Do About It?', *National Interest*, 13 September 2014; and Evan Braden Montgomery, 'China's Missile Forces Are Growing. Is It Time to Modify the INF Treaty?', *National Interest*, 2 July 2014.

Japan's Pacifism Is Dead

Karl Gustafsson, Linus Hagström and Ulv Hanssen

In September 2015, the Japanese government under Prime Minister Shinzo Abe passed a package of controversial security bills that made it possible for Japan to participate in collective self-defence – that is, to respond militarily to an attack on a 'friendly' country as though Japan itself had been attacked. The bills overturned the interpretation that Japan's constitution forbids the country from engaging in collective self-defence, a view the Japanese government had stood by for more than 60 years. The legislation removed a major legal obstacle to Japan's participation in war, as an attack on the Japanese homeland is no longer a necessary precondition for the country's use of force. This marks the latest and most dramatic instalment in a long line of changes to Japan's security policy since the end of the Cold War.

These developments have raised questions about whether Japan is 'abandoning pacifism',[1] with some media reports describing the passing of the security bills as the 'end of Japan's pacifism'.[2] The Abe government, for its part, has done its best to sell its changing security policy as 'proactive pacifism' (*sekkyokuteki heiwashugi*). This concept is alleged to herald a new era in which Japan's contribution to international peace and security will be commensurate with its economic power. Abe constantly uses familiar words such as 'pacifism' (*heiwashugi*) and 'peace state' (*heiwa kokka*) during

Karl Gustafsson is Associate Professor of Political Science and Senior Research Fellow at the Swedish Institute of International Affairs. **Linus Hagström** is Professor of Political Science at the Swedish Defence University and Senior Research Fellow at the Swedish Institute of International Affairs. **Ulv Hanssen** is a lecturer at Soka University, Japan. He is the point person for this article and can be contacted at hanssen@soka.ac.jp.

Survival | vol. 60 no. 6 | December 2018–January 2019 | pp. 137–158   DOI 10.1080/00396338.2018.1542803

deliberations in the Japanese Diet, apparently in a bid to signal that Japan is not abandoning pacifism, but rather implementing a security policy characterised by continuity.

While some scholars echo Abe in characterising Japan's security policy as essentially pacifist and current changes as merely incremental, others agree with media claims that Japan's pacifism is crumbling. By focusing only on capability and policy changes, however, even these analyses fail to capture the full extent of what is happening in Japan.

Japan's traditional pacifism was not merely about restricting the country's capabilities and adhering to policies limiting Japan's involvement in international security. More importantly, the country's pacifism has been an intrinsic part of a national identity that was seen to distinguish it from other countries. During the Cold War, there was a widespread understanding in Japan that the country had a unique responsibility to restrain its military more than other countries did, and that such restrictions were something to take pride in. This understanding enabled and normalised a number of concrete restrictions on Japan's security policy, which were both unusual for a surging economy such as Japan's and contrary to the expectations of realist international-relations theorists. The country's circumscribed security policy, in turn, reaffirmed Japan's self-identification as a particularly peace-loving people. This 'relative pacifism' did not require Japan to fully abolish its capacity to use force, only to restrain it compared to other states.

Relative pacifism reached its apex in the late 1970s and has since declined, slowly and steadily at first, but in recent years much more rapidly and dramatically. The legislation on collective self-defence means that Japan can now do more or less everything that other, more 'normal' countries do in the security field. Abe's attack on Japan's relative pacifism, as both a policy and an identity, has been so forceful and effective that we believe the time has come to declare Japan's pacifism dead.

Japan's security-policy change: incremental or radical?

Two principal schools of thought have emerged regarding Japan's security-policy trajectory under Abe. The first largely stresses continuity. While acknowledging that security-policy change is taking place, its proponents argue that this change has been incremental, predictable and largely constrained by pacifist, or anti-militarist, sentiments. Michael J. Green, for example, writes that 'Abe's national security agenda is *not*, in fact, a departure from the general trajectory established by his predecessors in the post-Cold War era. It represents far more continuity than change.'[3] Similarly, Jeffrey W. Hornung and Mike M. Mochizuki, while acknowledging that Japan's new security legislation will make it more proactive in the security realm, conclude that the country's pacifist restrictions remain largely intact, and that Japan is still an 'exceptional' – that is, not a 'normal' – US ally.[4] Adam P. Liff describes security reforms under Abe as 'evolutionary' and 'incremental', and denies that they constitute 'an abrupt transformation of Japan's defense policy'.[5] Leif-Eric Easley writes that 'Tokyo … is not aggressively remilitarizing';[6] while Andrew L. Oros writes that 'the effect of the postwar antimilitarist legacy remains strong even in contemporary Japan under Prime Minister Abe and even in the midst of a security renaissance'.[7]

In stark contrast to this 'incrementalist' view is the assessment that Japan's security policy under Abe constitutes a radical break with past practices. Christopher W. Hughes is perhaps the most vocal advocate of the 'radical change' view. He criticises the academic 'consensus' that Japan's security policy is characterised by 'stasis' and 'immobilism' – a view he sees as 'bordering on dogma'. More importantly, he believes it flies in the face of 'mounting signs of Japanese remilitarization'.[8] According to Hughes, the decision to allow collective self-defence should be seen as 'a watershed moment in Japan's development of a radical security trajectory'.[9] Bryce Wakefield and Craig Martin warn that Abe's reinterpretation of the constitution could have 'profound systemic ramifications' and may lead to Japan's involvement in wars 'sooner than Abe's defenders claim'.[10] Michael Auslin characterises Abe's security policies as 'Japan's new realism' and notes that Abe has 'distanced his country from its postwar pacifism'.[11]

We believe that this debate has been overly focused on changes in capabilities and policies, while neglecting more fundamental changes in Japan's national identity. Because Japan's relative pacifism is both a policy *and* an identity, overlooking the identity component risks underestimating the significance of changes in Japan's security doctrine. Indeed, we propose that changes in Japan's national identity were needed to facilitate changes in its policies.

Charles F. Hermann's seminal typology for assessing foreign-policy change is a useful starting point for gauging Japan's security trajectory since 1945. Hermann proposes four levels of change. Firstly, 'adjustment change' refers to changes that occur at 'the level of effort'.[12] These include minor budget increases or decreases, slight changes in the possession of certain capabilities and small adjustments to existing laws or standard operating procedures. Secondly, 'program change' encompasses changes 'in the methods or means by which the goal or problem is addressed'. This kind of change involves the acquisition or development of new capabilities, or the formulation of new laws or standard operating procedures, to deal with fundamentally unchanging problems or to meet fixed goals. Thirdly, 'problem/goal change' refers to a change in the goals, problems, objectives or purposes of national policies. Finally, 'international orientation change' involves changes in an 'actor's entire orientation toward world affairs', and in its 'relationship with external entities'.[13] Since the incrementalists contend that Japan's security-policy change has been moderate and evolutionary, they would arguably have to characterise it as adjustment change. Those who perceive a more radical change mostly refer to programme-level changes involving new budgets and the acquisition of new weapons systems; or to problem/goal-level changes, citing decisions, laws, policies and international agreements that have altered how problems and solutions central to Japan's security policy are formulated. We would suggest, however, that the changes Japan is undergoing represent an attempt to fundamentally reorient the country's role in world affairs through the reconfiguration of both its material capabilities and its identity. In other words, we are dealing with an example of international-orientation change.

There are two reasons why identity is neglected in most analyses of Japan's security policy. Firstly, observers who downplay the significance of the recent changes tend to do so with reference to the constraining effects of lingering anti-militarist or pacifist sentiments, thereby suggesting that identity change has been limited.[14] Secondly, analyses that deem changes to be more radical are generally informed by rationalist theories, most notably realism, which tend to ignore the identity factor. Those who do take identity into consideration tend to treat it as fixed and to conflate it with 'anti-militarism' – a factor typically employed to explain why post-war Japan deviated from the policy course that 'more rational states' would have taken.[15] Thus, incrementalists tend to understand changes as occurring within a largely static identity framework, while radicals appear to believe that recent developments have finally proved how flawed the identity perspective is, vindicating realism at last. As Martin Hollis and Steve Smith point out, realists often account for 'situations when states seem to behave in a way that undermines their power' by 'redefining the actions as mistakes or miscalculations'.[16] This arguably explains the proliferation of articles implying that Japan's changing security policy has finally become 'realist' now that the country has realised how misguided its brand of pacifism was.[17]

By contrast, a relational approach to identity holds that states and individuals construct identities by differentiating themselves from others.[18] This makes for an unfixed and malleable understanding of identity that is able to capture changes in a state's 'relationship with external entities'.[19] This approach is thus particularly well equipped for recognising changes at the level of international orientation, which antedate and facilitate changes that occur at other levels.

Japan's post-war international orientation: relative pacifism

To show that Japan is undergoing a change in its international orientation, it is necessary first to establish what kind of international orientation it is departing from. The establishment of Japan's euphemistically named Self Defense Force (SDF) in 1954 demonstrates that post-war Japanese security policy was never *absolutely* pacifist. However, that same year the Cabinet Legislation Bureau issued a landmark interpretation of Japan's constitution, which acknowledged the legality of the SDF for the purpose of self-defence, but that prohibited its use for the conduct of 'modern warfare'. In this way, the Cabinet Legislation Bureau ensured that the SDF was more restricted than the armed forces of other countries. As Richard J. Samuels points out, the SDF's 'war potential' thus became 'definable only in relation to other states' capabilities and international conditions'.[20]

In other words, rather than completely forsaking military capabilities, Japan simply opted for a security policy that was circumscribed *relative to that of other states*. In practice, this entailed a ban on aircraft carriers, long-range missiles and aircraft capable of in-flight refuelling. Moreover, the Cabinet Legislation Bureau's interpretation forbade Japan from sending the SDF abroad, and made participation in collective self-defence unconstitutional, as this was deemed to exceed the requirement that the 'use of defensive force is kept to the minimum necessary for self-defence'.[21] Since the right to collective self-defence is guaranteed by Article 51 of the UN Charter, this ensured that Japan's security policy was more restrictive than that of other countries. These early legal restrictions have become collectively known in Japan as 'exclusively defensive defence' (*senshu bōei*).

Japan added further security-policy restrictions in the 1960s and 1970s. In 1967, then-prime minister Eisaku Sato introduced two sets of three principles, one covering nuclear weapons and the other arms exports. Sato pledged that Japan would refrain from possessing and producing nuclear weapons, and from introducing them onto Japanese soil. On arms sales, he declared that Japan would not export arms to communist states, states under UN arms-exports sanctions, or those involved or likely to become involved in armed conflict. In 1976, the latter set of principles was effectively turned into a blanket ban on arms exports. Prime minister Takeo Miki justified this by stating that 'Japan, as a peaceful country, is to avoid promoting international conflicts by exporting arms'.[22] That same year, Miki also issued a cabinet decision limiting defence spending to 1% of GDP. Because this limitation was the last of Japan's major self-imposed security restrictions, 1976 can be regarded as the apex of Japan's relative pacifism. As one commentator wrote the following year, 'There are now no major political forces that are frontally opposed to the ideas and institutions of popular sovereignty, pacifism, and liberal democracy prescribed by the Constitution.'[23]

Another conspicuous feature of Japan's relative pacifism is that threat assessments were almost completely absent from the country's post-war defence debate. Until recently, Japanese policymakers went out of their way to avoid characterising other countries as threats, let alone enemies. This stance was evident in the 1957 Basic Policy on National Defense, the only document that could be considered an official Japanese grand strategy until the launch of the National Security Strategy in 2013.[24] The Basic Policy states that Japan shall 'build … up rational defense capabilities by steps within the limit necessary for self-defense in accordance with national strength and situation'.[25] In other words, economic performance and public opinion were to be the main determinants of Japan's defence capabilities.[26] Moreover, between Japan's independence in 1952 and the advent of Yasuhiro Nakasone's premiership in 1982, there was strong resistance to labelling other countries 'hypothetical enemies' (kasō tekikoku), as this was regarded as one of the practices that had encouraged Japan's pre-war military leadership to perceive war as inevitable.[27]

Taken together, these measures are often seen as proof that Japan in the post-war period developed especially 'peaceful cultural norms',[28] or an 'anti-militarist culture'.[29] 'Norm constructivists' believe that such internal factors constitute a 'pacifist' or 'anti-militarist' identity, which in turn explains why post-war Japan did not remilitarise in a way commensurate with its economic development.[30] By contrast, we see 'pacifist' Japan as having emerged as the country differentiated itself from others during the post-war period, both through the 'temporal othering' of Japan's own militarist past,[31] and the 'spatial othering' of contemporary great powers as they sought to maximise their military capabilities. As Japan contrasted itself both with its own past and with other countries, it constructed an identity according to which it was natural to take pride in military restrictions and far-reaching moderation in security matters. While Japan was not pacifist in the absolute sense, its restrictive security policy made it possible for the country to see itself as uniquely peaceful, replacing the militarist stigma it had borne since 1945 with the more attractive label of 'peace state' (heiwa kokka). Hence, Japan's relative pacifism was more than just a set of security-policy restrictions – it was also an identity that made these restrictions appear natural, while at the same time relying on them for legitimacy.

Throughout the 1970s, Japan's political leaders proudly proclaimed that even though Japan had become an 'economic great power' (keizai taikoku), it would never become a 'military great power' (gunji taikoku) – a stance that was said to be uniquely Japanese as every other economic great power had translated its economic prowess into military strength. This theme of exceptionalism through military moderation was repeated in successive versions of the *Diplomatic Bluebook* and the Defense White Paper, and in foreign-office and prime-ministerial speeches, such as this 1977 statement by prime minister Takeo Fukuda:

> What I really see as important is the question of peace. We are taking a unique stance in the world. If we had wanted to, we could have had powerful weaponry. But although we have that potential, we do not pursue it. Are we perhaps not the first country in world history to take such an approach? If one looks at history, economic great powers have almost unfailingly become military great powers. Japan does not choose that road.[32]

In sum, by 1976 Japan had developed and deepened its relative pacifism. This means that Japan deliberately held back its military potential. The Japanese understanding of pacifism, or *heiwashugi*, therefore differs from how the term is usually understood in the West, as entailing an absolute rejection of force. *Heiwashugi* can be literally translated as 'peace-ism'.[33] This differs from Western notions of pacifism in that, for the most part, it emerged not from Christian or Enlightenment thinking, but rather from the Japanese people's negative understanding of its war experience and unwillingness to repeat it.[34] Given the experience-based, non-philosophical origin of Japan's post-war pacifism, it is perhaps unsurprising that it mostly found expression in the rejection of Japan's pre-war and wartime militarist regime, and a *relative* rather than an *absolute* rejection of violence and force.[35]

The death of Japanese pacifism

Japan's international orientation of relative pacifism has been consistently challenged by those who argue that deliberately constraining a country's military capabilities is naive, irresponsible and dangerous. For most of the Cold War period, however, proponents of this view were largely relegated to the sidelines of political debate in Japan, although they gained some clout during the premiership of Nakasone in the 1980s. It was not until the premierships of Junichiro Koizumi and Shinzo Abe in the 2000s that their voices became dominant.

Adjustment, programme and problem changes

The first security constraint to be targeted for removal was the 1% ceiling on defence spending. In 1987, Nakasone managed to pass a defence budget that stood at 1.004% of GDP. This minimal hike was temporary, however, and Nakasone largely failed in his attempt, as Thomas Berger has described it, to 'rid the nation of the debilitating burden of the past and to approach national defence in the presumably more rational manner of other countries'.[36] His plans were opposed not only by the opposition parties, but also by many members of his own party, including several former prime ministers. By contrast, in March 2017, Abe not only referred to the security environment when discussing the defence budget – something that was anathema during the Cold War period – but also noted:

> We intend to secure the necessary budget to effectively defend our nation, taking into consideration the security environment in the Asia Pacific region, as well as the financial situation … There is no intention to limit [defence spending] to one per cent of the GDP.[37]

In stark contrast to Nakasone's experience, Abe's proclamation that the 1% ceiling was no longer in place seems to have attracted scant criticism from within his own Liberal Democratic Party (LDP).

Since 1987, attempts have been made to remove Japan's other self-imposed security restrictions as well. The 1954 ban on overseas SDF deployments was effectively removed in 1991, when Japan sent six minesweepers to the Persian Gulf in the aftermath of the Gulf War. In 1992, it sent the SDF to participate in a UN peacekeeping operation in Cambodia, and has since participated in similar operations in Mozambique, Rwanda, the Golan Heights, East Timor, the Indian Ocean, Iraq, Nepal, Sudan, Haiti and South Sudan. In response to the so-called US 'war on terror' after 9/11, Japan also sent the SDF to the Indian Ocean to conduct refuelling missions in 2001–10, and to Iraq to participate in various reconstruction efforts in 2004–08. While the latter deployments were carried out without UN authorisation, they upheld strict limitations on the use of force, as SDF members were only permitted to use arms in self-defence. To this day, no SDF member has fired a shot against an enemy while abroad. That track record may soon come to an end, however, since the Abe government in 2015 pushed through security legislation which, among other things, loosens the SDF's rules of engagement. The new legislation allows Japanese blue helmets to use force in order to rescue and assist UN peacekeepers and the staff of non-governmental organisations from any country. They are also permitted to participate in previously banned assignments, such as patrolling and carrying out vehicle inspections at checkpoints.[38]

Japan has also revised its ban on arms exports twice in recent years, in 2009 and 2014. The 2014 revision permits arms exports that: 1) do not violate UN resolutions or international agreements that Japan has entered into; 2) serve to promote peace and international cooperation, or enhance Japan's own security; and 3) involve full transparency by the recipient country. As long as transparency is assured, Japan can in principle export weapons and weapons technology to any country not under UN sanctions. The provision that arms exports must serve the promotion of peace or enhance Japan's own security is so vague that it is hard to imagine how it could ever function as a restraint if the other two conditions are met. Since most countries have adopted similar principles on transparency and UN sanctions, the arms-export principles have ceased to meaningfully differentiate Japan from other countries.

By far the most controversial element of the 2015 security legislation was the decision to lift the ban on collective self-defence. Abe pushed through this legislation in the face of massive protests from opposition parties and the general public. However, largely due to the apprehensions of the LDP's coalition partner (the Buddhist Komeito party), the legalisation of collective self-defence was somewhat watered down. Most significantly, it was conditioned on three specific criteria: 1) that an attack 'threatens Japan's survival and poses a clear danger to fundamentally overturn people's right to life, liberty and pursuit of happiness'; 2) that there are 'no other appropriate means available to repel the attack'; and 3) that Japan's use of force is limited to 'the minimum extent necessary'.[39] If these conditions are met, Japan can now legally participate in collective self-defence, which means that it can militarily come to the rescue of any foreign country 'in a close relationship with Japan' that has come under attack.[40] On the surface, the three conditions regulating Japan's exercise of the right to collective self-defence might appear strict, but it is not difficult to imagine how references to threats against the people's 'right to life, liberty and pursuit of happiness' might be applied loosely, and the meaning of the phrase 'minimum extent necessary' is unclear. Abe has promised that Japan will not become involved in foreign wars, but as Hughes points out, 'the only effective constraint appears to be his word and the prevailing political sentiment'.[41]

The ban on offensive weapons, another major security restriction, has been heavily diluted through the acquisition of equipment and technology that arguably have the capacity to project force, such as helicopter carriers and mid-air refuelling aircraft.[42] Furthermore, the technology used in Japan's ballistic-missile defence system, the implementation of which began in 2003–04, can also be used in missile systems built for offensive purposes. Before long, the offensive-weapons ban might be lifted altogether, as tensions with North Korea in 2017 spurred serious debate in the Diet about the acquisition of pre-emptive-strike capabilities. Japan has mulled such capabilities since the early days of its missile-defence project,[43] but their introduction now seems more likely than ever. On 30 March 2017, the ruling LDP's Policy Research Council delivered a proposal to the government calling for a 'swift and drastic' strengthening of Japan's defence against North Korean ballistic missiles. The single-page proposal stated that, in addition to strengthening missile defence, the Japanese government should 'immediately begin examining [the possibility] to acquire "retaliatory strike capabilities against enemy bases", starting with cruise missiles'.[44] An anonymous source with knowledge of Japanese military planning told Reuters that 'we have already done the groundwork on how we could acquire a strike capability'.[45] In November 2017, the Japanese newspaper *Yomiuri Shimbun* reported that the Ministry of Defense plans to start research on a Japanese version of the *Tomahawk* missile in fiscal year 2018.[46] The following month, Defense Minister Itsunori Onodera announced plans to acquire air-launched cruise missiles capable of reaching North Korea.[47] If LDP lawmakers go through with their proposal to develop or procure retaliatory-strike capabilities, they will probably face only limited resistance. A *Sankei Shimbun* poll found that 75% of respondents wanted Japan to either 'possess' or 'consider possessing' pre-emptive-strike capabilities.[48]

In sum, Japan in 2018 can dispatch the SDF abroad, use force during peacekeeping operations, engage in collective self-defence, sell arms and arms technology, and carry out limited force projection. It has also begun the process of allowing pre-emptive-strike capabilities. Furthermore, there is no longer a formal limit on Japan's defence spending, which is now overwhelmingly determined by 'threat assessments'. Indeed, the 2015 security legislation, and the 2014 Cabinet Resolution on which it is based, are replete with references to a 'security environment' that has been 'fundamentally transformed' for the worse.[49] There is now very little that Japan cannot do in terms of security policy that allegedly more 'normal' countries can. To be sure, the three non-nuclear principles from 1967 remain intact, although they were effectively breached in 1969 when the Japanese government secretly agreed to allow the United States to introduce nuclear weapons to Japan.[50] While nuclear weapons are still common among the world's major powers, the overwhelming majority of the world's countries have chosen to forswear them. It is thus highly debatable whether the possession of nuclear weapons is evidence of 'normality'. Japan's 'normalisation' project is therefore virtually complete.

International-orientation change

The developments outlined above can be described as changes at the adjustment, programme and problem levels. Nonetheless, we argue that they are intertwined with, and have been enabled by, an identity shift at the international-orientation level. Indeed, we believe that the increasing tendency to pinpoint 'threats', and the notion that Japan has been operating under 'abnormal' conditions and should strive for 'normality', cannot be separated from this shift.[51] Those who have done their utmost to transform Japanese security policy perceive Japan's identity in a fundamentally different way than did policymakers in the Cold War period. Back then,

Japan's security-policy constraints were infused with pride and exceptionalism, as they were believed to demonstrate Japan's unique peacefulness. In the Cold War period, a peace-loving Japan was contrasted with the militarist Japan of the 1930s and 1940s, along with other military-power-seeking states. However, those pushing for identity and policy changes today seek to distinguish contemporary Japan from post-war Japan, in all its alleged weakness, masochism and abnormality.[52] Hence, the country's deliberately constrained security policy has shifted from being predominantly an object of pride to becoming mostly an object of shame. Abe's call for Japan to 'break out of the postwar regime' is typical of this differentiation between a weak past and a strong future.[53] Masahisa Sato, an LDP parliamentarian with an SDF background, clearly expressed this temporal differentiation in a Diet session in 2013, saying, 'In the past, Japan was criticised for its one-country pacifism and its passive pacifism, so the mission of the Abe Cabinet is to reclaim a strong Japan which we can be proud of'.[54] Another conservative lawmaker differentiated between the 'passive pacifism' of the past and Abe's 'proactive pacifism' of the present and future, saying that the former stipulated 'ascetic self-restraint' (*kinyokuteki jikokisei*), while the latter called for 'altruistic self-sacrifice' (*ritateki jikogisei*).[55]

In this way, the pacifism of the past is depicted as shameful, while Abe's new pacifism is framed as a security policy that the Japanese can finally take pride in. According to this view, to achieve this sense of national pride, Japan must replace its pacifist security policy with a realist one determined by threat assessments. The rise of this political orientation has been so powerful, especially during the Abe government since 2012, that its proponents must now be seen as the mainstream, whereas the previously dominant pacifists have become peripheral.

Many observers argue that the recent changes in Japanese security policy have been adopted due to the external threats posed by China and North Korea. We do not dispute that external developments can at times seem unnerving to Japan. We do dispute, however, the suggestion that assessments of this kind are merely detached, objective descriptions of security problems that naturally lead to particular responses. Instead, we argue that Japanese threat assessments, and the policy changes that can accompany them, have been enabled by a changing understanding of the country's identity.

China has increasingly become an object of differentiation and securitisation in Japan.[56] This is often portrayed as a logical reaction to China's rise and 'aggressiveness'. However, this raises the question of why Japan did not respond in a similar way to the Soviet threat during the Cold War. The Soviet Union's destructive capacity far surpassed that of contemporary China, whose nuclear arsenal is far more modest. Moreover, the uncompromising rivalry between the American and Soviet superpowers produced international tensions that ran much higher than those present in the competitive but interdependent relationship between the US and China. The dangers posed by the Cold War could easily have been used by Japanese lawmakers to make a case for securitisation, as they were in many other countries. Yet this did not happen. The Soviet threat did not lead to the kind of military build-up in Japan that has been taking place in response to China's rise. On the contrary, Japan responded by adopting military restrictions. What is more, these restrictions evoked pride and exceptionalism. These widely differing responses appear mystifying if the changes in Japan's national identity are overlooked.

The Cold War example demonstrates that not all potentially threatening developments are necessarily construed as such. So too does Japan's differing response to the nuclear programmes of China and North Korea. After China conducted its sixth nuclear (first thermonuclear) test in 1967 – at the height of the markedly anti-Japanese Cultural Revolution – Japan responded by introducing the three non-nuclear principles. By contrast, Japan's response to North Korea's sixth nuclear (first thermonuclear) test in 2017 has been to push for pre-emptive-strike capabilities. This sums up the difference between an international orientation based on relative pacifism and one based on proactive pacifism. A self-constraining response along the lines of 1967 is simply unthinkable today.

It is also worth remembering that Japanese threat perceptions of North Korea have not principally been based on the latter's nuclear programme, but rather on North Korea's abduction of 17 Japanese citizens in the 1970s and 1980s.[57] Indeed, resolving the abduction issue is still officially designated 'the most important foreign policy issue' for the country.[58] Furthermore, annual public-opinion surveys by the Japanese Ministry of Foreign Affairs show that the abduction issue consistently ranks higher than the nuclear and missile issues as the North Korean problem of most concern to the Japanese people.[59] This indicates that national threat perceptions can be out of sync with the way that realists would frame threats. The fact that North Korea managed to kidnap Japanese citizens on Japanese soil has been interpreted as epitomising the perils of Japan's pacifist 'abnormality', providing emotional arguments for the country's 'normalisation' in security and defence terms.[60]

Finally, the 'aggressiveness' of North Korea and China cannot be viewed in isolation, but must be seen against the backdrop of Japan's already changing self-understanding, according to which Japan is perceived as peaceful, democratic and law-abiding, whereas China and North Korea are viewed as hostile, authoritarian and 'anti-Japanese'.[61] Japan understands China's and North Korea's actions not just with reference to these countries, but also to its own past. This understanding has changed tremendously in the 2000s, thereby enabling the recent far-reaching changes in Japanese security policy.

*   *   *

It is clear that Japan has moved away from its long-standing relative understanding of pacifism. Relative pacifism was characterised by a sense of pride in a security policy that was deliberately constrained compared to other countries. This self-constraint was taken as a symbol of Japan's exceptional peacefulness. Relative pacifism was thus both a policy and an identity. We have argued that the academic debate has failed to capture the full extent of the security-policy changes under the current Abe administration because debaters either insist that there has been only incremental change in both policy and identity, or acknowledge the radical policy change while ignoring the identity change. Today, almost every single security restriction Japan willingly imposed on itself during the Cold War period has been eliminated, with the result that there is very little Japan cannot do in the security sphere that other countries can.

Equally important, changes in material capabilities, policies and legal frameworks have been accompanied by, and intertwined with, identity change. The security restrictions of the past have increasingly come to be viewed as objects of shame rather than pride. What makes Japan pacifist according to Abe's doctrine of 'proactive pacifism' is a *lack* of restrictions that could inhibit the country's defence of peace at home and abroad. This is a far cry from the relative pacifism of the past, and indicative of a change in Japan's international orientation. The fierce attacks, particularly under Abe, on both the self-imposed security restrictions and the identity that took pride in them compel us to conclude that Japanese pacifism is dead.

The superficial continuity touted by the Abe government with respect to Japan's previous understanding of pacifism is unfortunate. If pacifism no longer means that Japan exercises more military moderation than other countries, but rather that it should defend peace much as other nations do, then the pacifist label will only serve to distinguish between peaceful and *un*peaceful countries. This could potentially lead to an increase in antagonistic sentiments towards those deemed unpeaceful, so that proactive pacifism legitimises not only a tougher military posture, but possibly also pre-emptive moves. In other words, pacifism can be warped into a justification for a more assertive security policy, and thus function in a polar opposite way to how it was previously understood and practised. This is arguably what we are now seeing with respect to Japan's security policy towards China and North Korea. The division of the world into peaceful and unpeaceful countries risks becoming an oversimplified lens through which balancing moves and deterrence strategies against those who fall on the outside are seen as the only sensible way to defend peace.

Notes

1   See, for example, 'Is Japan Abandoning Its Pacifism?', BBC, 23 September 2015, http://www.bbc.com/news/world-asia-34278846.

2   'End of Japan's Pacifism? Parliament Approves War Bills Allowing Troops to Fight Abroad', RT.com, 18 September 2015, https://www.rt.com/news/315893-japan-approve-war-pacifism/.

3   Michael J. Green, 'Japan Is Back: Unbundling Abe's Grand Strategy', Lowy Institute Analysis, 17 December 2013, p. 2, https://www.lowyinstitute.

org/publications/japan-back-unbun-dling-abe-s-grand-strategy. Emphasis in original.

4 Jeffrey W. Hornung and Mike M. Mochizuki, 'Japan: Still an Exceptional U.S. Ally', *Washington Quarterly*, vol. 39, no. 1, 2016, pp. 95–116.

5 Adam P. Liff, 'Japan's Defense Policy: Abe the Evolutionary', *Washington Quarterly*, vol. 38, no. 2, 2015, pp. 79–99.

6 Leif-Eric Easley, 'How Proactive? How Pacifist? Charting Japan's Evolving Defence Posture', *Australian Journal of International Affairs*, vol. 71, no. 1, 2017, p. 63.

7 Andrew L. Oros, *Japan's Security Renaissance: New Policies and Politics for the Twenty-First Century* (New York: Columbia University Press, 2017), p. 158. For additional examples of this incrementalist view, see Michael J Green and Jeffrey W. Hornung, 'Ten Myths About Japan's Collective Self-Defense Change', *Diplomat*, 10 July 2014, https://thediplomat.com/2014/07/ten-myths-about-japans-collective-self-defense-change/; and Jennifer Lind, 'Japan's Security Evolution', Policy Analysis, Cato Institute, 2016, https://object.cato.org/sites/cato.org/files/pubs/pdf/pa-788.pdf.

8 Christopher W. Hughes, 'Japan's "Resentful Realism" and Balancing China's Rise', *Chinese Journal of International Politics*, vol. 9, no. 2, 2016, p. 115.

9 Christopher W. Hughes, 'Japan's Strategic Trajectory and Collective Self-Defense: Essential Continuity or Radical Shift', *Journal of Japanese Studies*, vol. 43, no. 1, 2017, p. 93.

10 Bryce Wakefield and Craig Martin, 'Reexamining "Myths" About Japan's Collective Self-Defense Change: What Critics (and the Japanese Public) Do Understand About Japan's Constitutional Reinterpretation', *Asia-Pacific Journal* (n.d.), http://apjjf.org/-Bryce-Wakefield/4803/article.html.

11 Michael Auslin, 'Japan's New Realism: Abe Gets Tough', *Foreign Affairs*, vol. 95, no. 2, 2016, pp. 125–34.

12 Charles F. Hermann, 'Changing Course: When Governments Choose to Redirect Foreign Policy', *International Studies Quarterly*, vol. 34, no. 1, 1990, pp. 5–6.

13 *Ibid.*

14 See Liff, 'Japan's Defense Policy'; Lind, 'Japan's Security Evolution'; and Oros, *Japan's Security Renaissance.*

15 See, for example, Peter J. Katzenstein and Nobuo Okawara, 'Japan's National Security: Structures, Norms, and Policies', *International Security*, vol. 17, no. 4, 1993, pp. 84–118; Peter J. Katzenstein, *Cultural Norms and National Security: Police and Military in Postwar Japan* (Ithaca, NY: Cornell University Press, 1996); Thomas U. Berger, *Cultures of Antimilitarism: National Security in Germany and Japan* (Baltimore, MD: Johns Hopkins University Press, 1998); Andrew L. Oros, *Normalizing Japan: Politics, Identity and the Evolution of Security Practice* (Stanford, CA: Stanford University Press, 2007); and Andrew L. Oros, 'International and Domestic Challenges to Japan's Postwar Security Identity: "Norm Constructivism" and Japan's New "Proactive Pacifism"', *Pacific Review*, vol. 28, no. 1, 2015, pp. 139–60.

16 Martin Hollis and Steve Smith, *Explaining and Understanding International Relations* (Oxford: Clarendon Press, 1991), p. 63.

17 See Michael J. Green and Benjamin L. Self, 'Japan's Changing China Policy: From Commercial Liberalism to Reluctant Realism', *Survival*, vol. 38, no. 2, 1996, pp. 35–58; Christopher W. Hughes, 'The Democratic Party of Japan's New (but Failing) Grand Security Strategy: From "Reluctant Realism" to "Resentful Realism"?', *Journal of Japanese Studies*, vol. 38, no. 1, 2012, pp. 109–40; Hughes, 'Japan's "Resentful Realism"', p. 115; and Auslin, 'Japan's New Realism'.

18 See, for example, Roxanne Lynn Doty, *Imperial Encounters: The Politics of Representation in North–South Relations* (Minneapolis, MN: University of Minnesota Press, 1996); David Campbell, *Writing Security: United States Foreign Policy and the Politics of Identity* (Manchester: Manchester University Press, 1998); Iver B. Neumann, *Uses of the Other: 'The East' in European Identity Formation* (Manchester: Manchester University Press, 1999); and Linus Hagström and Karl Gustafsson, 'Japan and Identity Change: Why It Matters in International Relations', *Pacific Review*, vol. 28, no. 1, 2015, pp. 1–22.

19 Hermann, 'Changing Course', p. 6.

20 Richard J. Samuels, 'Politics, Security Policy, and Japan's Cabinet Legislation Bureau: Who Elected These Guys, Anyway?', JPRI Working Paper no. 99, March 2004, http://www.jpri.org/publications/workingpapers/wp99.html.

21 Japan Ministry of Defense, 'Fundamental Concepts of National Defense', http://www.mod.go.jp/e/d_act/d_policy/dp02.html.

22 Hideaki Kaneda et al., 'Japan's Missile Defense: Diplomatic and Security Policies in a Changing Strategic Environment', Japan Institute of International Affairs, 2007, p. 78, http://www2.jiia.or.jp/en/pdf/polcy_report/pr200703-jmd.pdf.

23 Kei Wakaizumi, 'Consensus in Japan', *Foreign Policy*, vol. 27, Summer 1977, p. 161.

24 Cabinet Secretariat, 'National Security Strategy', 17 December 2013, http://www.cas.go.jp/jp/siryou/131217anzenhoshou/nss-e.pdf.

25 Japan Ministry of Defense, 'Fundamental Concepts of National Defense'.

26 Isao Miyaoka, 'Military Change in Japan: National Defense Program Guidelines as a Main Tool of Management', in Jo Inge Bekkevold, Ian Bowers and Michael Raska (eds), *Security, Strategy and Military Change in the 21st Century: Cross-Regional Perspectives* (London and New York: Routledge, 2015), p. 40.

27 Ulv Hanssen, *Japan's Temporal Others: How the Past Has Shaped Japan's Postwar Security Policy*, PhD dissertation, Freie Universität Berlin, 2017, chapter 4.

28 Katzenstein, *Cultural Norms and National Security*.

29 Berger, *Cultures of Antimilitarism*.

30 See *Ibid.*; Katzenstein, *Cultural Norms and National Security*; Oros, *Normalizing Japan*; and Oros, 'International and Domestic Challenges'.

31 See Linus Hagström and Ulv Hanssen, 'War Is Peace: The Rearticulation of

"Peace" in Japan's China Discourse', *Review of International Studies*, vol. 42, no. 2, 2016, pp. 266–86; and Hanssen, *Japan's Temporal Others*.

32 Takeo Fukuda, statement 14, Budget Committee, Japanese parliament (upper house), 25 March 1977, translated into English by the authors of this article.

33 Mari Yamamoto, *Grassroots Pacifism in Post-War Japan: The Rebirth of a Nation* (London and New York: RoutledgeCurzon, 2004), p. 10.

34 Yamamoto, *Grassroots Pacifism*, pp. 9–10.

35 Obviously, there were 'absolute' pacifists in Japan too — especially in the Socialist Party — but by the 1960s the position of relative pacifism had become an acceptable compromise for most actors in the security debate.

36 Berger, *Cultures of Antimilitarism*, p. 141.

37 'Abe Shushō, Bōeihi Zōgaku ni Iyoku Sanin Yosani' (Prime Minister Abe Eyes Increased Defence Expenditures in the Upper House Budget Committee), *Nikkei*, 2 March 2017, http://www.nikkei.com/article/DGXLASFS02H3S_S7A300C1PP8000/.

38 Franz-Stefan Gady, 'Japan's Military Gets New Rules of Engagement', *Diplomat*, 30 September 2015, http://thediplomat.com/2015/09/japans-military-gets-new-rules-of-engagement/.

39 Cabinet Secretariat, 'Cabinet Decision on Development of Seamless Security Legislation to Ensure Japan's Survival and Protect its People', 1 July 2014, pp. 7–8, http://www.cas.go.jp/jp/gaiyou/jimu/pdf/anpohosei_eng.pdf.

40 *Ibid*.

41 Christopher W. Hughes, *Japan's Foreign and Security Policy Under the 'Abe Doctrine': New Dynamism or New Dead End?* (Basingstoke: Palgrave Macmillan, 2015), p. 57.

42 Linus Hagström and Jon Williamsson, '"Remilitarization", Really? Assessing Change in Japanese Foreign Security Policy', *Asian Security*, vol. 5, no. 3, 2009, pp. 251–2.

43 See Saadia M. Pekkanen, 'Japan Looks to Space Technology to Defend Itself from North Korea', *Forbes*, 28 January 2017, https://www.forbes.com/sites/saadiampekkanen/2017/01/28/japan-looks-to-space-technology-to-defend-itself-from-north-korea/#7686f897f4da; and Saadia M. Pekkanen, 'North Korea's Threats Revitalize Preemptive Strike Debate in Japan', *Forbes*, 25 April 2017, https://www.forbes.com/sites/saadiampekkanen/2017/04/25/north-koreas-threats-revitalize-preemptive strike debate in japan/#79cf67b36f7a.

44 Jiyū Minshutō Seimu Chōsakai (Policy Research Council of the LDP), 'Dandō Misairu Bōei no Jinsoku katsu Bapponteki na Kyōka ni Kan Suru Teigen' (Proposal for a Swift and Drastic Strengthening of Defences Against Ballistic Missiles), 30 March 2017, https://jimin.ncss.nifty.com/pdf/news/policy/134586_1.pdf. Translated into English by the authors of this article.

45 Tim Kelly and Nobuhiro Kubo, 'As North Korea Missile Threat Grows, Japan Lawmakers Argue for First Strike Options', Reuters, 8 March 2017, http://www.reuters.com/article/us-northkorea-missiles-japan-idUSK-BN16F0YE.

46 'Bōeishō, "Nihon-gata Tomahōku" kaihatsu kentō' (The Ministry of

Defense Considers Developing a 'Japanese Version of the Tomahawk'), *Yomiuri Shimbun*, 29 November 2017, https://www.yomiuri.co.jp/info/src/topic/20171127-OYT8T50134.html.

47 Robin Harding, 'Japan to Buy Cruise Missiles Capable of Striking North Korea', *Financial Times*, 8 December 2017, https://www.ft.com/content/a98b02da-dc05-11e7-a039-c64b1c09b482.

48 'Teki kichi kōgeki "yōnin" 75% chō, Kitachōsen ga hassha no gutaitekina kamae o misetara kōgeki mo 30% kosu' (More than 75% 'Approve' [Capabilities] to Attack Enemy Bases, More Than 30% also [Support] an Attack if North Korea Shows Signs of Launching), *Sankei Shimbun*, 17 April 2017, http://www.sankei.com/politics/news/170417/plt1704170037-n1.html.

49 Cabinet Secretariat, 'Cabinet Decision', pp. 1, 4, 7.

50 'Japan Officially Gave US Consent to Bring in Nuclear Weapons Ahead of Okinawa Reversion Accord: Document', *Japan Times*, 14 August 2017, https://www.japantimes.co.jp/news/2017/08/14/national/history/japan-officially-gave-u-s-consent-bring-nukes-ahead-okinawa-reversion-accord-document/.

51 See Linus Hagström, 'The "Abnormal" State: Identity, Norm/Exception and Japan', *European Journal of International Relations*, vol. 21, no. 1, 2015, pp. 122–45; and Hanssen, *Japan's Temporal Others*.

52 Hagström, 'The "Abnormal" State'.

53 Shinzo Abe, 'Ima koso "Sengo Rejīmu" no Dakkyaku o' (Now Is the Time to Break out of the 'Postwar Regime'), *Rekishi-tsū*, vol. 10, no. 1,

2011, pp. 69–76.

54 Masahisa Sato, statement 28, plenary session, Japanese parliament (upper house), 8 November 2013, translated into English by the authors of this article.

55 Manabu Matsuda, statement 226, cabinet committee, Japanese parliament (lower house), 24 October 2014, translated into English by the authors of this article.

56 Christian Wirth, 'Japan, China and East Asian Regional Integration: The Views of "Self" and "Other" from Tokyo and Beijing', *International Relations of the Asia-Pacific*, vol. 9, no. 3, 2009, pp. 469–96; Shogo Suzuki, 'The Rise of the Chinese "Other" in Japan's Construction of Identity: Is China a Focal Point of Japanese Nationalism?', *Pacific Review*, vol. 28, no. 1, 2015, pp. 95–116; Taku Tamaki, 'The Persistence of Reified Asia in Japan's Foreign Policy Narratives', *Pacific Review*, vol. 28, no. 1, 2015, pp. 23–45; Kai Schulze, 'Risks of Sameness, the "Rise of China" and Japan's Ontological Security', in Sebastian Maslow, Ra Mason and Paul O'Shea (eds), *Risk State: Japan's Foreign Policy in an Age of Uncertainty* (Farnham and Burlington: Ashgate, 2015), pp. 101–16; and Karl Gustafsson, 'Identity and Recognition: Remembering and Forgetting the Postwar in Sino-Japanese Relations', *Pacific Review*, vol. 28, no. 1, 2015, pp. 117–38; Karl Gustafsson, 'Routinised Recognition and Anxiety: Understanding the Deterioration in Sino-Japanese Relations', *Review of International Studies*, vol. 42, no. 4, 2016, pp. 613–33.

57 Linus Hagström, 'Normalizing Japan:

Supporter, Nuisance, or Wielder of Power in the North Korean Nuclear Talks?', *Asian Survey*, vol. 49, no. 5, 2009, pp. 831–51.

58 Ministry of Foreign Affairs of Japan, *Diplomatic Bluebook* (Tokyo: Ministry of Foreign Affairs, 2017), p. 33.

59 Ministry of Foreign Affairs, 'Gaikō ni kan suru yoron chōsa' (Public Opinion Survey on Diplomacy), 2002–17, https://survey.gov-online.go.jp/index-gai.html.

60 Linus Hagström and Ulv Hanssen, 'The North Korean Abduction Issue: Emotions, Securitisation and the Reconstruction of Japanese Identity from "Aggressor" to "Victim" and from "Pacifist" to "Normal"', *Pacific Review*, vol. 28, no. 1, 2015, pp. 71–93.

61 Linus Hagström, '"Power Shift" in East Asia? A Critical Reappraisal of Narratives on the Diaoyu/Senkaku Islands Incident in 2010', *Chinese Journal of International Politics*, vol. 5, no. 3, 2012, pp. 267–97; and Wrenn Yennie Lindgren and Petter Y. Lindgren, 'Identity Politics and the East China Sea: China as Japan's "Other"', *Asian Politics and Policy*, vol. 9, no. 3, 2017, pp. 378–401.

Implementing Safe Areas: Lessons from History

Astrid Stuth Cevallos and Bryan Frederick

It has been more than seven years since Syria plunged into civil war, and the situation there remains grim. Both government forces and insurgent groups have targeted civilians. President Bashar al-Assad's government has used chemical weapons against them, starved them by placing cities under siege, and detained them in prisons where they have been tortured, neglected and even executed. Insurgent groups, including the Islamic State (ISIS), have also used chemical weapons against Syrian civilians, attacked them with artillery, kidnapped them and executed them. In response, many civilians have fled their homes: the United Nations has registered more than five million Syrian refugees, including 3m in neighbouring Turkey alone.[1]

The Obama administration conducted airstrikes against ISIS strongholds under *Operation Inherent Resolve*, which has continued under the Trump administration. Yet the Obama White House declined, after significant analysis and debate, to create safe areas to protect internally displaced Syrians and slow refugee flows.[2] Last year, US President Donald Trump said he would 'absolutely do safe zones in Syria for the people'.[3] While these have yet to materialise, in May 2017, Russia, Iran and Turkey pledged to build four 'de-escalation zones' in which a ceasefire between government and insurgent forces would be enforced, though how or by whom remains

Astrid Stuth Cevallos is an adjunct policy analyst at the RAND Corporation. **Bryan Frederick** is a political scientist at the RAND Corporation.

Survival | vol. 60 no. 6 | December 2018–January 2019 | pp. 159–180   DOI 10.1080/00396338.2018.1542805

unclear.[4] The Pentagon has previously estimated that a safe area in Syria would require between 15,000 and 30,000 ground troops to defend civilians from ground attacks, but officials continue to review resource requirements, rules of engagement and potential consequences.[5]

Safe areas were a staple of peacekeeping missions in the early 1990s, when policymakers perceived them as a means of protecting civilians and limiting refugee flows at less cost compared with a full-scale military intervention. But after a few high-profile failures in which belligerents breached safe areas to commit atrocities against civilians who had sought protection within them, the approach fell out of favour. It has since found its way back into policy debates as a result of the situation in Syria. History shows that a safe area's ability to protect civilians depends on the resources committed by the intervening state and its willingness to suffer casualties; the rules of engagement under which the forces guarding the safe areas operate; and the geographic concentration of the population being protected.

Why safe areas?

Safe areas are a policy option that states may choose in order to protect civilians during an armed conflict. This article is based on a study[6] that reviewed the creation and efficacy of five safe areas and four no-fly zones (the latter of which are more limited policy tools) that were declared over the past three decades and were created:

- during a war;
- to protect civilians – that is, unarmed non-combatants – and not just to provide aid;
- by external actors that deployed ground troops to defend the relevant population;
- within the borders of a country experiencing conflict; and
- within a limited geographic area.

Historically speaking, most safe areas have been established through United Nations Security Council (UNSC) resolutions that authorise troops to protect civilians and humanitarian-aid operations by denying warring parties access to a designated geographic area.[7] This approach was most widely used in the early 1990s. The Cold War had both fuelled many civil wars and prevented the UN from taking steps to minimise their consequences; its end permitted new efforts to mitigate the costs of war. In 1992, the UNSC noted that 'the absence of war and military conflicts amongst States does not in itself ensure international peace and security'.[8] Whereas the UNSC authorised 18 peacekeeping missions in the 44 years from 1945 to 1989, it authorised 49 such missions in the 24 years between 1990 and 2014.[9]

Post-Cold War civil conflicts have tended to kill fewer civilians, in both absolute and relative terms, than Cold War-era proxy conflicts.[10] Yet without external support from superpowers, warring parties in many post-Cold War civil conflicts depend on looting civilian possessions and raw materials, which may induce more civilians to leave their homes.[11] Indeed, the number of civilians displaced as a result of civil conflict increased between 1990 and 1994, before declining from 1995 to 1999.[12] By providing shelter and protection for displaced civilians within their home countries, safe areas can help to limit refugee flows. This may help to prevent conflict spillover and may even shorten a conflict by removing a source of rebel funding. Refugees in neighbouring states are an important source of support for rebel groups, particularly if refugees share the groups' ethnicity.[13]

In cases where external powers did not perceive a sufficient national interest to intervene decisively to end civil wars, safe areas have served the political and humanitarian function of channelling concerns regarding violence against civilians into action intended to protect them, and to contain the underlying conflict. Establishing such areas is not without risk, however. In some cases, they may serve as unintended sanctuaries for a belligerent party. They may also lead to mission creep or escalation.

Historical cases

The five post-Cold War conflicts that meet the five criteria listed above are northern Iraq (1991–2003), Liberia (1992–96), Somalia (1993–94), Bosnia (1993–95) and Rwanda (1994).[14] In addition, air forces have created no-fly zones – which aim to protect civilians by banning military and sometimes even civilian flights in a defined airspace – in four post-Cold War conflicts: northern Iraq (1991–2003), southern Iraq (1992–2003), Bosnia (1992–95) and Libya (2011).[15] In Bosnia and Iraq, no-fly zones covered the airspace above safe areas. Table 1 captures essential aspects of these civilian-protection operations.

The following summaries sketch the circumstances in which each safe area or no-fly zone was established, and the outcomes of each civilian-protection effort.

Table 1. **Civilian-protection areas (safe areas and no-fly zones)**

Country	Years	Main enforcers	Operation name	Maximum troops	Aircraft	Total sorties
Northern Iraq	1991–2003	US, UK, France	**SA:** *Provide Comfort* **NFZ:** *Northern Watch*	20,000 (US: >10,000)	45	>75,000
Southern Iraq	1992–2003	US	**NFZ:** *Southern Watch*	25,000 (air personnel)	270	150,000
Liberia	1992–96	ECOWAS, UN	**SA:** ECOMOG	19,000	N/A	N/A
Somalia	1992–93	UNITAF, US, UN	**SA:** *Restore Hope*	38,000 (US: 26,000)	N/A	N/A
Bosnia	1993–95	UN, NATO	**SA:** UNPROFOR **NFZ:** *Sky Monitor, Deny Flight, Deliberate Force*	11,500 5,000 (air personnel)	>400	109,000
Rwanda	1994	UN, France	**SA:** UNAMIR, *Operation Turquoise*	500–3,000	N/A	N/A
Libya	2011	NATO	**NFZ:** *Odyssey Dawn, Unified Protector*	8,000 (air personnel)	260	26,500

SOURCES: Daniel L. Haulman, 'Crisis in Iraq: Operation PROVIDE COMFORT', in A. Timothy Warnock (ed.), *Short of War: Major USAF Contingency Operations, 1947–1997* (Maxwell AFB, AL: Air University Press, 2000), p. 181; Linda D. Kozaryn, 'Patrolling Iraq's Northern Skies', American Forces Press Service, 1 June 1998, http://archive.defense.gov/news/newsarticle.aspx?id=43185; Karl P. Mueller, *Denying Flight: Strategic Options for Employing No-Fly Zones* (Santa Monica, CA: RAND Corporation, 2013), pp. 4–5; William J. Allen, 'Crisis in Southern Iraq: Operation SOUTHERN WATCH', in Warnock (ed.), *Short of War*, p. 193; Human Rights Watch, 'Waging War to Keep the Peace: The ECOMOG Intervention and Human Rights', 1 June 1993, https://www.hrw.org/report/1993/06/01/liberia-waging-war-keep-peace/ecomog-intervention-and-human-rights; Quentin Outram, 'Cruel Wars and Safe Havens: Humanitarian Aid in Liberia, 1989–1996', *Disasters*, vol. 21, no. 3, 1997, p. 195; Daniel L. Haulman, 'Crisis in Somalia: Operations PROVIDE RELIEF and RESTORE HOPE', in Warnock (ed.), *Short of War*, p. 210; US General Accounting Office, 'Peace Operations: Cost of DOD Operations in Somalia', March 1994; US General Accounting Office, 'Peace Operations: Heavy Use of Key Capabilities May Affect Response to Regional Conflicts', March 1995; IISS, *The Military Balance 1994–1995* (London: Brassey's for the IISS, 1994), pp. 274–5; IISS, *The Military Balance 1995–1996* (Oxford: Oxford University Press for the IISS, 1995), p. 304; Richard L. Sargent, 'Aircraft Used in Deliberate Force', in Robert C. Owen (ed.), *Deliberate Force: A Case Study in Effective Air Campaigning* (Maxwell AFB, AL: Air University Press, 2000), p. 200; Kurt Miller, 'Deny Flight and Deliberate Force: An Effective Use of Airpower?', US Army Command and General Staff College, June 1997, p. 47; Donald C. F. Daniel, Bradd C. Hayes and Chantal de Jonge Oudraat, *Coercive Inducement and the Containment of International Crises* (Washington DC: United States Institute for Peace, 1999), p. 130; 'Operation UNIFIED PROTECTOR Final Mission Stats', NATO, 2 November 2011, https://www.nato.int/nato_static/assets/pdf/pdf_2011_11/20111108_111107-factsheet_up_factsfigures_en.pdf.

Northern Iraq

A week after *Operation Desert Storm* concluded in February 1991, Iraqi Kurds rebelled against Saddam Hussein's Ba'athist regime.[16] When the Iraqi government began to retaliate against the insurgents, at least 400,000 – and perhaps up to 2m[17] – Kurds fled to Turkey. In response to the targeting and displacement of this population, US forces launched *Operation Provide Comfort*. This created a safe area in northern Iraq that encompassed the cities of Zakho, Amadiyah, Suri and Duhok.[18] To protect Kurdish civilians, as well as coalition aircraft and troops providing humanitarian assistance, the United States Air Force also established a no-fly zone that banned fixed-wing and rotary-wing aircraft north of the 36th parallel. From April to July 1991, more than 200 aircraft and 20,000 coalition troops pushed Iraqi troops out of the safe area, to which, under the cover of US forces, hundreds of thousands of Kurdish refugees then returned to occupy internally displaced person (IDP) camps.[19]

US ground troops departed northern Iraq in July 1991, leaving the UN High Commissioner for Refugees in charge of the IDP camps. A major test of the safe area's efficacy came in late 1996, when one of the two main Kurdish factions allied with Iraqi government troops to seize control of a city within the area's borders. The US punished the Iraqi government for its incursion by launching cruise missiles at radar installations in southern Iraq and extending the southern no-fly zone to the 33rd parallel. In January 1997, *Operation Northern Watch* replaced *Operation Provide Comfort*. The no-fly zone remained in effect through the US invasion of Iraq in March 2003.[20]

The northern Iraq safe area and the no-fly zone above it enabled hundreds of thousands of Kurdish refugees to return to their homes, and defended them against Iraqi government attacks.[21] These efforts also eased Turkey's concerns about the effects of an influx of Kurdish refugees. As a result, *Operation Provide Comfort* is generally regarded as the most successful implementation of the safe-area concept to date.

Southern Iraq

Like the Kurds in northern Iraq, Shi'ites in southern Iraq rebelled against Saddam's Sunni-dominated Ba'athist regime in early 1991. As the Iraqi government attempted to quell the uprising, many Shi'ites fled to Saudi Arabia and Iran. Yet US forces did not create a safe area in southern Iraq. Instead, beginning in August 1992, they worked with forces from the United Kingdom and France to implement a no-fly zone south of the 32nd parallel, in part to prevent the Iraqi government from targeting Shia civilians with aerial attacks.[22] In 1996, coalition forces extended the southern no-fly zone to the 33rd parallel after Iraqi ground forces engaged in operations within the northern safe area.

Operation Southern Watch defended against most Iraqi air incursions into the southern no-fly zone and destroyed many Iraqi surface-to-air missile sites. But Iraqi government forces adapted, substituting artillery fire for airpower. Without robust rules of engagement or a safe area defended by ground forces, the coalition was unable to stop many of these attacks against Shia civilians.[23] Hussein's forces remained largely in control.[24]

Bosnia

In April 1992, Bosnia – the most ethnically diverse of the Yugoslav republics, with a population that was roughly half Muslim (Bosniak), one-third Orthodox Serb and one-fifth Roman Catholic Croat[25] – seceded from Yugoslavia and declared independence. Bosnian Serbs rejected the declaration and allied with Serb troops from the Yugoslav National Army to capture Bosnian territory. More than a million civilians were displaced as the newly established Bosnian Serb Army (BSA) embarked on a mission to 'cleanse' regions of Bosnia of non-Serbs.[26] To protect them, the UNSC created a no-fly zone over Bosnia before any safe areas were established. NATO airborne early-warning aircraft monitored the no-fly zone, but were not authorised to engage the approximately 500 flights that illegally entered the zone between October 1992 and April 1993.[27] In March 1993, the UNSC expanded the no-fly zone and changed the rules of engagement to permit 'all necessary measures' to enforce it. Before launching an airstrike, however, NATO forces were required to receive approval from the UN, in what came to be known as the 'dual-key' process.[28]

Alarmed about actions that US secretary of state Warren Christopher described as 'tantamount to genocide',[29] but reluctant to get involved in a costly, protracted conflict,[30] US policymakers worked with other members of the UNSC to create safe areas in six cities – Srebrenica, Sarajevo, Zepa, Gorazde, Tuzla and Bihac. Bosnian Serb paramilitary units were required to leave these areas, which were established in April and May 1993, and to end all armed attacks.[31] In June, the UN Protection Force (UNPROFOR) was deployed 'to deter attacks against the safe areas'. UNPROFOR was authorised to use force against attacking troops, and UN member states could support UNPROFOR and defend the safe areas using airpower.[32] But this did not change the BSA's behaviour. It refused to withdraw its heavy weapons from the areas surrounding the designated cities, and it continued to bomb them, specifically targeting 'civilian-inhabited areas, often in ways calculated to maximize civilian casualties', as reported by the UN at the time.[33]

Although UNPROFOR requested an additional 32,000 ground troops to defend civilians within the safe areas, UNSC members initially declined to contribute any additional troops. It eventually authorised only an extra 7,600.[34] In 1994 and 1995, there were approximately 5,000 UNPROFOR troops defending Sarajevo and Zepa; 5,000 defending Tuzla and Srebrenica; 1,000 defending Bihac; and 500 defending Gorazde.[35] Over the course of the war, the BSA – claiming that Bosniak militias used the safe areas as sanctuaries and staging grounds for assaults on the BSA – attacked them all. There was some truth to BSA claims: in October 1994, the Bosniak Fifth Corps of the Army of Bosnia and Herzegovina launched an attack from the Bihac safe area.[36] Ultimately, Sarajevo, Tuzla, Bihac and Gorazde (the largest areas) were successfully defended against the BSA. But in July 1995, BSA forces breached Srebrenica and Zepa, while most of the meagre UNPROFOR troops defending them withdrew. In addition, the dual-key process necessitating clearance from both NATO and the UN for airstrikes prevented these areas' timely aerial defence. In a matter of days, the BSA slaughtered more than 8,000 Bosnian Muslim men and boys who had taken shelter in Srebrenica.[37] A month later, a BSA artillery attack killed 37 people in Sarajevo. NATO responded to these developments with an air campaign to deter further BSA attacks. Throughout September 1995, NATO aircraft flew sorties attacking BSA ammunition bunkers and surface-to-air missile sites. This mission crippled the BSA and compelled it to come to the negotiating table less than six months later.[38]

Liberia

From 1989 to 1997, the rebel forces of Charles Taylor's National Patriotic Front of Liberia (NPFL) waged a civil war against president Samuel Doe's regime. The conflict claimed 200,000 lives and displaced 1.2m people. In late 1990, the Economic Community of West African States Military Observer Group (ECOMOG) deployed 3,000 troops to Monrovia to help keep the peace during a ceasefire. Through its intervention, ECOMOG hoped to stem refugee flows, stop the killing of Nigerian citizens in Monrovia, and limit the conflict's spillover into neighbouring countries, including Sierra Leone, where the Revolutionary United Front (RUF) rebel group was receiving support from Taylor's NPFL. But fighting flared again in October 1992, when Taylor's NPFL began directly attacking ECOMOG forces during what became known as the 'siege of Monrovia'. In response, ECOMOG adopted more robust rules of engagement to protect civilians against attack and created a de facto safe area in Monrovia.[39]

The civil war in Liberia continued until 1996, when Taylor felt sufficiently confident that he would win the presidency in the following year's elections to rein in the violence. During the conflict, ECOMOG had protected approximately 700,000 IDPs who sought sanctuary in the capital.[40] But ECOMOG's operation was not without flaws. Throughout the intervention, ECOMOG troops were underpaid and often resorted to looting the possessions of the people they were meant to be protecting. In addition, ECOMOG forces were accused of cooperating with and providing sanctuary to forces fighting against Taylor's NPFL.[41] These groups – and ECOMOG forces – were accused of human-rights violations, including the bombing of civilian targets.[42]

Somalia

In January 1991, riots against the dictatorship of Mohammed Siad Barre erupted into civil war. Violence between Somali warlords and their militias exacerbated the effects of an ongoing drought and fuelled a famine that left hundreds of thousands starving and convinced a million people to flee the country.[43] In April 1992, the UNSC authorised the first United Nations Operation in Somalia (UNOSOM) mission to provide humanitarian relief.[44] But fighters hijacked food supplies and the famine grew worse. To defend humanitarian-relief workers, supplies and recipients in Mogadishu, the US contributed airlift capabilities to the mission in August 1992, and deployed troops in December 1992. The US-led United Task Force (UNITAF) of 38,000 heavily armed soldiers from 23 nations also helped bring about a ceasefire between two of the strongest warring parties.[45] By May 1993 – after saving an estimated 250,000 lives – UNITAF handed over its responsibilities to the UN under UNOSOM II.[46]

Eager to build on UNITAF's successes, UNOSOM II took on the new mission of bringing the conflict to an end by compelling the belligerents to come to a negotiated political settlement. The 16,000 troops left over from UNITAF were not enough to enforce the brief ceasefire, however. On 3 October, Somali militiamen shot down two MH-60 *Black Hawk* helicopters with rocket-propelled grenades. In total, 18 US soldiers and between 500 and 1,500 Somalis died in the ensuing battle. The US soon deployed a joint special-operations task force to Mogadishu to help UN forces capture one of the main militia leaders as the conflict grew more violent. By March 1994, most US troops had withdrawn from Somalia, having failed in their expanded 'nation-building' mission.

Rwanda

Within hours of Rwandan president Juvénal Habyarimana's apparent assassination in April 1994, Hutu extremists calling themselves the Interahamwe slaughtered ten Belgian peacekeepers stationed in Kigali as part of the UN Assistance Mission in Rwanda (UNAMIR). The Interahamwe hoped the violence would prompt UN forces to leave Rwanda just as US forces had withdrawn from Somalia following the Battle of Mogadishu. Hutu militants went on to kill 20,000 Tutsis in just three days.[47] In response to the carnage, UNAMIR commander Romeo Dallaire asked for 2,500 additional troops and more robust rules of engagement to protect civilians. Instead, the UNSC voted to withdraw 2,000 peacekeepers, leaving Dallaire with approximately 500 troops authorised to use force in self-defence. In response to the UNSC's vote to reduce UNAMIR's strength, a few of the council's non-permanent members attempted to establish a new mission with 5,000 well-armed troops that would take control of Kigali and create safe areas around the country. But no additional peacekeepers deployed to Rwanda during the conflict.[48]

As members of the Tutsi Rwandan Patriotic Front gained control of Rwandan territory in June, France – a long-time supporter of the Hutu government in Rwanda – sent 2,500 soldiers to set up a *zone humanitaire sûre*, or safe area, in southern Rwanda. Most of those who found refuge within its confines were Hutus who had perpetrated the genocide against their Tutsi countrymen.[49] By the time troops deployed under France's UN-approved *Operation Turquoise* arrived, most of the Tutsi victims of the genocide had already been killed.[50] Estimates suggest that at least half a million Rwandans – including 75% of the Tutsi population in Rwanda prior to the conflict – were killed in 100 days.[51] Still, the safe area saved tens of thousands of lives and prevented some Hutu IDPs from becoming refugees in Zaire (now the Democratic Republic of the Congo). The 500 remaining UN soldiers also managed to dissuade the Hutus from attacking some 20,000 to 25,000 Rwandan Tutsis in de facto safe areas in major buildings and landmarks around Kigali.[52]

Libya

When Libyan dictator Muammar Gadhafi retaliated against civilians in the wake of popular uprisings in February 2011, the Arab League voted for a no-fly zone over Libya, one of its members. The UNSC authorised the zone with the explicit mandate to 'take all necessary measures … to protect civilians'. The rules of engagement allowed for airstrikes against Libyan-government ground forces and military installations.[53] In mid-March, American, British and French troops initiated *Operation Odyssey Dawn*. British and French aircraft flew most of the sorties and struck Libyan tanks and air-defence systems. The US provided most of the missiles, precision-guided munitions, air-refuelling and aerial-surveillance capabilities, as well as all electronic-warfare capabilities.[54] At the end of March, NATO assumed responsibility for enforcing the no-fly zone under *Operation Unified Protector*, which ended after Gadhafi's death in October 2011.

The initial no-fly zone and air campaign in Libya lasted seven months. Because the mission prevented the mass killing of civilians, NATO analysts and policymakers viewed it as a success, especially because of its low human and financial cost.[55] The intervention failed to bring stability to the country, however. Between the end of the operation and August 2016, the country had nine different prime ministers. Moreover, al-Qaeda and ISIS found sanctuary in Libya's substantial ungoverned spaces, prompting additional US airstrikes.[56] Although NATO interpreted the UN mandate to include regime change, NATO forces decided not to pursue stabilisation operations following the intervention.[57] In retrospect, the deployment of ground troops might have improved the chances of a stable post-war recovery.[58]

Lessons and implications

While it may be impossible to assess whether, or to what extent, implementing safe areas protects more civilians than not doing so, these historical cases suggest that their success or failure depends on the resources and resolve of the forces that implement them, the rules of engagement and geography.[59]

Resolve and capabilities

More than any other factor, the intervener's resolve and capabilities determine a safe area's ability to protect the civilian population. While threatening to use force may deter some attacks, belligerents are likely to test the credibility of such threats. To defend the civilians within a safe area, foreign military forces must be willing and able to enforce their promises of protection.[60] The consequences of not doing so can be dire. In May 1995, after Bosnian Serbs took 370 UN peacekeepers hostage in response to NATO airstrikes on a BSA ammunition depot, the UN held off on requesting additional NATO airstrikes.[61] Two months later, Bosnian Serbs overran the Srebrenica safe area while the 300 UN peacekeepers charged with protecting it stepped aside, unwilling to challenge the better-equipped BSA. In about a week, the BSA rounded up and killed 8,000 Bosnian Muslim men and boys.[62] In Rwanda, the 500 troops that remained after most UN troops withdrew failed to prevent the genocidal slaughter of over half a million Tutsis and moderate Hutus.

The extent to which the capabilities and resolve of the intervener are tested depends on a variety of factors, including the location and size of the safe area, and the capabilities and resolve of the parties targeting civilians. Symmetric, non-conventional wars in which weak rebel groups face weak governments will involve different weapons and doctrine than will conventional, internal wars in which professional armies split into factions.[63] In Rwanda, which experienced a symmetric, non-conventional conflict involving poorly disciplined and equipped forces, 'even a minor presence could save many lives', according to Taylor Seybolt, because 'militiamen who were very good at bludgeoning unarmed civilians melted away when confronted by soldiers'.[64] In the few months that it took the Rwandan Patriotic Front to drive Hutu forces out of Rwanda, the small UN force that remained in Kigali protected thousands of civilians. In such cases, the intervener's willingness to tolerate casualties may be just as important as its military capabilities. While a few hundred UN peacekeepers in Rwanda intimidated Hutu militiamen armed with machetes, thousands of UN peacekeepers in Bosnia – supported by NATO airpower – failed to defend two of the six safe areas in the country against better-trained and -organised forces fighting a conventional internal conflict. In such cases, effective safe areas require sizeable and well-equipped ground forces, and may benefit from being located within a no-fly zone enforced by air forces that are authorised to use airstrikes, as in Bosnia and Iraq. Those examples also make clear, however, that airpower alone is not enough to protect civilians targeted by artillery and ground troops.

Mustering sufficient ground forces with the training, equipment and resolve necessary to defend civilians in safe areas is a persistent problem. This difficulty may be less acute in conflicts in which foreign powers have a clear interest in the outcome, and may therefore be more willing to intervene directly. Should this interest be lacking, however, foreign governments are likely to hesitate to commit resources and bear the costs of protecting safe areas even as they condemn the killing of civilians. In the cases discussed here, UN forces that were reliant on a diverse set of member countries for troops were often the least willing to accept casualties. In Somalia and Rwanda, several member countries withdrew their troops after suffering casualties, leaving behind a small, under-resourced force. In Bosnia, the Bosnian Serb tactic of taking UN troops hostage made UN forces reluctant to defend safe areas against BSA incursions.

The 'Brahimi Report' published by the UN in 2000 acknowledged that these incidents have made it more difficult for UN member states to foster the domestic support needed to endorse UN peace operations. It also noted that 'developed States tend not to see strategic national interests at stake' in the kind of conflicts the UN often seeks to address, which exacerbates the problem of getting well-trained and well-equipped forces to participate in UN peace operations in a timely manner.[65] In contrast, US-led efforts in Iraq and NATO efforts in Libya arguably were more effective because forces were able to deploy rapidly with sufficient force, and were willing to suffer costs, including casualties. Safe areas appear more likely to succeed if they are created by a UN mandate, but defended by a coalition of states under the leadership of a single, powerful state with unified command and control.[66] In recognition of this, the UN sometimes puts a highly capable troop-contributing country in charge of potential flashpoints. In the Democratic Republic of the Congo, the European Union-led International Emergency Multinational Force deployed in 2003 to re-establish control when the weak UN Mission in the Democratic Republic of Congo (MONUC, now MONUSCO) faltered. But despite the widespread recognition of previous shortcomings, gaps in the quantity and quality of the troops deployed by UN member states to protect civilians still exist.[67]

Robust rules of engagement
To be effective, safe areas also require a mandate that explicitly authorises the use of force to protect civilians. UN peacekeeping missions with clear mandates to protect civilians using 'all means necessary' can reduce rebel attacks against civilians, but those without such mandates have tended to provoke an *increase* in rebel attacks against civilians.[68] UN peace operations in the 1990s aspired to 'impartiality'. The need for safe areas, however, is greatest in more violent civil conflicts in which at least one party deliberately targets civilians. In these cases, the mission to protect civilians demands that interventions not remain neutral. Moreover, the costs of attempting

to maintain neutrality could be high. In order to limit collateral damage and decrease the risk of escalation, UN operations in Bosnia had extremely restrictive rules of engagement and, as noted, complicated command-and-control systems for approving NATO airstrikes. These rules led to a three-day delay in approving Dutch peacekeepers' requests for NATO close air-support missions over Srebrenica. In the event, the BSA captured the town and slaughtered thousands of civilians.[69]

The Brahimi Report noted that 'no failure did more to damage the standing and credibility of United Nations peacekeeping in the 1990s than its reluctance to distinguish victim from aggressor'.[70] To remedy this, the report argued that 'mandates should specify an operation's authority to use force' and – as discussed above – that UN operations should consist of larger and better-equipped forces capable of acting as a 'credible deterrent'.[71] Most importantly, it concluded that 'peacekeepers – troops or police – who witness violence against civilians should be presumed to be authorized to stop it'.[72]

Geographically concentrated populations

Safe areas appear to be most useful when violence is carried out against a particular sub-population, particularly one that is located in what Barry Posen describes as 'geographically limited areas', or that is 'too weak militarily to defend itself'.[73] The US Army War College's handbook *Mass Atrocity Response Operations* describes safe areas as 'an appropriate approach when violence against particular victim concentrations is imminent and when the [intervening force's] land force strength is limited'.[74] Concentrated populations are easier to protect with relatively limited troops. More widely dispersed populations, by contrast, require greater resources to protect – resources that may not be available when the intervening state has already ruled out decisive intervention to end the conflict. Iraqi Kurds, for example, were concentrated in cities and villages north of the 36th parallel, and the safe area and no-fly zone created under *Operation Provide Comfort* offered Kurds protection throughout the entire region of northern Iraq even though ground forces were concentrated near three main cities. In contrast, Rwandan Tutsis were dispersed across the country, living in both urban and rural areas. Even a much larger force than the one available at the time would have struggled to adequately protect members of this population from their neighbours.

A costly solution

While safe areas can be a useful policy option to prevent atrocities against civilians, the prominent failures of the 1990s demonstrate that safe areas require substantial resources and a commitment to use force in order to be effective. Accordingly, advising and implementing safe areas should be done with considerable caution.

Since 2011, there have been repeated calls for US and NATO forces to create a safe area or a no-fly zone in Syria to protect civilians targeted by the Assad regime and ISIS forces, and to stem the tide of refugees entering Turkey and Europe. In February 2016, for example, this suggestion was made by two former US diplomats writing in the *Washington Post*.[75] Past experience suggests that such a mission would need a substantial US commitment to be effective, however. A 2013 RAND analysis of the options for using US airpower in Syria evaluated the possibility of creating no-fly zones to defend safe areas and concluded that 'negating Syrian airpower would have only a marginal direct effect on civilian casualties, which have mostly been caused by ground forces'.[76] Therefore, although 'airpower could play a major role in defending designated safe areas against attack by regime forces … there is a need for effective defensive forces on the ground'.[77] Most importantly, the report concluded that defending safe areas would be equivalent to 'full intervention on the side of the opposition'.[78] As such, it 'could become a prolonged and demanding commitment' that 'might well lead to even deeper involvement in the war'.[79]

Safe areas and no-fly zones carry a risk of mission creep or escalation for two main reasons. Firstly, they may inadvertently provide sanctuary for belligerents, enabling them to expand the fight.[80] Within the confines of the safe area, belligerents may take advantage of humanitarian aid and civilian resources (food, money and potential recruits), and use the opportunity to regroup before launching attacks of their own. This dynamic occurred in safe areas in Bosnia, Liberia, Rwanda and Libya. Furthermore, in some cases, safe areas may also contribute to conflict spillover by providing sanctuary to the militias of transnational ethnic groups. The Turkey-based Kurdistan Workers' Party (PKK) used the safe area in northern Iraq as a base from which it recruited new members, gathered financial resources (often through illegal trafficking) and launched military operations against Turkey.[81]

Secondly, any failure to defend a safe area may call into question the reputation and resolve of the intervener, and thereby encourage it to take more decisive action against the perpetrators of the attack.[82] The fall of Srebrenica led to an intensified air campaign designed to bring Serbs to the negotiating table in the hopes of ending the conflict. The no-fly zones in Iraq established after the 1991 Gulf War did not end until after the 2003 US invasion. In most cases, then, safe areas are not likely to remain limited efforts. From this perspective, safe areas may be preferable as a complement to, rather than a substitute for, robust military intervention into a conflict.

Judging from the historical record, operations to protect civilians during war are often much costlier and carry much greater risk than anticipated. No-fly zones are attractive in that they minimise risk to the intervening state, but they seldom provide substantial protection to civilians without additional and significant military efforts on the ground. Safe areas defended by ground forces can be effective in protecting civilians, especially when the populations to be protected are highly concentrated. But such areas usually require major military commitments – in terms of both capabilities and resolve – to succeed. Efforts to create safe areas 'on the cheap' have often resulted in disaster. It would be better not to repeat this mistake.

Notes

1   United Nations High Commissioner for Refugees, 'Syria Regional Refugee Response Inter-agency Information Sharing Portal', 1 May 2017, http://data.unhcr.org/syrianrefugees/regional.php.

2   Mark Mazzetti and Peter Baker, 'U.S. Is Debating Ways to Shield Syrian Civilians', *New York Times*, 22 October 2015, https://www.nytimes.com/2015/10/23/world/middleeast/us-considering-ways-to-shield-syrian-civilians.html.

3   'Trump Says He Will "Absolutely Do Safe Zones" in Syria', Reuters, 27 January 2017, http://www.cnbc.com/2017/01/25/trump-says-he-will-absolutely-do-safe-zones-in-syria.html.

4   Andrew Roth and Karen DeYoung, 'Putin Pushes Syrian Safe Zone Proposals in Talks with Turkish Leader', *Washington Post*, 3 May 2017, https://www.washingtonpost.com/world/putin-pushes-syrian-safe-zone-proposals-in-talks-with-turkish-leader/2017/05/03/b75d003a-2ffc-11e7-a335-faoae1940305_story.html.

5   See Justin Fishel, 'Up to 30,000 Troops Needed for Syria Safe Zone, Kerry Says', ABC News, 24 February 2016, http://abcnews.go.com/International/30000-troops-needed-syria-safe-zone-kerry/story?id=37173697; and Lolita C. Baldor, 'Would "Safe Zones" Help Syria? Defense Secretary Mattis Calls for Review of Russia Proposal', Associated Press, 8 May 2017, http://www.pbs.org/newshour/rundown/safe-zones-help-syria-defense-secretary-mattis-calls-review-russia-proposal/.

6   Stephen Watts et al., *Limited Intervention: Evaluating the Effectiveness of Limited Stabilization, Limited Strike, and Containment Operations* (Santa Monica, CA: RAND Corporation, 2017). This research was conducted within the RAND Arroyo Center, a federally funded research and development centre sponsored by the United States Army.

7   There are two variations on safe areas. 'Safe zones' are larger safe areas that physically protect civilians where they normally live, while 'safe havens' are smaller safe areas that protect IDPs in specific places within the borders of their country. See Barry R. Posen, 'Military Responses to Refugee Disasters', *International Security*, vol. 21, no. 1, 1996, pp. 77–8, 93–104, 110. Posen argues that 'safe havens should be viewed as analytically distinct from safe zones. They are primarily refuges, not places of normal existence. They are an expedient to be adopted only in the most dire circumstances. They are very demanding of every aspect of military power, ground and air, and logistics.' In this essay, the two types are discussed together under the rubric of 'safe areas', since both aim to protect a civilian population by denying belligerents access to a specific area through the threat or use of military force.

8   United Nations Security Council, 'Note by the President of the Security Council', S/23500, 31 January 1992, p. 3.

9   Bruno Stagno Ugarte and Jared Genser, 'Evolution of the Security Council's Engagement on Human Rights', in Jared Genser and Bruno Stagno Ugarte (eds), *The United Nations Security Council in the Age of Human Rights* (New York: Cambridge University Press, 2014), pp. 14–15. See also Stathis N. Kalyvas and Laia Balcells, 'International System and Technologies of Rebellion: How the Cold War Shaped Internal Conflict', *American Political Science Review*, vol. 104, no. 3, August 2010, p. 417.

10   See Laia Balcells and Stathis N. Kalyvas, 'Does Warfare Matter? Severity, Duration, and Outcomes of Civil Wars', *Journal of Conflict Resolution*, vol. 58, no. 8, 2014, pp. 17–18. According to Kalyvas and Balcells (see pp. 421–3), during the superpower rivalry that characterised the Cold War, the United States and

the Soviet Union often channelled material support to opposing sides of a civil conflict, increasing the relative power of both weak governments and weak rebel groups. As a result, many rebel groups succeeded in mounting lengthy insurgent campaigns – two-thirds of the civil wars during the Cold War were irregular wars. Once the Cold War ended, civil wars lost their appeal as proxy wars, and both sides reduced their support for governments and rebel groups. But civil wars did not disappear. After the collapse of the Soviet Union, well-armed post-communist armies waged conventional wars for territorial and governmental control, and weak governments no longer receiving superpower support fought symmetric, non-conventional wars with similarly weak rebel groups.

11 See Erik Melander, Magnus Oeberg and Jonathan Hall, 'Are "New Wars" More Atrocious? Battle Severity, Civilians Killed and Forced Migration Before and After the End of the Cold War', *European Journal of International Relations*, vol. 15, no. 3, 2009, p. 530; and Daniel Byman et al., *Trends in Outside Support for Insurgent Movements* (Santa Monica, CA: RAND Corporation, 2001). See also Stathis N. Kalyvas, '"New" and "Old" Civil Wars: A Valid Distinction?', *World Politics*, vol. 54, no. 51, October 2011, p. 117.

12 Melander, Oeberg and Hall, 'Are "New Wars" More Atrocious?', p. 528.

13 See Idean Salehyan and Kristian Skrede Gleditsch, 'Refugees and the Spread of Civil War', *International Organization*, vol. 60, no. 2, Spring 2006, pp. 335–66; and Halvard Buhaug and Kristian Skrede Gleditsch, 'Contagion or Confusion? Why Conflicts Cluster in Space', *International Studies Quarterly*, vol. 52, no. 2, June 2008, pp. 215–33.

14 There were two 'near miss' cases from the 1990s that we examined, but that did not qualify based on our criteria: Sri Lankan 'open relief centres' (ORCs) from 1990 to 2002, and Afghan IDP camps from 1994 to 1996. Neither of these had a military component. Rather, both were run by the UNHCR, and were successful as long as the belligerents agreed not to fight in the safe areas. According to Phil Orchard, security in the Sri Lankan ORCs was 'relative': one ORC 'was shut down by government forces for a year', and the government 'routinely removed people' from another ORC to torture them. Similarly, in the Afghan case, a 'lack of security and the hazard of land mines [were] a major impediment to effective relief delivery'. See Phil Orchard, 'Revisiting Humanitarian Safe Areas for Civilian Protection', *Global Governance*, vol. 20, no. 1, January–March 2014, pp. 55–75.

15 See Alexander Benard, 'Lessons from Iraq and Bosnia on the Theory and Practice of No-fly Zones', *Journal of Strategic Studies*, vol. 27, no. 3, 2004, p. 455.

16 See Samantha Power, *'A Problem from Hell': America and the Age of Genocide* (New York: Harper Perennial, 2003), pp. 189, 237.

17 For the former figure, see Bill Frelick, 'Down the Rabbit Hole: The Strange Logic of Internal Flight Alternative', in US Committee for

Refugees, 'World Refugee Survey 1999', p. 23. For the latter figure, see David M. Malone, *The International Struggle Over Iraq* (New York: Oxford University Press, 2006), p. 85.

18 See Daniel L. Haulman, 'Crisis in Iraq: Operation PROVIDE COMFORT', in A. Timothy Warnock (ed.), *Short of War: Major USAF Contingency Operations, 1947–1997* (Maxwell AFB, AL: Air University Press, 2000), p. 181.

19 See 'War and Humanitarian Action: Iraq and the Balkans', in UNHCR, *The State of the World's Refugees 2000: Fifty Years of Humanitarian Action* (Oxford: Oxford University Press, 2000), pp. 216–17. See also Taylor B. Seybolt, *Humanitarian Military Intervention: The Conditions for Success and Failure* (New York: Oxford University Press/SIPRI, 2007), p. 192; and J.R. McKay, *Shifting Sands: Air Coercion and Iraq, 1991–2003* (Ottawa: Canadian Forces Aerospace Warfare Centre Production Section, 2014), p. 80.

20 See Malone, *The International Struggle Over Iraq*, pp. 89–90, 93–5.

21 See 'War and Humanitarian Action: Iraq and the Balkans', p. 217.

22 See Malone, *The International Struggle Over Iraq*, p. 98; and McKay, *Shifting Sands*, p. 93.

23 See McKay, *Shifting Sands*, pp. 97–8.

24 See Malone, *The International Struggle Over Iraq*, pp. 98–9.

25 See Power, *'A Problem From Hell'*, p. 247; and Jennifer Hyndman, 'Preventive, Palliative, or Punitive? Safe Spaces in Bosnia-Herzegovina, Somalia, and Sri Lanka', *Journal of Refugee Studies,* vol. 16, no. 2, 2003, p. 173.

26 See Hyndman, 'Preventive, Palliative, or Punitive?', p. 173; and Power, *'A Problem From Hell'*, pp. 249–50.

27 See Ronald M. Reed, 'Chariots of Fire: Rules of Engagement in Operation Deliberate Force', in Robert C. Owen (ed.), *Deliberate Force: A Case Study in Effective Air Campaigning* (Maxwell AFB, AL: Air University Press, 2000), pp. 396–7; and Daniel L. Haulman, 'Resolution of Bosnian Crisis: Operation DENY FLIGHT', in Warnock, *Short of War*, p. 220.

28 See Reed, 'Chariots of Fire', pp. 397, 399–402; and Haulman, 'Resolution of Bosnian Crisis', pp. 220–1.

29 As quoted in Power, *'A Problem From Hell'*, p. 298.

30 *Ibid.*, p. 284.

31 See United Nations Security Council, Resolution 819, 16 April 1993, https://documents-dds-ny.un.org/doc/UNDOC/GEN/N93/221/90/IMG/N9322190.pdf; and United Nations Security Council, Resolution 824, 6 May 1993, https://documents-dds-ny.un.org/doc/UNDOC/GEN/N93/262/07/IMG/N9326207.pdf.

32 United Nations Security Council, Resolution 836, 4 June 1993, https://documents-dds-ny.un.org/doc/UNDOC/GEN/N93/330/21/IMG/N9333021.pdf.

33 United Nations General Assembly, 'Report of the Secretary-General Pursuant to General Assembly Resolution 53/35: The Fall of Srebrenica', A/54/549, 15 November 1999, p. 25.

34 *Ibid.*, p. 26.

35 See IISS, *The Military Balance 1994–1995* (London: Brassey's for the IISS, 1994), pp. 274–5; and IISS, *The Military Balance 1995–1996* (Oxford: Oxford University Press for the IISS, 1995), p. 304.

36 See United Nations General Assembly, 'Report of the Secretary-General Pursuant to General Assembly Resolution 53/35: The Fall of Srebrenica', pp. 38–9; and Michael Barutciski, 'Safe Areas in Bosnia-Herzegovina: Some Reflections and Tentative Conclusions', *Refuge*, vol. 14, no. 10, March 1995, pp. 18–19.

37 See United Nations General Assembly, 'Report of the Secretary-General Pursuant to General Assembly Resolution 53/35: The Fall of Srebrenica', pp. 40, 68; Reed, 'Chariots of Fire', p. 403; and Power, *'A Problem From Hell'*, p. 406.

38 See Power, *'A Problem From Hell'*, pp. 439–40; and Seybolt, *Humanitarian Military Intervention*, p. 240.

39 See Human Rights Watch, 'Waging War to Keep the Peace: The ECOMOG Intervention and Human Rights', *Africa Watch*, vol. 5, no. 6, 1993, https://www.hrw.org/reports/1993/liberia/.

40 See Quentin Outram, 'Cruel Wars and Safe Havens: Humanitarian Aid in Liberia, 1989–1996', *Disasters*, vol. 21, no. 3, 1997, p. 194.

41 See Christopher Tuck, '"Every Car or Moving Object Gone": The ECOMOG Intervention in Liberia', *African Studies Quarterly*, vol. 4, no. 1, 2000, pp. 1–16.

42 See Human Rights Watch, 'Waging War to Keep the Peace'.

43 See Richard W. Stewart, 'Historical Overview: The United States Army in Somalia, 1992–1994', in *United States Forces, Somalia: After Action Report and Historical Overview: The United States Army in Somalia, 1992–1994* (Washington DC: Center for Military History United States Army, 2003), pp. 3–4.

44 United Nations, 'Somalia – UNOSOM I: Mandate', undated, http://www.un.org/en/peacekeeping/missions/past/unosom1mandate.html.

45 See 'Somalia – UNOSOM I: Mandate'; United Nations; and 'Somalia – UNOSOM II: Mandate', undated, http://www.un.org/en/peacekeeping/missions/past/unosom2mandate.html.

46 See Chester A. Crocker, 'The Lessons of Somalia: Not Everything Went Wrong', *Foreign Affairs*, vol. 74, no. 3, May–June 1995, p. 3; and Stewart, 'Historical Overview', pp. 6–8.

47 See Power, *'A Problem From Hell'*, pp. 329–32, 336–7, 353.

48 See *ibid.*, pp. 378–81.

49 See Larry Minear and Philippe Guillot, *Soldiers to the Rescue: Humanitarian Lessons from Rwanda* (Paris: Organization for Economic Cooperation and Development, 1996), pp. 103–8.

50 See Power, *'A Problem From Hell'*, pp. 380–1.

51 See Alison Desforges, 'Leave None to Tell the Story: Genocide in Rwanda', Human Rights Watch Reports, 1999, https://www.hrw.org/reports/1999/rwanda/Geno1-3-04.htm.

52 See *ibid.*, pp. 367–9; and Seybolt, 'Humanitarian Military Intervention', pp. 206–7.

53 See United Nations Security Council, S/RES/1973, 17 March 2011; and Karl P. Mueller, *Denying Flight: Strategic Options for Employing No-Fly Zones* (Santa Monica, CA: RAND Corporation, 2013), p. 5.

54 See Christopher S. Chivvis, *Toppling Qaddafi: Libya and the Limits of Liberal Intervention* (Cambridge: Cambridge University Press, 2014), pp. 79–81, 89.

55 See *ibid.*, pp. 174–7.

56 See Dominic Tierney, 'How Not to Plan for "The Day After" in Libya', *Atlantic*, 9 August 2016, http://www.theatlantic.com/international/archive/2016/08/-libya-isis-obama-doctrine-nato/495002/.

57 See Chivvis, *Toppling Qaddafi*, pp. 90–1. One effect of the choice to use the UN mandate to oust Gadhafi has been that China and Russia have refused to support UNSC resolutions to authorise the use of force to protect civilians in Syria. See Sarah Brockmeier, 'Lessons in Statecraft Still to Be Learned 5 Years After the Libya Intervention', *War on the Rocks*, 16 March 2016, http://warontherocks.com/2016/03/lessons-in-statecraft-still-to-be-learned-5-years-after-the-libya-intervention/.

58 See Chivvis, *Toppling Qaddafi*, p. 184.

59 This analysis has been informed by a UN-sponsored, independent study of the UN's approach to peace operations following its failures to protect civilians in safe areas from mass atrocities in the 1990s. In 2000, the chairman of the panel, distinguished UN diplomat Lakhdar Brahimi, summarised the study's findings, identifying several causes of these missions' shortcomings and making suggestions for updating the doctrine and strategy of UN peace operations in a document that came to be known as the 'Brahimi Report'. See 'Report of the Panel on United Nations Peace Operations', A/55/305 S/2000/809, 13 November 2000, available at http://www.un.org/en/events/pastevents/brahimi_report.shtml.

60 See Posen, 'Military Responses to Refugee Disasters', pp. 82, 86; and Seybolt, *Humanitarian Military Intervention*, p. 180.

61 See Haulman, 'Resolution of Bosnian Crisis: Operation DENY FLIGHT', p. 225.

62 See United Nations General Assembly, 'Report of the Secretary-General Pursuant to General Assembly Resolution 53/35: The Fall of Srebrenica'; and Reed, 'Chariots of Fire', p. 403.

63 See Kalyvas and Balcells, 'Does Warfare Matter?'.

64 Seybolt, *Humanitarian Military Intervention*, p. 208.

65 United Nations General Assembly and Security Council, 'Report of the Panel on United Nations Peace Operations', pp. 17–18.

66 See Seybolt, *Humanitarian Military Intervention*, p. 273.

67 See Ray Murphy, 'UN Peacekeeping in the Democratic Republic of the Congo and the Protection of Civilians', *Journal of Conflict and Security Law*, vol. 21, no. 2, 2016, pp. 217–18.

68 See Lisa Hultman, 'Keeping Peace or Spurring Violence? Unintended Effects of Peace Operations on Violence Against Civilians', *Civil Wars*, vol. 12, nos 1–2, March–June 2010, p. 42. Hultman argues that this happens because the presence of peacekeepers alerts rebels to the possibility that the conflict will end soon and spurs them to improve their bargaining position before a settlement is reached. These rebel groups may attack civilians to gain control over territory, weaken government or other adversary troops, or seize loot in order to finance further fighting.

69 See Reed, 'Chariots of Fire', p. 403.

70 United Nations General Assembly and Security Council, 'Report of the Panel on United Nations Peace Operations', p. ix.

71 *Ibid.*, p. 9.

72 *Ibid.*, p. 11.

73 Posen, 'Military Response to Refugee Disasters', pp. 95–6.

74 Sarah Sewall, Dwight Raymond and Sally Chin, *Mass Atrocity Response Operations: A Military Planning Handbook* (Scotts Valley, CA: CreateSpace, 2010), pp. 77–80, 86.

75 Nicholas Burns and James Jeffrey, 'The Diplomatic Case for America to Create a Safe Zone in Syria', *Washington Post*, 4 February 2016, https://www.washingtonpost.com/opinions/the-diplomatic-case-for-america-to-create-a-safe-zone-in-syria/2016/02/04/f3c7c820-caa9-11e5-88ff-e2d1b4289c2f_story.html.

76 Karl P. Mueller, Jeffrey Martini and Thomas Hamilton, *Airpower Options for Syria: Assessing Objectives and Missions for Aerial Intervention* (Santa Monica, CA: RAND Corporation, 2013), p. 1.

77 *Ibid.*, p. 2.

78 *Ibid.* For the authors' detailed treatment of the possibility of having both a safe area and no-fly zone in Syria, see pp. 10–12.

79 *Ibid.*, p. 12.

80 See Neil Narang, 'Assisting Uncertainty: How Humanitarian Aid Can Inadvertently Prolong Civil War', *International Studies Quarterly*, vol. 59, no. 1, March 2015, pp. 184–95. Narang writes that 'aid can prolong war by creating protected space for combatants to launch attacks with relative immunity. For decades, groups have used protected camps and aid enclaves as safe havens for rest, recuperation, and recruitment. During the Bosnian War, for example, analysts argued that the humanitarian safe zones prolonged fighting and protected Bosnian forces.' See also Hultman, 'Keeping Peace or Spurring Violence?', especially p. 38, where she writes, 'The conflicts that have had the most one-sided violence [against civilians] while peacekeepers were present are also the cases that are usually mentioned as failures of the international community, most notably Rwanda 1992–96 and Bosnia 1992–95. In these conflicts, the peacekeepers did not have enough forces or the mandate to protect the civilian population.'

81 See Megan A. Stewart and Yu-Ming Liou, 'Do Good Borders Make Good Rebels? Territorial Control and Civilian Casualties', *Journal of Politics*, vol. 79, no. 1, December 2016, pp. 294–9.

82 See Andrew Radin, 'The Misunderstood Lessons of Bosnia for Syria', *Washington Quarterly*, Winter 2015, pp. 56–60, 64–5. According to Radin, 'the first lesson from Bosnia – concerning the link between intervention and reputation – suggests that the US use of military force in Syria will eventually lead to the United States attacking the Assad regime directly'.

Review Essay

A Patriot's Farewell

Kori Schake

The Restless Wave: Good Times, Just Causes, Great Fights, and Other Appreciations
John McCain and Mark Salter. London and New York: Simon & Schuster, 2018. £25.00/$30.00. 402 pp.

> Nothing in his life became him like the leaving it; he died as one that had been studied in his death.
>
> William Shakespeare, *Macbeth*

Sitting in the solemnity of the National Cathedral amid US Senator John McCain's fellow prisoners of war, listening as two presidents extolled his contributions to American life in what was for all intents and purposes a state funeral, feeling the emotional wallop of the senator's careful cultivation of reminders that we are a better and more united country than our current behaviour would suggest, I heard the resonance of Shakespeare's Malcolm describing the Thane of Cawdor. *The Restless Wave* is part of the senator's orchestrated departure; written with Mark Salter, who has long given poignant voice to the best angels of John McCain's nature, it is McCain's last political will and testament.

Kori Schake is Deputy Director-General of the IISS. Her most recent book is *Safe Passage: The Transition from British to American Hegemony* (Harvard University Press, 2017).

Survival | vol. 60 no. 6 | December 2018–January 2019 | pp. 181–188   DOI 10.1080/00396338.2018.1542809

The opening chapter is titled 'Accumulated Memories', and that elegiac feel colours the book. There are tender portraits of campaigning in Gee's Bend, Alabama, soldiers re-enlisting in Iraq during the surge, and McCain apologising to a victim of American torture. He gently teases Senate colleague Hillary Clinton for dragging out a lengthy briefing on Afghanistan, and recalls Michael Bloomberg asking 'are you sure about this?' when being vetted for the vice-presidential slot in 2008. He shares his own trepidation during the Iraq War when he was approached by a Gold Star mother, fearing that 'she would hold me responsible for her loss, and she would be right to' (p. 24).

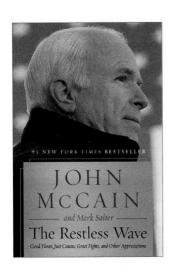

The passage from the book that best conjures McCain occurs early on:

What a privilege it is to serve this big, boisterous, brave, magnificent country. With all our flaws, all our mistakes, with all the frailties of human nature as much on display as our virtues, with all the rancor and anger of our politics, we are blessed. We are living in the land of the free, the land where anything is possible, the land of the immigrant's dream, the land with the storied past forgotten in the rush to the imagined future, the land that repairs and reinvents itself, the land where a person can escape the consequences of a self-centered youth and know the satisfaction of sacrificing for an ideal, where you can go from aimless rebellion to noble cause, and from the bottom of your class to your party's nomination for President. (p. 8)

The Restless Wave is more than an encomium, however. It is also a political accounting. In it, a consequential figure of the past 40 years in American politics makes the case for the policies he believed in, recounted through a memoir of the last stage of his life. His central message is that 'We will not thrive in a world where our leadership and ideals are absent. We wouldn't deserve to' (p. 9). It is a simple, ringing call to duty.

A man of conviction

The book starts with the 2008 campaign. I was senior policy advisor on that campaign, and can confirm that the account in *The Restless Wave* does not pretty up the mistaken strategy of spending like a front-runner early on; lingering too long over the refusal of Republican Party leaders to countenance the selection of former Democratic senator Joe Lieberman as McCain's running mate; rushing the vetting of governor Sarah Palin; not adequately preparing her for the intensity of national scrutiny; emphasising the strength of the economy during the collapse of Lehman Brothers; and then suspending the campaign but failing to deliver a policy solution as the financial crisis burgeoned. What also comes through in the book is the best thing about McCain: he never shirked responsibility for his mistakes.

His resentment of Barack Obama's campaign, and occasionally of Obama's choices as president, smoulders. He reveals that senator Obama pledged his support for immigration reform to gain Ted Kennedy's endorsement, but then did not keep his end of the deal. McCain describes the Syria red line as 'the worst decision' of Obama's presidency (p. 189), and condemns him as commander in chief: 'his approach to world leadership, however thoughtful and well-intentioned, was negligent, and encouraged our allies to find ways to live without us, and our adversaries to try and fill the vacuums our negligence created' (p. 192).

But McCain also demonstrates a lighter touch when describing the ennobling decisions he made during the campaign not to let racial animus have any place, and perhaps his best moment in public life: his 2008 presidential concession speech. He writes 'the moral values and integrity of our nation, and the long, difficult, fraught history of our efforts to uphold them at home and abroad, are the test of every American generation' (p. 104). John McCain showed us all how to pass that test.

He could be impetuous, as when he declared that 'today we are all Georgians' when Russia invaded that country in 2008. He often over-committed to politicians in transitional countries that turned out to be undemocratic or corrupt. But he believed fervently that it wasn't good enough to strengthen the West at its core. He understood that revolutions often fail, that learning the reflexes of democratic practice is hard, that political and financial temptations are many where the rule of law and confining institutions are weak or new – and that it is important to strengthen the politicians and civil societies of nations in transition by standing beside them, shielding them and helping them to make good choices by investing them with the West's strength and confidence. He would rather have been wrong believing in a country's potential than in excluding from American protection those who might, with the right conditions and support, become forces for propagating the values he believed in.

McCain's unflinching commitment to American values comes through most vividly in the chapter of the book titled 'About Us', which recounts his fury at the use of 'enhanced interrogation techniques' by the United States after 9/11, and his successful legislative efforts to expose American atrocities and foreclose the use of torture by any future US government. As is well known, John McCain spoke with unmatched stature about torture, having himself been the victim of it while in North Vietnamese captivity. He doesn't make himself the centre of the story, instead extolling Americans like Captain Ian Fishback, who revealed the abuses at Abu Ghraib, and Jack Goldsmith, who repudiated the Justice Department's torture memos. But without McCain's stature and commitment, those practices would never have been acknowledged and stopped; the Bush administration and the Republican Party would have continued to profess that torture produced such valuable information that it could be countenanced. McCain thunders in reply:

> Will we act in this world with respect for our founding conviction that all people have equal dignity in the eyes of God and should be accorded the same respect by the laws and governments of men? That is the most important question history ever asks of us. Answering in the affirmative by our actions is the highest form of patriotism. (p. 104)

His personal stature as a torture victim helped shield others who would stop torture from the accusation that they were not protecting the country in a time of war.

The Restless Wave shows the remarkable degree to which Senator McCain used the means available to an American legislator to practise foreign policy: by participating in bipartisan congressional delegations; attending meetings with military commanders and dissidents; funding the International Republican Institute; making his annual pilgrimage to the Munich Security Conference; holding committee hearings; engaging journalists; and writing opinion pieces in newspapers (including *Pravda*, in which he argued, 'I'm more pro-Russian than the regime that rules you today'). He used those tools to inform himself and his legislative colleagues, to cudgel several presidents for their failures of international leadership, and to model the values of moral outrage and concern for the oppressed – values he considered important to America's role in the world. While his engagement with dissidents often brought no change in American policy, he thought it essential to send the message that 'we hear them, we acknowledge the justice of their cause, they aren't forgotten' (p. 288).

There are long chapters making the case for adopting a counterinsurgency approach in Iraq, describing what McCain saw on the many trips he made to war zones, and expressing admiration for the unfussy patriotism of soldiers. He goes a fair way to recanting his support for the Iraq War, acknowledging that it was a mistake because Iraq did not have any weapons of mass destruction, but reiterating his belief that the invasion would have been justified if it had possessed them, and that replacing the government of Saddam Hussein was a 'just cause' (pp. 107–8). He interestingly observes that 'Iraq was a grimmer, more oppressive place than Afghanistan' (p. 110). He poignantly describes a re-enlistment ceremony for 600 soldiers at the nadir of the Iraq insurgency, at which 161 soldiers also became naturalised US citizens, emphasising caustically that 'immigrants, many of them having entered the country illegally, are making sacrifices for Americans that many Americans would not make for them' (p. 20).

His account of the long and unsuccessful effort to pass a bipartisan immigration bill, and his discussion of the political challenges and policy implications of immigration issues, represents the very best part of the book. It is in these passages that the senator's beliefs about America's promise come together most powerfully. 'We live in a land made from ideals, not blood and soil', he writes. 'We are custodians of those ideals at home, and their champion abroad. We have done great good in the world because we believed our ideals are the natural aspiration of all mankind, and that the principles, rules, and alliances of the international order we superintended would improve the security and prosperity of all who joined us' (p. 9).

His concerns for our current path resonate throughout the book, in chapters on the opportunities missed during the Arab Spring, on Republican efforts to repeal healthcare legislation, on the solipsism of many of Obama's foreign policies, and on the narrow nationalism American conservatives have adopted. 'Decisions made in the last ten years and the decisions made tomorrow might be closing the door on the era of the American-led world order', he warns (p. 192).

Friends and foes

The book runs to 325 pages before any mention is made of President Donald Trump. McCain clearly worries about Trump's character, observing that 'a reality show facsimile of toughness seems to matter more than any of our values' (p. 325). But he was less excoriating than I expected, still giving the president the benefit of the doubt on policies. He is more derisory about the people around Trump, saying of Steve Bannon and Sebastian Gorka, 'bigger misfits haven't been seen inside a White House since William Taft got stuck in his bathtub' (p. 327). That slap brought John McCain vividly back to life.

Senator McCain was a famously sharp-tongued man, and he is derisive about fellow Senator Rand Paul, torture supporters, former CIA director John Brennan, the Coalition Provisional Authority, Ambassador Chris Hill, former secretary of state Rex Tillerson, Ambassador Nikki Haley, Congressman Steve King, senator Obama's perfidy on immigration, and former French president Nicolas Sarkozy's claim in 2009 that Russia poses no military threat to the West. He says of Russian despot Vladimir Putin, 'I've got plenty of things wrong in a long political career. Putin isn't one of them' (p. 244).

One of the senator's most wonderful habits was referring to both allies and adversaries as 'my friends'. It is a beautiful convention that I encourage us all to adopt as we fight for what we believe is right. It was a reminder, as much to himself as to us, that there are boundaries to be respected even as we litigate our differences. It also signified his relish in doing so. He writes:

> Many an old geezer like me reaches his last years wishing he had lived more in the moment, had savoured his days as they happened. Not me, friends. Not me. I have loved my life. All of it … I have lived with a will. I served a purpose greater than my own pleasure or advantage, but I meant to enjoy the experience, and I did. I meant to be amazed and excited and encouraged and useful, and I was. (pp. 5–6)

Which is not to say that John McCain did not have enemies. He not only had them, he cultivated them, nourishing his wrath against them. He was obdurate in nursing grudges, many of which leap off the page as he writes of the Obama campaign, three CIA directors who excused torture (George Tenet, Porter Goss and Michael Hayden), the CIA itself, former secretary of defense Donald Rumsfeld, General George Casey, Obama's withdrawal from Iraq (and his stinginess toward Afghanistan), Faiza Abou el-Naga (Egypt's national security adviser) and most of all Vladimir Putin. He remains furious about the 'bad tactics, bad strategy, and bad leadership in the highest ranks of uniformed and civilian defense leadership' in the Iraq War (p. 16).

John McCain's funeral was nearly concurrent with that of another great American, Aretha Franklin. The route of her funeral cortège was lined with pink Cadillacs by the mayor of Detroit. She, too, had presidents to eulogise her; celebrated artists performed, and her corpse's clothing changed four times, her crossed ankles showcasing fabulous shoes. Senator McCain would have been delighted that her final send-off rivalled his own in prompting civic jubilation, because these celebrations also embodied the America John McCain fought for, suffered for, worked for and loved. *The Restless Wave* is a beautiful reminder of an American life well lived.

Some political commentators described McCain's funeral as a gathering of 'the resistance'. That both politicises and diminishes what Senator McCain was aiming for, in life and in death. He was trying to do so much more than pull together the president's opponents – he was trying to remind us who we are as a nation. As he put it,

> I would like to see us recover our sense that we are more alike than different. We are citizens of a republic made of shared ideals forged in a new world to replace the tribal enmities that tormented the old one. Even in times of political turmoil such as these, we share that awesome heritage and the responsibility to embrace it. (p. 379)

That is what washed over his funeral as we stood weeping and singing 'America the Beautiful' together – John's call to live bigger and do better.

Review Essay

Staining the Flag

Russell Crandall

The True Flag: Theodore Roosevelt, Mark Twain, and the Birth of American Empire
Stephen Kinzer. New York: Henry Holt and Co., 2017. $28.00.
306 pp.

> The situation seems to me this. An immense democracy, mostly ignorant and completely secluded from foreign influence, finds itself in possession of enormous power and is eager to use it in brutal fashion against anyone who comes along, without knowing how to do it, and is therefore constantly on the brink of some frightful catastrophe.

> E.L. Godkin, editor of the *Nation*, 1895[1]

Territorial expansion was a key element of the American project from the beginning. Thomas Jefferson started the expansionist game when, in 1803, he bought all 827,000 square miles of the Louisiana Territory from France for the measly sum of $15 million, or $309m in today's money.[2] In the following decades, the mostly forcible removal of Native Americans from their traditional lands, and the Mexican–American War from 1846–48, brought ever larger portions of North America under what many saw as Washington's

Russell Crandall is a professor of American foreign policy at Davidson College in North Carolina, and a contributing editor to *Survival*.

Survival | vol. 60 no. 6 | December 2018–January 2019 | pp. 189–198   DOI 10.1080/00396338.2018.1542810

divinely sanctioned control. The 1867 purchase of Alaska from Russia completed the expansion.

Yet despite the United States' catastrophic success in achieving its continental aspirations, it wasn't until the 1890s that Uncle Sam began to lift his gaze overseas. In 1891, Americans were outraged by revelations that American sailors from the USS *Baltimore* had been killed during a drunken bar fight in the port city of Valparaíso, Chile. Complained future president Theodore Roosevelt, 'We are actually at the mercy of a tenth-rate country!' (p. 25). The *Baltimore* affair, which provided a foretaste of the role that big business would come to play in spreading American power abroad, was

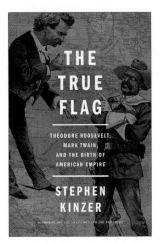

as much about Washington's desire to safeguard the profits of American mining interests in Latin America as it was a rebuke of the decidedly not tenth-rate Chilean navy. A year later, an increasingly confident US government dispatched several warships to ensure American cargo was kept safe in civil-war-ravaged Brazil. In the mid-1890s, the administration of president Grover Cleveland appointed itself the arbiter of an especially hostile boundary dispute between Venezuela and British Guiana.

Stephen Kinzer, author of *The True Flag*, characterises these late-nineteenth-century episodes as 'practice runs, psychic preparations for the explosion of American intervention that lay ahead' (p. 25). In 1896, the Republican candidate for president, Ohio governor William McKinley, offered the following solution for the effects of the depression that had been afflicting the United States since 1873: 'We want a foreign market for our surplus products' (p. 25). As Kinzer sees it, McKinley's stance was not especially surprising given that he had received large contributions from capitalist barons – a first for an American presidential candidate. Even so, in his January 1897 inaugural address, McKinley claimed that he 'cherished the policy of non-interference with affairs of foreign governments', adding that, 'We want no war of conquest; we must avoid the temptation of territorial aggression' (p. 27).

McKinley's ascension to the presidency prompted Henry Cabot Lodge, a senator from Massachusetts, to ask him for 'one personal favor' in recognition of Lodge's having supported his campaign for president: to appoint Lodge's political ally, Theodore Roosevelt, as assistant secretary of the navy (p. 27). According to Kinzer, both Lodge and Roosevelt 'believed two things passionately: that the United States must become one of the world's great powers, and that it could do so only by taking foreign lands' (p. 19). Once Roosevelt was duly appointed, the two men 'did all they could to promote the building of warships, expansion of naval bases, and better conditions for seamen' (p. 28).

Their efforts would pay off in 1898, when the defeat of the Spanish fleet in Manila Harbour and in Cuba – and the resulting annexation fever – allowed the United States to gain control over 'five far-flung lands' encompassing more than 10m subjects: Guam, the Philippines, Cuba, Puerto Rico and Hawaii (p. 66). Although the campaign against Spain had initially been fuelled by American outrage at Madrid's colonial behaviour in Cuba, 'fervor for the new idea of overseas expansion' soon captivated a country whose very self-identity was predicated on the notion of self-determination (p. 6). According to Kinzer, although Roosevelt, who had resigned his naval post to battle as a Rough Rider in Cuba, was the 'public face' of American expansionism, Lodge deserves at least as much credit for the policy's success. As the anti-imperialist Edward Atkinson put it, 'Lodge [was] the Mephistopheles whispering poison in [Roosevelt's] ear all the time' (p. 67). Kinzer also makes the case that it was the conflict in the Philippines, where the United States carried out a dirty counter-insurgency campaign against Filipino nationalists, and not Cuba, where the Americans had initially sided with the pro-independence rebels to oust their Iberian masters, that galvanised the theretofore insignificant anti-imperialist movement.

By the end of the year, the newly formed American Anti-Imperialist League had categorically demanded that Congress end the military campaign in the Philippines and concede to Filipinos 'the independence for which they have so long fought and which of right is theirs' (p. 153), thus helping to plunge the US into one of the most wrenching national debates in its history. 'Only once before', writes Kinzer, referring to the very founding of the United States, had 'so many brilliant Americans so eloquently debated a question so fraught with meaning for all humanity' (p. 3). In Kinzer's view, the imperialist debate was even more significant than the polarising question of slavery because of its importance not just to the United States but to other countries, too. Itself a former colony established on the principle that all nations must be ruled by 'the consent of the governed', the US now was debating the question of whether it ought to 'project power into faraway lands' (pp. 2–3). Some thought that it should, 'to guarantee our prosperity, save innocent lives, liberate the oppressed, and confront danger before it reaches our shores', while others believed that 'intervention brings suffering and creates enemies' (p. 3). It was a question, Kinzer convincingly argues, that would determine nothing less than the type of country the United States would become in the subsequent decades, and even centuries.

Anti-imperialists viewed their cause as defending America's founding principles and allowing native peoples to govern themselves. They 'hated war and believed liberty was America's greatest gift to humanity' (p. 13). The New England patrician theologian and Unitarian minister Charles Ames admonished the nation lest it 'sacrifice the principles on which the Republic was founded' (p. 6), adding:

> The policy of imperialism threatens to change the temper of our own people, and to put us into a permanent attitude of arrogance, testiness, and defiance towards other nations … Once we enter the field of international conflict as a great military and naval power, we shall be one more bully among bullies. We shall only add one more to the list of oppressors of mankind. (p. 6)

Expansionists had no patience for such thinking. They believed that notions of liberty and democracy were only appropriate for stable Western countries – 'that is, nations populated and governed by white people. Others, they asserted, were too primitive to rule themselves and must be ruled by outsiders' (pp. 11–12). Moreover, they 'considered war a purifying, invigorating, unifying force. In their imagined future, humanity would be guided by a virtuous United States and disciplined by American military power' (p. 13). American intervention would bring the 'material blessings' of education, public health, 'orderly systems of justice' and infrastructure to countries that lacked them (p. 230).

The events of 1898 dealt a blow to the anti-imperialists, but they were quick to strike back. One particularly influential voice belonged to Carl Schurz, a German immigrant who had served as a general in the Civil War before becoming a senator and then secretary of the interior under president Rutherford B. Hayes. Speaking in Chicago on 17 October 1899, Schurz denounced the Philippine war as 'unnecessary as it is unjust – a wanton, wicked, and abominable war' (p. 153). He attacked the imperialist argument that the United States needed to 'restore order' in the Philippines, accusing Washington of having 'carried riot and death and desolation into peaceful communities whose only offense was not that they did not maintain order and safety among themselves, but that they refused to accept us as their rulers'.[3] 'This "order"', he continued, 'is the kind that has been demanded by the despot since the world had a history' (p. 155).

Kinzer's sense is that the imperialists, having assumed that the political war had been won with the Treaty of Paris in December 1898 that ended the war with Spain, failed to anticipate how the bleeding ulcer in the Philippines would only worsen, pushing legions of Americans away from imperialism. Lodge sought to counter the charges of the anti-imperialists by accusing them of complicity – intentional or otherwise – in the killing of Americans through their support for Filipino rebel fighters:

> I cannot understand, when our soldiers are in the field, face to face with an enemy, that there should be any part or any organization of men in this country ready to cry out 'Surrender!' The soldiers of the United States in the Philippines – where they have the right to be by the laws of nations, by the laws of this country, and by the laws of sound morals – are fighting with the public enemies of the United States ... I vote with the army that wears the uniform and carries the flag of my country. When the enemy has yielded and the war is over, we can discuss other matters! (pp. 154–5)

It is an argument that has been made many times since in defence of American conduct in overseas wars.

Two kinds of patriot

A significant subplot in Kinzer's narrative is the outsized roles played by Roosevelt and Mark Twain in the imperialist debate. Kinzer contrasts Roosevelt's American chauvinism and Twain's cosmopolitanism, gained from years spent travelling abroad to places such as Australia, Fiji, Mozambique and South Africa. Yet he describes the two men as 'deliciously matched' in terms of their sharp wit, lust for the limelight and overlapping social circles (p. 12):

> Both were fervent patriots who believed the United States had a sacred mission on earth – though they defined that mission quite differently. Both were writers and thinkers as well as activists. Most important, both were relentless self-promoters, born performers who carefully cultivated their public images. (p. 13)

Each was also viscerally aware of the other's fame, even if they publicly denounced each other. Roosevelt told acquaintances he'd be only too glad to 'skin Mark Twain alive', while Twain described his rival as the 'most formidable disaster that has befallen the country since the Civil War' (p. 13).

When the crisis with Spain initially erupted in the first half of 1898, Twain was in Vienna, a member of a 'luminous circle' that included Johann Strauss, Gustav Mahler, Gustav Klimt and Sigmund Freud (p. 49). Initially, he supported the American campaign against Spain, writing to a friend back home,

> I have never enjoyed a war – even in written history – as I am enjoying this one. For this is the worthiest one that was ever fought, so far as my knowledge goes. It is a worthy thing to fight for one's freedom; it is another sight finer to fight for another man's. And I think this is the first time this has been done. (p. 50)

Within months, however, his enthusiasm had given way to revulsion:

> When the United States sent word that the Cuban atrocities must end, she occupied the highest position ever taken by a nation since the Almighty made the earth. But when she snatched the Philippines and butchered a

poverty-stricken, priest-ridden nation of children, she stained the flag. That's what we have today – a stained flag. (pp. 160–1)

Twain's inimitable rhetoric helped him to become one of the most visible anti-imperialists of the era. No imperialist was too powerful to be spared Twain's criticism. During a reception in late 1900 for a young Winston Churchill, who had found fame while reporting on the Boer War, Twain's 'rambling salute' to shared American and British principles included the following observation:

England sinned when she got herself into a war in South Africa which she could have avoided, just as we sinned in getting into a similar war in the Philippines. England and America – yes, we are kin. And now that we are also kin in sin, there is nothing more to be desired. The harmony is complete, the blend is perfect. (p. 185)

Just months later, Twain hosted an event at his adored Lotos gentlemen's club at which Roosevelt, now vice president, was in attendance. Twain took the opportunity to defend himself against the accusation by a certain 'reverend gentleman' that he was a 'traitor' for not supporting the war in the Philippines:

It would be an entirely different question if the country's life was in danger, its existence at stake. Then – that is one kind of patriotism – we would all come forward and stand by the flag, and stop thinking about whether the nation was right or wrong. But when there is no question that the nation is in any way in danger, but some little war away off, then it may be that on the question of politics the nation is divided, half patriots and half traitors – and no man can tell which from which. (p. 185)

Roosevelt appears to have been unmoved by Twain's rebukes. Unlike the latter, who 'saw nobility in many peoples, and found much to admire abroad', Roosevelt held that 'the man who loves other countries as much as he does his own is quite as noxious a member of society as a man who loves the other women as much as he loves his wife' (p. 12).

Accusations and rebuttals

Throughout most of his book, Kinzer approaches his subject – a passionate debate that in many ways continues to this day – with a commendable degree of balance and disinterest. This changes in his long concluding chapter.

Kinzer acknowledges that American empire has had some benefits, in 1898 no less than in subsequent decades. For example, he notes that towns and cities in Cuba became cleaner and safer, and that the scourge of yellow fever was checked by the United States' nineteenth-century adventures. Yet he is certain that *most* American interventions abroad have been unmitigated failures. The war in the Philippines, he claims, 'set off waves of nationalism across East Asia that contributed to the Communist takeover of China in 1949, and can also be seen as a progenitor of disasters from Pearl Harbor to Vietnam' (p. 246). He criticises later American interventions for producing 'terrible results that their planners never anticipated. From Iran and Guatemala to Iraq and Afghanistan, intervention has devastated societies and produced violent anti-American passion' (p. 246). Kinzer's ultimate conclusion is that lofty American rhetoric about defending freedom 'rarely matches the facts on the ground'. Instead, many interventions are launched simply to 'prop up predatory regimes' and increase US power, especially its economic power (p. 248).

Kinzer is a former journalist who covered the Reagan administration's controversial policies in Central America, and who has written several widely read general histories of mostly Cold War-era episodes featuring covert American action, among them *Bitter Fruit: The Story of the American Coup in Guatemala*, *All the Shah's Men: An American Coup and the Roots of Middle East Terror*, and *The Brothers: John Foster Dulles, Allen Dulles, and Their Secret World War*. Another book, *Overthrow*, chronicles a century of American-led regime change from Hawaii to Iraq. It would be admittedly difficult to conclude from these accounts that the United States was not guilty of moral outrages and strategic failings in Cold War episodes such as 1950s Guatemala and Iran, and 1970s Chile.

Yet these episodes, and even the Philippines in 1898, are not fully representative of the American experience overseas. Obvious counterexamples include the overthrow and subsequent occupation of fascist Germany and

Japan in the 1940s. Moreover, even the defence of South Korea after 1950 and the ousting of the domestically despised Marxist regime in Grenada in 1983 are at the very least more ambiguous than Kinzer's critique might suggest. He seems to have an easy time connecting the dots from American covert operations to deleterious outcomes, but not to more positive ones. It may be that Kinzer simply wishes to ensure that the United States atones for its sins. But moral shaming does not ensure historical accuracy. The US may be guilty of great crimes, but this is not the full story.

Kinzer contends that anyone who questions the 'deeply embedded assumptions' of US foreign policy are not 'welcome in the corridors of power in Washington' (p. 242), but he seems to have forgotten about Jimmy Carter, Bill Clinton and Barack Obama, to say nothing of high-profile dissenters like Mark Twain, who may not have held office in Washington, but whose criticisms were clearly heard by those who did. There have also been several instances in which, fearing a Vietnam-like morass, Washington failed to enact regime change (or did so only belatedly), in places such as Rwanda, the Balkans and Somalia. In each of these cases, inaction was likely more catastrophic than action. A sage reporter, Kinzer must have a sense of this. He begins his book with the observation that Americans 'want to guide the world, but … also believe every nation should guide itself' (p. 1). On that, I think, we can all agree.

Notes

1   Quoted by Stephen Kinzer in *The True Flag* (New York: Henry Holt and Co., 2017), p. 246.
2   See Robert Lee, 'The True Cost of the Louisiana Purchase', *Slate*, 1 March 2017, http://www.slate.com/articles/news_and_politics/history/2017/03/how_much_did_the_louisiana_ purchase_actually_cost.html.
3   Carl Schurz, 'The Policy of Imperialism', address at the Anti-Imperialistic Conference, Chicago, IL, 17 October 1899, available at https://en.wikisource.org/wiki/The_Policy_of_Imperialism.

Review Essay

Rhodesia's Improbably Dirty War

Kathleen M. Vogel

**Dirty War: Rhodesia and Chemical Biological Warfare
1975–1980**
Glenn Cross. Solihull: Helion & Company, 2017. £25.00. 248 pp.

In March 2018, former Russian spy Sergei Skripal and his daughter Yulia were made gravely ill in an attempted assassination with a chemical nerve agent known as Novichok in Salisbury, United Kingdom. The UK government has accused two Russian military-intelligence agents of carrying out this attack, and of causing the unintended death of Dawn Sturgess, who succumbed to the nerve agent after unexpectedly coming into contact with it, as well as severe illness in Charlie Rowley, her partner. There are ongoing deliberations by the Organisation for the Prohibition of Chemical Weapons (OPCW), the implementing body of the Chemical Weapons Convention, to determine an international response to this breach of the global norm against chemical-weapons use. The Salisbury incident has underscored long-standing domestic and international concerns about the use of chemical and biological (CB) agents by state and non-state actors.

Chemical weapons, including chlorine, phosgene and mustard gas, were of course widely used in the First World War. Although it is not extensive, there is also a historical record of CB agents being developed or used for

Kathleen M. Vogel is an associate professor at the School of Public Policy, University of Maryland. She is the author of *Phantom Menace or Looming Danger? A New Framework for Assessing Bioweapons Threats* (Johns Hopkins University Press, 2013).

Survival | vol. 60 no. 6 | December 2018–January 2019 | pp. 199–206   DOI 10.1080/00396338.2018.1542811

assassinations and unconventional military purposes. The United States, the Soviet Union, South Africa and Iraq had assassination programmes utilising chemical or biological agents.[1] More recently, North Korean operatives used VX nerve agent to murder Kim Jong-nam, the half-brother of North Korean leader Kim Jong-un, in Malaysia in February 2017.[2] CB weapons were also employed to counter insurgencies in Spain (1921–27), Italy (1935–36), Yemen (1963–67), South Africa (1980s), Iraq (1988) and Syria (2013–18), and by Iraq in the Iran–Iraq War (1982–88).[3] CB agents have also been pursued by non-state actors such as the Japanese religious sect Aum Shinrikyo.[4] Although the use of these agents as weapons has been limited, some actors, in certain contexts, could still find them expedient in attempting to accomplish political, religious or social goals.

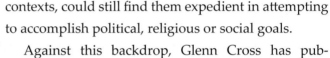

Against this backdrop, Glenn Cross has published a useful book, *Dirty War: Rhodesia and Chemical Biological Warfare 1975–1980*. He painstakingly details the development and use of CB agents by Rhodesia's white colonial minority government in the 1970s against the majority black population to counter the guerrilla insurgency that was seeking to overthrow that government. Eventually, of course, the insurgency succeeded: Rhodesia became what is now the Republic of Zimbabwe in 1980. Through in-depth research, a close parsing of available sources and personal interviews, Cross explains how the Rhodesian military came to its decision to use CB weapons.

The central reason was practical desperation: the white regime was unable to defeat the insurgency through conventional arms and existing Rhodesian military manpower. Having unilaterally declared its independence from the UK in 1965 after refusing to accede to London's requirement that it transition to majority rule, the Rhodesian government was considered an illegal racist regime by the UN, politically isolated and subject to sanctions, drained of manpower through white emigration, and largely without external political or material support. In this case, then, the decision to use CB agents was not frivolous but rather was reached in a specific political and military context that gave rise to an operational need that they seemed to meet.

The Rhodesian CB programme was a small-scale, low-cost effort operated by a small, secretive branch of the army's Selous Scouts – an elite special-operations force set up specifically to engineer the clandestine elimination of insurgents, whom the government characterised as terrorists. The programme employed relatively crude materials such as toxic agricultural and industrial chemicals, and available biological agents like *vibrio cholerae* – the causative agent of cholera. Using intermediaries, the Rhodesian military planned and executed a variety of CB attacks involving the contamination of guerrillas' water, food, medicine and clothing. The programme did not have a sophisticated design, and was conducted on a trial-and-error basis. Ultimately, its overall effectiveness was constrained by its limited scope and application, the kinds of agents the military used and its crude dissemination methods. Cross and others (including members of the Rhodesian military) have determined that the attacks had no effect on the war's ultimate outcome. Even so, Cross finds that the Rhodesian military believed that the use of CB agents had killed perhaps a few thousand black African nationalists and significantly disrupted guerrilla efforts. Eventually, the guerrillas got wise to the CB attacks and developed countermeasures, which rendered further attacks useless.

Cross's book is certainly a fascinating examination of a relatively little-known aspect of a post-colonial conflict. But it's fair to ask how an understanding of the rather obscure Rhodesian CB programme is helpful today. There are three key takeaways for the contemporary audience. Firstly, Cross's book helps scholars and policy analysts ascertain what circumstances and conditions motivate regimes that decide to act against the international norm barring the military use of CB agents. The Rhodesian case, based on Cross's detailed explanation of the government's decision-making, provides a nuanced, well-documented and concrete example of how regimes that are existentially threatened may resort to CB use. In addition to the regime's survival being at stake, key factors shaping Rhodesia's decision to use CB agents included a deficient number of military personnel compared to its adversary; Rhodesia's status as a rogue nation regarded as operating outside of international law; the dehumanisation of enemy combatants; know-how; infrastructure; and available materials. The larger point is that a wide range of social, political and economic factors can intertwine with scientific and technological means to determine how and when state or non-state actors decide to pursue a CB weapons programme. Cross's work also supports Gregory Koblentz's argument that states will acquire and use chemical and biological weapons if they believe their regime is at risk of an internal threat.[5]

Secondly, the book raises troubling questions about the strength of international norms, taboos and regimes against the development and use of CB weapons, and how states can be deterred from going down this path when they see it as an expedient way of advancing important political ends.[6] It also prompts consideration of difficult issues involving what international actors and non-governmental organisations should do when revelations of CB use come to light – particularly if the perpetrators are not signatories to international conventions against CB acquisition, development or use. (Rhodesia was never a signatory, and Zimbabwe did not sign the Biological and Toxin Weapons Convention until 1990 and the Chemical Weapons Convention until 1993.) Information about the Rhodesian use of CB agents was slow to emerge, and there was no trial, 'truth and reconciliation' process, or punishment of any of the scientists, military personnel or government officials suspected of participating in the programme. This sobering fact is particularly salient in light of the Syrian regime's serial use of chemical weapons in Syria's ongoing civil war, and the recent accusations that the Russian and North Korean governments used chemical agents against their enemies; it remains to be seen how the OPCW and the UN might address these breaches of proscriptions against CB use.

There was no trial or punishment

Thirdly, Cross's book illustrates the inherent difficulties of collecting intelligence on CB weapons programmes – especially those using off-the-shelf materials (such as commercially available pesticides) and personnel already on hand. The Soviet Union had the largest and lengthiest bioweapons programme in history; it originated in the 1920s and expanded in the 1980s. Although US and British intelligence suspected that the Soviets had a sizeable bioweapons capability, they were unable to prove it until defectors emerged in the 1980s and 1990s and provided detailed accounts of the programme. Much smaller in scale, the Rhodesian programme was able to operate in secret for several years and was not known to Western intelligence agencies until the creation of the new Zimbabwean government in the 1980s, when former Rhodesian security personnel came out with their own revelations. For example, Rhodesian intelligence chief Ken Flower disclosed elements of the Rhodesian CB programme in his 1987 autobiography.[7] More details later materialised through the uncovering of South Africa's CB weapons programme, 'Project Coast', in the 1990s. Cross outlines some important technology and knowledge transfers between Rhodesia and South Africa during this period.

Also relevant to the challenges of developing good intelligence is Cross's look at the Rhodesian anthrax outbreak that started in 1978, during the last stages of the war. This has long been a controversial case. Some scientists and intelligence experts insist that it was a bioweapons attack by the Rhodesian military, while others argue that it was more consistent with a natural outbreak of disease.[8] Assessing the available clinical and epidemiological data, Cross concludes that the anthrax outbreak occurred naturally and was exacerbated by the collapse of Rhodesia's veterinary and public-health services in rural areas due to the deteriorating security situation. More broadly, however, he notes that intentional human involvement cannot be decisively ruled out – or, for that matter, confirmed – absent first-hand human testimony about the circumstances of infection. To date, no one from the nationalist insurgency or the black African population in Zimbabwe has alleged that the Rhodesian military intentionally disseminated anthrax bacteria. And while Cross carefully interrogated and triangulated military sources, he takes pains to alert readers to the limitations of the available sources and the dubious reliability of some of his interviewees. Overall, the fact that information about Rhodesia's programme came to light via individuals' disclosures rather than technical means suggests the ongoing importance of developing human intelligence with respect to CB programmes, and not relying exclusively on technical intelligence.

Finally, Cross highlights the importance of understanding the organisational and managerial context in which Rhodesia's CB efforts arose. Sonia

Ben Ouagrham-Gormley's book *Barriers to Bioweapons* discusses the differences between the US and Soviet bioweapons programmes, and why the US government's different organisational and managerial approach led to greater innovation.[9] Under the US model, administrators devoted time, effort and resources to coordinate and integrate individuals and teams through all stages of development, production and weaponisation. Cross provides an interesting gloss on this subject by showing how a dysfunctional Rhodesian security bureaucracy actually facilitated the CB programme by allowing informal hierarchies and personal networks to flourish in which essentially rogue elements keen to weaponise CB agents could operate with little or no oversight or accountability. But while significant de facto compartmentalisation of information may have enabled the Rhodesian programme to get off the ground, it later inhibited innovation. The Soviets, Iraqis and South Africans encountered comparable problems.

Tight organisational and managerial structures are required to create an environment conducive to a sophisticated and innovative CB weapons enterprise and sustain it over the long term. But Cross points out that a high-end CB programme is not required to cause significant harm. The Rhodesian military was able to launch a series of attacks affecting between several hundred and several thousand individuals using largely low-tech means of contamination. In scale, its operations were roughly comparable to the Rajneeshi religious sect's biological attack involving salmonella bacteria in the 1980s, from which 970 people became ill (though all survived); and the anthrax attacks in the US in 2001, which killed only five people but necessitated the decontamination of dozens of buildings costing several hundred million dollars and the preventative prophylaxis of more than 30,000 people who might have come in contact with the *anthracis* spores.[10] Seth Carus has documented many other examples of contamination by way of other low-tech attacks using CB agents since 1900.[11]

These examples suggest that when dispersed on a relatively small scale, CB agents function primarily as weapons of mass *disruption*. One lesson may be that intelligence agencies should devote more attention to collecting and analysing information regarding low-tech CB attacks, particularly by non-state actors, in generating threat assessments. To date, at least in the

United States, the focus has been almost exclusively on higher-end threats involving advanced CB weapons agents, with little attention paid to cruder weapons and attacks. In addition, Cross warns that 'we need to be mindful that although some nations may no longer perceive [chemical and biological weaponry, or CBW] as having the same utility it did during the 1950s and 1960s as a battlefield weapon against opposing armies, some countries may perceive use of CBW by Special Forces or in counterinsurgencies as a valuable addition to their arsenal' (p. xxxv).

*   *   *

Carus has noted that, 'even if the past is not prologue', detailed histories of unconventional-weapons programmes are useful because they illuminate the kinds of motivations, challenges and trade-offs that might more generally inform decisions that produce weapons programmes in the future.[12] Cross provides one such history, and does it well and to a sound purpose. While the use of CB weapons in a late-colonial African conflict was itself improbable, and that conflict separated by some distance from contemporary situations, such insidious, threshold-crossing weapons remain attractive as expedient military equalisers and means of psychological intimidation. Just look at Syria.

Notes

[1]   See Milton Leitenberg, Raymond A. Zilinskas and Jens H. Kuhn, *The Soviet Biological Weapons Program: A History* (Cambridge, MA: Harvard University Press, 2012); Marlene Burger and Chandre Gould, *Secrets and Lies: Wouter Basson and South Africa's Chemical and Biological Warfare Programme* (Cape Town: Struik Publishers, 2002); Charles Duelfer, 'Comprehensive Report of the Special Advisor to the DCI on Iraq's WMD', 30 September 2004, https://www.cia.gov/library/reports/general-reports-1/iraq_wmd_2004/; US Senate, *Hearings Before the Select Committee to Study Governmental Operations with Respect to Intelligence Activities of the United States Senate* [Church Committee], *Ninety-fourth Congress, First Session, Volume I: Unauthorized Storage of Toxic Agents, September 16, 17 and 18, 1975* (Washington DC: US Government Printing Office, 1976), https://nsarchive2.gwu.edu/NSAEBB/NSAEBB58/RNCBW25.pdf.

[2]   Rick Gladstone, 'U.S. Slaps Sanctions on North Korea Over Use of Nerve

Agent in Assassination', *New York Times*, 6 March 2018, https://www.nytimes.com/2018/03/06/world/asia/north-korea-vx-kim-sanctions.html.

3   See Glenn Cross, *Dirty War: Rhodesia and Chemical Biological Warfare 1975–1980* (Solihull: Helion & Company, 2017); and Seth W. Carus, 'The History of Biological Weapons Use: What We Know and What We Don't', *Health Security*, vol. 13, no. 4, 2015, pp. 219–55.

4   See Yasuo Seto, 'The Sarin Gas Attack in Japan and the Related Forensic Investigation', *Synthesis*, 1 June 2001, https://www.opcw.org/news/article/the-sarin-gas-attack-in-japan-and-the-related-forensic-investigation/; and Milton Leitenberg, 'Aum Shinrikyo's Efforts to Produce Biological Weapons: A Case Study in the Serial Propagation of Misinformation', *Terrorism and Political Violence,* vol. 11, no. 4, Winter 1999, pp. 149–58.

5   Gregory D. Koblentz, 'Regime Security: A New Theory for Understanding the Proliferation of Chemical and Biological Weapons', *Contemporary Security Policy*, vol. 34, no. 3, 2013, pp. 501–25.

6   See Richard M. Price, *The Chemical Weapons Taboo* (Ithaca, NY: Cornell University Press, 2000).

7   Ken Flower, *Serving Secretly: Rhodesia's CIO Chief On Record* (Alberton: Galago, 1987).

8   See Meryl Nass, 'Anthrax Epizootic in Zimbabwe, 1978–1980: Due to Deliberate Spread?', *Physicians for Social Responsibility Quarterly*, vol. 2, no. 4, 1992, pp. 198–209; and J.C. Davies, 'A Major Epidemic of Anthrax in Zimbabwe: The Experience at the Beatrice Road Infectious Disease Hospital, Harare', *Central African Journal of Medicine,* vol. 31, no. 9, 1985, pp. 176–80.

9   Sonia Ben Ouagrham-Gormley, *Barrier to Bioweapons: The Challenges of Expertise and Organization for Weapons Development* (Ithaca, NY: Cornell University Press, 2014).

10   Edward A. Belongia et al., 'Demand for Prophylaxis after Bioterrorism-related Anthrax Cases, 2001', *Emerging Infectious Diseases*, vol. 11, no. 1, January 2005, pp. 42–7, https://wwwnc.cdc.gov/eid/article/11/1/04-0272_article.

11   Seth W. Carus, *Bioterrorism and Biocrimes: The Illicit Use of Biological Agents Since 1900*, CSWMD Working Paper (Washington DC: Center for Counter Proliferation Research, National Defense University, 2001), http://wmdcenter.ndu.edu/Portals/97/Documents/Publications/Articles/Bioterrorism-and-Biocrimes.pdf.

12   Carus, 'The History of Biological Weapons Use: What We Know and What We Don't', p. 219.

Book Reviews

Europe
Hanns W. Maull

Journey into Europe: Islam, Immigration, and Identity
Akbar Ahmed. Washington DC: Brookings Institution Press,
2018. $34.99. 573 pp.

This massive tome is the fourth and final work in a project undertaken by the leading Islamic thinker Akbar Ahmed. An anthropologist and former Pakistani high commissioner to the UK and Ireland, Ahmed holds the Ibn Khaldun Chair of Islamic Studies at American University in Washington DC. The project, conceived in the days after the 9/11 terrorist attacks, sought to examine the relationship between Islam and the Western world in the context of globalisation; previous volumes explored the present situation in the Islamic world, the position of Islam in the United States, and the American 'war on terror' as experienced by the tribal peoples on the receiving end of that war. *Journey into Europe* probes the ominous escalation of tensions within Europe between Muslims and non-Muslims through the prism of what the author calls a 'European dialectic', which brings together Max Weber's and Ibn Khaldun's very different takes on collective identity. Weber held that modernity had profoundly shaped and transformed societies along the lines of rationality and reason. For him, citizenship was ideally nested in a democratic order in which the rule of law guaranteed equality for all. Ibn Khaldun, by contrast, was more concerned with the nature of social solidarity (*asabiyya*). Having himself experienced the disintegration of Islamic societies in North Africa in the fourteenth century, he sought to discover what held tribal societies together and prevented them from descending into violent self-destruction. Each vision reflected the views of those who dominated the two men's respective societies, while neglecting the role of minorities.

Survival | vol. 60 no. 6 | December 2018–January 2019 | pp. 207–215   DOI 10.1080/00396338.2018.1542812

Ahmed argues that a synthesis is needed between the ideals of tribal cohesion and modern plurality – one that might be able to hold societies together under conditions of globalisation.

To assess the condition of Islam in contemporary Europe, the author and his team engaged in extensive fieldwork over four years, visiting 50 cities and towns in eight European countries. What they found was the opposite of synthesis: a 'perfect storm' whipped up by 'terrorism, immigrants, ISIS, and Islamophobia' (p. 414). Their analysis looks at the various European nations through the lens of tribal societies, distinguishing between 'primordial', 'perverted' and 'pluralist' tribal identities. According to Ahmed, the Germanic tribes lie at the core of Europe's primordial identity: 'tribal pride', he writes, 'permeates the worldview of Germanic Europeans' (p. 42). Honour and revenge are seen as important political motivations and identified, somewhat dubiously, as 'prime causes' of the Second World War, 'which was seen by Germans as an imperative to restore German honor and dominance' (p. 47). Nazi Germany stands for the ultimate perversion of primordial tribalism into an extreme, predatory tribalism that seeks to murderously eliminate minorities, but predatory tribalism is also seen as pervasive in the Islamic world. By contrast, pluralist tribalism, as expressed by the 'Andalusian model' of 'convivencia' (p. 22), offers ways to achieve the peaceful, creative cohabitation of different tribes within a single polity.

Part Two, which focuses on the experiences of Muslims in Europe, is subdivided into three chapters that document the views and experiences of Muslim immigrants, European Muslims (such as Bosniaks) and converts. Part Three draws 'lessons from Europe', which includes historical reflections and empirical data on the close links between anti-Semitism and Islamophobia (chapter seven), and an assessment (in chapter eight) of 'the current predicament of contemporary European society', which the author sees as afflicted by a range of problems, including:

> angry and noisy young Muslims, unresolved issues concerning immigration, frequent violence and extremism, often inspired by ISIS, the rise of the Far Right and its dangerous rhetoric of religious hatred, and rampant Islamophobia. To compound matters, leadership across the different communities is marked by pusillanimity that creates a sense that society is out of control. (p. 415)

These problems make for a significant obstacle to achieving convivencia in Europe. The author offers a number of sensible but largely familiar recommendations for overcoming this obstacle, urging Europeans to 'acquire knowledge and think for yourself' (p. 507), 'focus on youth' (p. 510), 'support Muslim women' (p. 510), 'facilitate the training of Imams' (p. 511), 'recognize the importance of interfaith dialogue' (p. 514) and 'recognize that Muslims tend to view the European Union favorably' (p. 515).

Overall, this is an important book, which contains a wealth of fascinating detail, both historical and contemporary, on an issue that is of critical importance to Europe's future. It impresses with its noble spirit and intentions, as well as with its close, unshrinking look at what are often ugly truths. There are also a few weaknesses and omissions, however. Analysing European societies through the lens of tribalism, while stimulating, risks overlooking the impact of the massive social change that occurred as Europe modernised through the centuries, thus producing distorted and misleading images. Moreover, the author frequently relies on his own personal experiences – for example, we are told, complete with photographic evidence, that he once lectured Princess Diana on Islam, making headlines in both the *Daily Mail* and the *Daily Express* – as well as his reputation and contacts. This may have resulted in a somewhat biased selection of interlocutors and sources, favouring dignitaries over other voices. Perhaps most important, there is next to no reference to the role played by governments, such as those of Saudi Arabia and Turkey, in promoting their preferred versions of Islam in Europe. These are minor blemishes, however, on what is otherwise a tremendous accomplishment: a book that provides us with a comprehensive, authentic picture of Islam in European societies.

Continent by Default: The European Union and the Demise of Regional Order

Anne Marie Le Gloannec. Ithaca, NY: Cornell University Press, 2017. $29.95. 266 pp.

Can the European Union survive in a post-liberal world? This question lies at the heart of Anne Marie Le Gloannec's *Continent by Default*, which was published against the background of a crumbling pan-European regional order. The cracks have been apparent since 2014 at the latest, when Russia invaded and annexed Crimea. Rather than being surrounded by well-governed states, as the European Security Strategy of 2003 postulated, the EU now finds itself, if not quite encircled by 'a ring of fire' (as Carl Bildt once put it), then certainly confronted with a number of sullen and hostile authoritarian regimes, failed states, civil wars and military aggression among its neighbours to the east and south. Clearly, the EU has been unable to ensure security and stability in its immediate geopolitical environment – it has, in the words of the author, failed 'as a model and an anchor' of stability (p. 201), both in Eastern Europe and on the southern and eastern shores of the Mediterranean.

Continent by Default dissects the EU's strategy and resources since 1990, identifying the shortcomings and failures of the Union's approach to enlargement (which Le Gloannec aptly calls, on p. 201, a 'makeshift foreign policy'), its European Neighbourhood Policy, and its separate strategy towards Russia. The policy tools the EU deployed assumed that Europe's neighbours could be rebuilt in the name of European integration as post-modern, peace-loving liberal democracies. Meanwhile, the EU initially tried to create security and stability in its neighbourhood without any security policy at all; the Balkan wars of the 1990s, which the EU completely failed to prevent or contain, finally persuaded the Europeans to establish the European (later the Common) Security and Defence Policy, whose origins, evolution and deficiencies are discussed in chapter three under the telling heading of 'Peace, War and Confetti: An Elusive Security Policy' (p. 77). In dealing with conflict and violence, the EU has largely relied on what the author calls 'the Irish tool kit' (p. 91). This reflected the experience of conflict transformation in Northern Ireland, an experience 'the EU has tried to transfer … to other terrains from Cyprus to Moldova, from the Middle East to the Caucasus' (p. 91). The results have often been difficult to gauge, but decidedly mixed.

Le Gloannec underlines the 'tremendous accomplishment' (p. 6) of the project of European integration in overcoming the division of the continent after 1990, but she also unblinkingly exposes its failures while putting her finger on their causes. Among these, she identifies the internal fragmentation of the EU resulting from its enlargement, a sense of hubris, difficulties in coping with power politics and violence, a lack of military power and coherence, and a willingness to compromise the Union's own moral convictions, for example by cosying up to authoritarian regimes to stem the flow of migrants to Europe. Still, Le Gloannec acknowledges the tragic dimensions of Europe's demise, prefacing her conclusion with a quote from William B. Yeats's 'The Second Coming' ('Things fall apart; the centre cannot hold'), and discussing, in chapter five, how the continent was overwhelmed by a refugee crisis that it did little to cause.

Sadly, Le Gloannec died in 2017. This thoughtful, wide-ranging and lucid account of Europe's engagement with its geopolitical environment is a reminder that her voice will be missed among those who care about the future of the European experiment.

The Decline of European Naval Forces: Challenges to Sea Power in an Age of Fiscal Austerity and Political Uncertainty
Jeremy Stöhs. Annapolis, MD: Naval Institute Press, 2018.
$36.95. 290 pp.

Jeremy Stöhs focuses on a specific aspect of Europe's capabilities as a global power in this comprehensive assessment of European naval power. As one might expect, his survey of how European navies have fared since the end of the Cold War offers a glum outlook, with only a very few rays of light. Case studies (in Part Two) discussing the navies of the United Kingdom, France, Italy, Spain, Turkey and Greece, Germany, Denmark and the Netherlands, and Sweden and Norway form the core of the book; Part One discusses the principles of sea power and presents the basic assumption of the study – that 'powerful naval fleets [are] a guarantor of economic wealth and prosperity', in the present and future no less than in the past (p. 15). The overall picture that emerges from the author's survey is one of naval forces that have not only shrunk dramatically (the British fleet has been reduced by 60%, while France has seen the strength of its navy halved since 1990), but have also been substantially restructured in ways that neglect the basic function of naval power: to deter or defeat an enemy. Thanks to political neglect and fiscal stringency, European navies are now desperately overextended and often 'unable to provide sufficient means to conduct their daily tasks' (p. 184). With political and fiscal neglect have come severe shortages of qualified personnel – in trying to make ends meet, navies have also tended to neglect training and readiness, degrading traditional naval prowess. Stöhs approvingly quotes British Rear Admiral Christopher Parry as saying, 'The peace dividend was spent a long time ago and, in some cases, many times over' (p. 185).

There are, as noted, a few glimmers of hope. Stöhs finds that the UK may just be able to hang on to a multidimensional navy on the basis of the second aircraft carrier that is scheduled to come into service in the next decade. By working together, European companies and navies have been able to develop and deploy warships that 'can rightfully be considered among the best in the world' (p. 187). Inter-operability has made great strides, and there has also been a shift towards more specialised navies with niche capabilities in the context of bi- and multilateral naval cooperation. Yet these advances are, in the author's view, a mixed blessing. Specialised naval forces will have to rely on others to supplement their own capabilities, which will involve considerable political risks. They will also find it more difficult to adapt to new circumstances. Broadly based, multipurpose navies, on the other hand, will be less dependent on allies and more versatile in adapting to a changing security environment.

Overall, European naval forces will be hard pressed to meet their basic military function. Yet this function, Stöhs argues, underpins the other important roles that naval power can play, in diplomacy and in policing the global commons at sea. With the relative decline of US predominance, the rise of new naval powers (particularly in Asia), and the renewed challenges posed by Russia's resurgent navy, this neglect may come to haunt Europe. As Stöhs concludes: 'Although utterly dependent on trade by sea, it is questionable to what extent European states can contribute to … the freedom of the sea outside their immediate sphere of influence' (p. 195).

NATO and Article 5: The Transatlantic Alliance and the Twenty-First-Century Challenges of Collective Defense
John R. Deni. Lanham, MD: Rowman & Littlefield, 2017. $40.00. 167 pp.

Beyond NATO: A New Security Architecture for Eastern Europe
Michael E. O'Hanlon. Washington DC: Brookings Institution Press, 2017. $14.99. 155 pp.

These two books offer two rather different solutions to NATO's problems with Russia. Since mid-2017, with the arrival of the first rotating troop contingents in the Baltic states and Poland, the Alliance has been working toward a familiar goal: to reinforce collective deterrence and defence, and to protect member states against possible Russian encroachment. John Deni explains how this came about, exploring the hurdles NATO is facing in its struggle to refocus on collective defence as its most important task, and sketching a new strategy towards Russia that would aim to weaken its power to threaten European NATO members. Michael O'Hanlon, by contrast, wants to work with Russia to rebuild a pan-European regional security order. The central idea of his strategy is to create a large buffer zone of permanent neutrality between NATO and Russia stretching from Scandinavia to the Mediterranean.

After the end of the Cold War, the West tried hard to avoid the mistakes of the 1919 Versailles peace settlement that imposed punitive measures on former adversaries and thus stoked the flames for another world war. Through instruments such as its Strategic Concept (revised in 1991), the North Atlantic Cooperation Council (established in 1991), the Partnership for Peace (1994) and the NATO–Russia Council (2002), the West sought ways of integrating the former members of the Warsaw Pact, says Deni. This implied that NATO was now engaged in the business of cooperative security, a project that superseded the traditional task of collective defence. At the same time, it acquired a third mission, crisis management. Thus, NATO aircraft flew their first combat missions in the skies over Bosnia in 1994, soon to be followed by ground troops. A focus on crisis management continued with NATO's intervention against Serbia in Kosovo in 1999. From 2003 onward, NATO assumed responsibility for pacifying Afghanistan, and in 2011 it took over the operations in Libya that led to the demise of Muammar Gadhafi and his regime.

Deni shows how the severe shortcomings within the Alliance revealed by the Kosovo war persuaded NATO to change track. Beginning in 2000, it engaged in a decade-long, far-reaching effort to restructure its doctrine, its forces, its command structures, its training and even its equipment with a view to enhancing its ability to conduct robust crisis-management and peacekeeping operations beyond the European continent. This effort caused NATO to lose sight of its original mission of collective self-defence, says Deni. The Alliance's material foundations were also allowed to erode. Meanwhile, the strategy of co-opting Russia into a new pan-European order, the success of which the Alliance was counting on to offset its neglect of collective defence, looked less and less promising. As Deni concludes: 'The alliance and its leading member states ... pursued this strategy with Moscow despite uneven results at best and obvious indications that Russia [was] largely uninterested in the kind of partnership that NATO favors' (p. 8). By 2014, the annexation of Crimea, and Russia's support for secessionists in eastern Ukraine, served as the straws that broke the strategy's back.

Deni places responsibility for this development squarely on Russia's (and not just President Vladimir Putin's) shoulders. In his view, Russia's zero-sum approach to East–West relations is the result of domestic political dynamics that reflect the reverberations of a vulnerable geopolitical position among Russia's elites. This leads him to argue for a new approach towards Russia – a 'competitive strategy' (p. 123) intended to reduce Russia's power to threaten NATO security. Such a strategy would require member states to form a 'unified front' (p. 123), and to engage with the strategy across the whole spectrum of their foreign policies, not limiting themselves to the usual political and military measures. Thus, Deni suggests that NATO members encourage emigration from Russia; end high-visibility bilateral summits and state visits to weaken Russia's soft power; facilitate the entry of Sweden into NATO should Stockholm wish to apply; and permanently bar Russia from the Group of Seven highly developed Western democracies (at present, its membership is suspended). Militarily, Deni advocates that NATO dramatically scale down the number of Russian observers in NATO exercises, and refrain from military-to-military contacts that do not provide demonstrable intelligence benefits to the West or help avoid the risks of escalation (such as the contacts over Syria). The most important element of this new strategy, however, would be economic sanctions to limit the development of the Russian economy and thus eventually weaken Russia's power in a decisive way.

Will NATO find not only the resolve, but also the money to stand up to Russia? Deni presents some good news concerning long-standing concerns about Alliance burden-sharing in chapter four, noting that European member states seem to have experienced a change of heart with regard to defence spending, which has recently increased throughout Europe. Yet Deni worries, on the basis of his detailed analysis of European defence expenditure and its determinants in chapter five, that European governments will spend the additional money mostly on equipment and personnel, neglecting training and exercises, and hence the combat readiness of their armed forces. His policy recommendations thus include not only higher defence spending, but also measures to ensure appropriate funding of readiness.

For O'Hanlon, NATO's present stance in Europe represents 'the worst of all worlds'. In principle, the Alliance has invited Georgia and Ukraine to join, without offering any clear indication as to when or how that might happen. From Russia's perspective, the threat of further NATO expansion is 'an insult' offered by 'a psychologically and politically imposing former enemy that has approached right up to [its] border' (p. 5). 'Vladimir Putin', O'Hanlon writes, 'therefore has every incentive to keep [Georgia and Ukraine] weak and unstable so they will not become eligible for NATO membership' (pp. 2–3). To resolve this problem, O'Hanlon suggests that Russia and the West negotiate a zone of permanent neutrality consisting of Sweden and Finland to the north; Belarus, Moldova and Ukraine in Eastern Europe; Georgia, Armenia and Azerbaijan in the Caucasus; and Cyprus, Serbia and possibly other Balkan states in the Mediterranean. For all these countries, NATO membership would be indefinitely ruled out. Russia would have to withdraw its troops, and guarantee these countries' security together with NATO. The neutral countries would be free to choose their own form of government and to join the European Union.

This suggestion may smack of appeasement – a criticism that the author tries to refute through the specifics of his proposal, which calls on NATO to 'stay strong and resolute in defense of existing members' (p. 5), and in its insistence on verification and compliance. Options for tougher policies should be retained in case Russia refuses to negotiate or breaks its commitments. O'Hanlon also accepts that an agreement, even an informal one, might not be achieved, but he insists that an attempt should still be made, since nothing would be lost if that effort failed.

O'Hanlon's proposal is thoughtful, knowledgeable, carefully argued and developed in considerable detail. Yet it also assumes a degree of inner stability and coherence, and a commitment to a rational and reasoned foreign policy, in all the countries concerned. This seems like an unsafe assumption at present. O'Hanlon may also have failed to recognise that for Putin, Russia's security threats do not stem from what the West does but from what it represents. The fact that several NATO governments are busily demolishing what the West stands for may in the end turn out to be the Alliance's greatest weakness.

United States
David C. Unger

We Were Eight Years in Power: An American Tragedy
Ta-Nehisi Coates. New York: One World, 2017. $28.00. 367 pp.

This lucid and thought-provoking volume shines a penetrating light on the enduring role of white racism in American history. As Ta-Nehisi Coates tells it, white racism practically defines American history. This provocative contention is at once the book's greatest strength and its greatest weakness. While Coates demonstrates the pervasiveness and explanatory power of this central theme of American history, he also falls victim to the inevitable one-dimensionality of his identity politics.

There is a steadily growing scholarly literature on these themes (one thinks, in particular, of the deeply researched and highly readable books by Jacqueline Jones on black labour, male and female, slave and free), but Coates's writing falls into a different genre. His potent mixture of journalism, witnessing and personal reflection recalls James Baldwin. But Coates is his own man, and well worth reading for his own sake. His unerring prose style, which he tells us is inspired by hip-hop lyrics and rhythms, is sometimes spare, sometimes explosive. His tone is passionate and compelling.

We Were Eight Years in Power strings together eight long essays Coates wrote for the *Atlantic*, one for each year of Barack Obama's presidency. An epilogue frames the rise of Donald Trump as being primarily driven by a white-American backlash against the Obama experience. Coates has supplied new introductions for each of his Obama-era essays, written from his chastened and embittered vantage point in 2017 and offering his radically changed view on the prospects for black America. Coates had allowed himself a measure of cautious optimism in the wake of the astonishing election of America's first black president in 2008, an optimism which subsequent events caused him to shed. He allows that he might have known better given America's long history of white racism, but he explains why a degree of hopefulness once seemed justified.

Some of the most interesting parts of this book examine the long-term damage wreaked by the 1965 Moynihan Report on the black family, and by some of author Daniel Patrick Moynihan's subsequent political advice to president Richard Nixon. Coates's argument is concerned less with Moynihan's overall analysis and prescriptions than with how they were selectively edited and transformed in the political arena, a process that Coates argues Moynihan was very much complicit in. Also particularly good is Coates's discussion of how discriminatory mortgage-lending practices by banks and the federal government widened the racial wealth gap by denying African Americans access to what for whites was the single-biggest intergenerational wealth multiplier, (federally subsidised) home ownership. Coates's accounts of the damage done to black families and neighbourhoods by bipartisan policies of mass incarceration are searing, and he rightly takes to task continual efforts to render white racism and its consequences less visible – even *in*visible – in the stories white Americans tell themselves about American life.

By the final chapter, however, much of which consists of an exit interview with Obama himself at the close of his presidency, Coates's argument begins to falter, as does his previously vibrant prose. This is even more true of the epilogue, in which Coates tries to systematically eliminate every possible argument other than white racism for the swing of previously Obama-voting counties in the Rust Belt of the Upper Midwest to Trump. Not content to indict every Trump voter as a white racist, Coates paints any white pundit offering alternative explanations as an apologist for white racism through some kind of imagined racial solidarity.

White racism can explain a great deal that would otherwise be unexplainable. But insisting that it explain *everything* requires dismissing the otherwise obvious role played by other factors that do not fit into the chosen single-gunman theory. By doing so, particularly in his epilogue, Coates traps himself in a kind of explanatory cul-de-sac. This is no reason, however, not to savour and learn from the brilliant insights and arguments of the preceding chapters.

Republic in Peril: American Empire and the Liberal Tradition
David C. Hendrickson. Oxford and New York: Oxford University Press, 2018. $34.95. 287 pp.

This ambitious book argues that, since the end of the Cold War, the makers of US foreign policy have cast aside many of the built-in restraints of the liberal internationalism they claim as their guiding principle, such as a respect for international law and a preference for non-military over military solutions. Thus unbound, says author David Hendrickson, policymakers have embarked on a new, destructive and unattainable quest for global military hegemony. The result, he argues, has been an era of endless wars abroad and the serious erosion of republican government at home.

Hendrickson teaches political science at Colorado College and has written eight books on America's international relations past and present. He supports his arguments with a thorough recounting and analysis of recent US foreign-policy adventures, laced with thoughtful invocations of the writings of relevant political philosophers and international jurists of the distant, and more recent, past.

Hendrickson reminds us that, strictly speaking, liberal internationalism is classical liberalism as applied to the international arena, and thus shares its distrust of leviathan states and governmental coercion. Instead, liberal internationalism values diversity, pluralism, rule of law, national self-determination and a peaceful, unfettered competition of ideas as well as commodities. How can all this be consistent, Hendrickson asks, with a US government that spends trillions of dollars creating a military force premised on global force projection and global geopolitical ambitions; that keeps essential aspects of its national-security agenda secret from its own voters; and that disregards UN Security Council votes, the Geneva Conventions and other international norms at will, even as it claims a right to invade and sanction others for violating these same standards?

Hendrickson acknowledges that this inconsistency has been in evidence for a long time, often excused in the name of American exceptionalism. He rightly dates the United States' full break-out from the norms of liberal internationalism to the end of the Cold War, which left the country as the world's sole superpower. American political leaders of the late 1980s and early 1990s chose to respond to this unipolar moment not by reverting to liberal-internationalist norms but with bursts of military spending and military activism meant to extend the country's accidental unipolarity indefinitely. In Hendrickson's view, a military–industrial constituency has since steered US foreign policy in directions inimical to the interests and preferences of American capitalism itself.

After largely making his case, Hendrickson succumbs, in the book's final sections, to a species of overreach himself, yielding to the understandable but unfortunate temptation of proposing alternative approaches to almost every errant contemporary policy he criticises. While this could potentially serve as a constructive intellectual exercise, in practice, it leaves him tangled in counterfactual hypotheticals that seek to reconcile alternative prescriptions with today's goals and assumptions. (An example of this would be his proposals for a reduced but ongoing US security role on the Korean Peninsula.) None of this undermines Hendrickson's basic argument, but he might have better served his readers by limiting himself to identifying and critiquing current distortions of liberal internationalism while offering broad suggestions for getting American foreign policy back on track.

Foreign Service: Five Decades on the Frontlines of American Diplomacy
James F. Dobbins. Washington DC and Santa Monica, CA:
Brookings Institution Press and The RAND Corporation, 2017.
$29.99. 329 pp.

For a half-century, from the presidency of Lyndon Johnson through to that of Barack Obama, James Dobbins was in the thick of America's major foreign-policy crises and melodramas, witnessing – if not contributing to – key episodes such as the escalation of the Vietnam War and the peace negotiations that ended it; US–Soviet arms-control talks; the winding down of the Cold War in Germany and Europe; and US interventions in Haiti, the Balkans, Iraq and Afghanistan. In this enlightening memoir, he shares his insider's view on the evolution of US policy since the 1960s, coming across as an intelligent, thoughtful and articulate foreign-policy professional. A diplomat in every sense, he was more consistently true to America's professed liberal-internationalist values than some of the administrations he loyally served.

Dobbins's take on internal White House disputes about strategies and tactics provides a useful sense of the broad continuity of American aims and assumptions, along with the sharp variations in political outlook and personal dynamics that accompanied every change in executive leadership. Missing are any fundamental critiques of America's basic foreign-policy assumptions during these years, such as the reasons why Washington increasingly chose to pursue a strategy of global hegemony rather than offshore balancing, especially after the end of the Cold War deprived globalism of its originally stated rationale. Nor is there any real questioning of the return to all-out Cold War competition after the brief Nixon–Ford–Kissinger interlude of detente; or of Washington's bipartisan commitment, even after the Cold War, to the fiscally ruinous pursuit of global military dominance, with its resulting chronic mismatch of mission and resources; or of the expectation that even the closest American allies yield some of their sovereignty to larger American purposes.

Such decisions were made well above Dobbins's pay grade (as the saying goes), and offering far-reaching critiques is generally not compatible with long-running foreign-service careers, as critical thinkers like George Kennan learned the hard way. But Kennan, to his great credit, rarely hesitated to examine and re-examine the basic assumptions of American policy, particularly in the speeches, articles and memoirs he produced after his retirement from active State Department service.

Dobbins's inside stories of policy debates over Somalia, Rwanda, Haiti, the Balkans, Iraq and Afghanistan are insightful and illuminating. And he is admirably candid in describing some of his own crisis-management advice, revealing not just whether more senior policymakers went along with his suggestions, but whether, looking back, he thinks it was for the best that in some cases his ideas were ignored or overruled. Yet his accounts sometimes left this reviewer feeling regretful that challenging perspectives were so often absent from the inner sanctums of policymaking.

The Fifty-Year Rebellion: How the U.S. Political Crisis Began in Detroit
Scott Kurashige. Oakland, CA: University of California Press, 2017. $18.95. 178 pp.

Scott Kurashige is an American Studies professor at the University of Washington's Bothell campus, but this is not a conventional academic book. Writing from an avowedly radical-left perspective and inspired by the community-organising philosophy of long-time Detroit activist Grace Lee Boggs (with whom he co-authored *The Next American Revolution: Sustainable Activism for the Twenty-First Century* in 2011), Kurashige argues that Detroit's explosion of racial violence in summer 1967 was not just a one-off urban riot during a long, hot summer, as it was mostly portrayed at the time, but a highly political rebellion rooted in the city's history. He also sees it as a critical moment in a much longer struggle that continues to this day, one pitting the neoliberal models of governance imposed on Detroit by Michigan's Republican governor and legislature against the democratically expressed preferences of the city's largely African American population.

Long-standing trends such as the decline of Detroit's auto industry, white flight to the suburbs and tensions provoked by racist policing all contributed to the four-day eruption of violence that July. In its wake came greater political empowerment for the city's African American residents, but also intensified white fear and repression. Coleman Young, Detroit's left-leaning Democratic mayor from 1974 to 1994, instituted police reforms and attempted to attract corporate development. But the city's economic and demographic decline continued, culminating in the municipal bankruptcy of 2013, the largest in American history.

Kurashige's purpose is advocacy as much as exposition, but he presents compelling details on what led up to, and what followed, Detroit's bankruptcy, including the forms of state administration that were imposed on the city, a story barely covered by the national press (as compared, for example, to the water-safety crisis unfolding at the same time in nearby Flint). He reveals the often shocking class and racial biases on display in the state's administration of

Detroit's public schools, finances and parks, even in cases where the administrators were themselves African American. Some of Kurashige's stories recall
Naomi Klein's concept of a 'shock doctrine', in which technocratic ideologues
take advantage of economic or political traumas to impose new structures of
governance and economic power on unwilling, but temporarily numbed and
defenceless, populations.

Kurashige makes a number of proposals, such as greatly expanding today's
modestly successful, small-scale community-farming experiments by acquiring
former industrial and residential lands with low market values, and boosting
political education 'on healthy eating … food justice and black culture' in the
style of the old Black Panther free-breakfast programmes (p. 129). While these
ideas may be instructive and appealing alternatives to the current emphasis on
for-profit speculative redevelopment, they seem unlikely to succeed without
the kind of government sponsorship or financial backing that is not now available. Moreover, Kurashige's attempt, at the end of this short book, to situate his
Detroit-centred lessons within a broader national and global context is unper-
suasive to this reviewer.

Nevertheless, this book, like others of its kind, usefully spotlights the cruel
and destructive political choices often made in the name of seemingly bland
neoliberal and technocratic dogmatism, and the sometimes inspiring resilience
of affected communities.

The Left Behind: Decline and Rage in Rural America
Robert Wuthnow. Princeton, NJ: Princeton University Press,
2018. $24.95. 192 pp.

America's culturally conservative rural voters generally vote Republican, so
their having done so, as usual, in 2016 plainly did not throw that year's election
to Donald Trump. Shifting allegiances among urban and suburban voters in
the Rust Belt of the Upper Midwest did that. But the 'decline and rage' of rural
America as described by Robert Wuthnow in *The Left Behind* is a key feature of
an America that too many shell-shocked Hillary Clinton voters still either do
not understand or wrongly dismiss as a declining demographic of deplorables.
America's electoral machinery, from the Electoral College system for presidential elections to the constitution's allotment of two senate seats to every state,
large or small, is designed to amplify the voice of rural voters, and will continue
to do so for many electoral cycles to come.

The economic and demographic facts of rural decline may be obvious, but
the reasons for rural rage are not. Like the white, working-class inhabitants of
many suburban Rust Belt communities, the rural voters Wuthnow spoke with

feel that the America they knew and loved has been slipping away, through urbanisation, immigration and Washington-centred big government. For many of them, the country they long for is an explicitly white, Christian, heterosexual and English-speaking one. Most of them seem convinced that the politicians who have been running the United States do not want to listen to them, or know them, or attend to the needs of their communities.

Wuthnow writes about these issues from an unusual and valuable perspective. He is a Princeton sociologist and an avowed Hillary Clinton liberal, giving him an intellectual and political outlook that many of his interview subjects would identify as a source of their rage. But Wuthnow, who grew up in rural Kansas, also feels a personal connection to rural America, seeing it as part of a single, diverse, political community that mutually determines America's political destiny. Rural Americans, he reminds us, may think differently, but they are not crazy. He might have added that they are not deplorables, but fellow voters.

Wuthnow says that the political likes and dislikes of the 'left behind' are rooted in their self-perception as members of what he calls moral communities, which usually coincide with the towns in which they live. They tend to see themselves as proudly self-reliant, or at least family- and community-reliant, and to feel that this kind of self-reliance is morally preferable to a reliance on outside help. This is not to say that they would necessarily refuse government help or attention, but they believe that they have little chance of receiving any, which adds to their sense that the country is run for the benefit of others.

The rural Americans profiled in this book recognise that their desire to keep on living in the rural communities in which they grew up, at a time when many of these communities are shrinking and lack the economic and infrastructural advantages of larger, growing communities, contributes to their problems. Some of them stay because of family responsibilities, such as a need to care for ageing parents. Others stay because they are attached to their moral communities despite the material disadvantages and dim prospects that accompany this choice.

The left behind understand the trade-offs they are making, but are by no means resigned to them. They feel, understandably, that they have a right to remain in the communities they have always considered home without being penalised for doing so. This kind of thinking may make some sense in moral terms, but the American capitalist economy is not known for emphasising morality. Rural decline – and its political companion, rural rage – will likely be with us for some time to come.

Counter-terrorism and Intelligence
Jonathan Stevenson

22 July (film)
Paul Greengrass, writer and director. Distributed by Netflix, 2018.

This inevitably harrowing and usually riveting film recounts Norwegian right-wing extremist Anders Behring Breivik's terrorist attacks in Norway on 22 July 2011, in which he killed 77 people and injured more than 300. From an operational standpoint, the movie demonstrates just how much carnage one competent and determined terrorist can wreak on an unsuspecting population. Disguised as a policeman, Breivik initially targeted the government quarter of Oslo with a van bomb made from fertiliser and fuel, killing eight people and injuring 209. This focused the counter-terrorism response on the capital, leaving him free to divert to a Workers' Youth League summer camp on Utøya Island, 38 kilometres northwest of Oslo, where two hours later he killed 69 people, mostly teenagers, and wounded at least 110 with automatic weapons. In 2011, Western governments were worried almost exclusively about Islamist terrorist threats. Such threats are still the most salient ones, and Breivik himself was assessed to be mentally disturbed (though legally sane) and to have acted alone despite his claims of networked support. In retrospect, however, his militantly anti-Islamic and anti-immigrant agenda appeared to telegraph a reactively right-wing fascist disposition that would become more widespread, especially in Europe, due partly to the rising influx of mainly Muslim refugees on account of persistent unrest in the Middle East.

Paul Greengrass is one of the world's best action directors, with a distinct vocation for chronicling political violence (he helmed *Bloody Sunday*, *United 93* and *Captain Phillips*, as well as three of the Jason Bourne movies, and wrote *Omagh*). He starts the film with the terrorist attacks, rather than making them the climax, and devotes the remainder of the narrative to their legal and psychological aftermath. This choice diminishes the opportunity to explore Breivik's character and circumstances, and he is left somewhat underdeveloped and two-dimensional – a fatuous egomaniac whose motivations are relegated to a few set-piece declamations during interrogation sessions, conversations with his lawyer, flashbacks and the criminal trial. But Greengrass's narrative strategy does afford him the chance to zone in on Breivik's victims – in particular, Viljar Hanssen, evidently a very brave young man whom Breivik shot five times and left on the beach to die. Frustrated by his infirmities, Hanssen is torn between ignoring Breivik and simply trying to move on, on the one hand, and addressing

Survival | vol. 60 no. 6 | December 2018–January 2019 | pp. 223–230   DOI 10.1080/00396338.2018.1542821

him in court alongside other survivors, on the other. Ultimately, he chooses confrontation. In a poignant scene, he shows that as long as he isn't dead he will resist spiritual defeat and embrace what life still has to offer – family, friends, dreams and hope. This, of course, is the terrorist victim's classic upbeat, inspirational dispensation. It is admirable and salutary. But not all victims can muster that kind of psychological resilience. It seems a simpler course when the perpetrator is a monster devoid of moral standing, as Breivik is, and a more complicated one when he or she has a plausible grievance, notwithstanding the despicable methods employed.

The Future of Terrorism: ISIS, Al-Qaeda, and the Alt-Right
Walter Laqueur and Christopher Wall. New York: Thomas
Dunne Books, 2018. $26.99. 268 pp.

**The Rage: The Vicious Circle of Islamist and Far-Right
Extremism**
Julia Ebner. London: I.B. Tauris, 2017. £11.99. 271 pp.

This century, Islamist extremism has dominated counter-terrorism agendas, and with good reason: the transnational sweep and mass-casualty aims of groups like al-Qaeda and the Islamic State (ISIS) make them more formidable threats than ethno-nationalist groups, such as the Provisional Irish Republican Army (IRA) and Eskudi ta Askatasuna (ETA), that had once preoccupied Europe, but were fading even before 9/11. In the United States, the Ruby Ridge stand-off, the Waco shoot-out and even the massively lethal Oklahoma City bombing did not spell a lasting trend of domestic right-wing terrorism, and any residual worries about it gave way to concerns about al-Qaeda's and later ISIS's threats. But those very threats have helped to produce a virtually global shift rightward towards a strain of politics that tends to be populist, illiberal, nativist and racist, and directed, to a significant extent, against Muslims. Some fear it could spawn substantial right-wing terrorist activity.

Two new books examine this possibility. Walter Laqueur (who died on 30 September at age 97) and Christopher Wall, in a wide-ranging and erudite study, explore the history of terrorism and contemporary jihadism before considering what the future holds. Notwithstanding the book's subtitle, they devote rather little space to the prospect of a far-right terrorist backlash. But what they do have to say about it is probative; noting that US President Donald Trump's signature 'America First' slogan harks back to 1930s anti-Semitism, they observe that the president has made retrograde alt-right ideas such as white nationalism and supremacism 'part of modern-day Republican orthodoxy. Though many Republicans will not buy into many of the alt-right's ideas, nevertheless, it would take only a small grouping of individuals to stumble upon its thinking, to radicalize, and then to take up arms' (p. 171). Infrastructure already exists in the form of 'sovereign citizens' groups and armed militias. The authors recognise similar trends in Europe, but appear relatively optimistic that the continent can 'limit the contagion of Trump's policies and rhetoric' (p. 252).

Julia Ebner, an investigative journalist from Austria who has devoted her entire book to investigating the pernicious synergy (she calls it 'reciprocal radicalisation') between jihadist and far-right extremism, is more alarmed about the trajectory of right-wing terrorism. She writes in a shrill, almost polemical tone:

> I call it 'The Age of Rage'. This era is characterised by a vicious circle of emotional actions and reactions. Whether on social media or in the streets, anger and fear are omnipresent: online and offline hate crimes are at an all-time high. Brexit and Trump are among the products of this global rise of rage. So are terrorist attacks. (p. 12)

But she also marshals facts well, identifies trends clearly, endeavours to contextualise her viewpoint and has a flair for the illustrative anecdote. Policy analysis is not Ebner's forte – she tends to default to platitudes – but her core lesson is creditable: 'the louder moderate voices get, the harder it will become to intimidate and silence them' (p. 204). The problem, of course, is that moderates, almost by definition, are inclined to speak more softly.

Rules for Rebels: The Science of Victory in Militant History
Max Abrahms. Oxford: Oxford University Press, 2018. £35.00.
285 pp.

Why Terrorist Groups Form International Alliances
Tricia Bacon. Philadelphia, PA: University of Pennsylvania
Press, 2018. $69.95. 344 pp.

The strategy and tactics of non-state militant groups, particularly since the rise of al-Qaeda and other transnational jihadist groups, have been vigorously debated. 'Old' ethno-nationalist and ideological outfits, such as the IRA and Italy's Red Brigades, are generally cast as constraining their levels of violence in order to preserve a place at a notional negotiating table, at which they might one day exert sufficient leverage to attain their political goals. 'New' jihadist terrorists' seeming lack of compunction about mass casualties has made this analysis appear inapposite: given their unforgivable carnage and uncompromising political goals, such as the expulsion of the United States and its allies from entire regions, they could not seriously be contemplating a sit-down with their adversaries. While al-Qaeda in Iraq's and ISIS's unilateral declarations of caliphates might appear to present a plausible alternative, their overall military inferiority makes their ultimate success unlikely, as US-led counter-terrorism campaigns have shown.

Political scientist Max Abrahms seeks to extend this line of analysis in his bold and ambitious book, *Rules for Rebels*. His leading premise is that jihadists, in their political and operational absolutism, are simply 'stupid'. He cheekily purports to offer 'the first book to identify a cohesive set of actions to enable militant leaders to win' (p. 1), as well as 'the first to show how militant leaders affect the caliber of decisions and hence the prospects of victory' (p. 198). He analytically develops three rules that incorporate the aforementioned actions. In essence, they are to leave civilians alone, to restrain lower-level operatives and to disavow the actions of those who flout directives of restraint. With gratuitous swagger (ISIS's strategy 'stinks', p. 89) and an inordinately snarky penchant for calling out fellow analysts, Abrahms applies regression analysis, arrays an abundance of charts and graphs, and knowingly holds forth on the principal–agent problem. He impressively compiles and shapes information and scholarship, and makes a few smart observations; for instance, acts routinely characterised as effective terrorism often do not really fit the definition. An apt example he cites is Hizbullah's 1983 bombing of the US Marine barracks in Lebanon, which targeted military personnel as opposed to innocent civilians and therefore does not align with the standard definition of terrorism (p. 43). Ultimately, though, his book comes to little more than a pernickety and self-congratulatory gloss on the distinction between new and old terrorism, which is by now orthodoxy.

In contrast, Tricia Bacon's systematic and authoritative study of alliances among transnational terrorist groups is a measured and practical contribution to our understanding of what makes them tick. A former counter-terrorism practitioner at the US State Department who now teaches at American University, she starts by pointing out that such groups are by nature insular, suspicious and averse to increasing their exposure to uncertainties, and consequently have a built-in reluctance to forge bonds with relatively unfamiliar groups. Accordingly, for a terrorist group to enter into an alliance, the projected benefits must outweigh the considerable risks. The primary inducements that Bacon identifies and tests through empirical examination are 'organizational needs, identity affinity, and trust', in that order of priority (p. 256). The fact that these are also intuitive only reinforces their validity, and Bacon's syntheses generally comport with common sense. Referring to al-Qaeda in the 1990s, she notes that 'for alliance hubs, success attracts because it projects their ability to address others' deficiencies' (p. 275). The book also has the not inconsiderable virtue of acute policy relevance. Bacon recommends, as a straightforward corollary of her findings, that counter-terrorism efforts concentrate more heavily than they presently do 'on degrading hubs' ability to fulfil other groups' needs' (p. 280). Especially potent means of doing this would be to curtail terrorist groups' capacity to provide sanctuary, to publicly stress their differences rather than their similarities, and to impede inter-group communications. Overall, this book is a fine example of academic research assiduously designed and calibrated to advance counter-terrorism in practice.

The Ghosts of Langley: Into the CIA's Heart of Darkness
John Prados. New York: The New Press, 2017. $28.95. 466 pp.

Principled Spying: The Ethics of Secret Intelligence
David Omand and Mark Phythian. Oxford: Oxford University
Press, 2018. £20.00. 295 pp.

In *Legacy of Ashes*, Tim Weiner's prize-winning history of the CIA, he argued in part that the agency's penchant for covert action undermined its effectiveness in collecting and analysing intelligence. The dramatic eruption of transnational, mass-casualty terrorism on 9/11 impelled the George W. Bush administration – which established renditions, black sites, torture and large-scale surveillance of the US population as counter-terrorism tools – to drag the intelligence community over to what Dick Cheney, then vice president, called 'the dark side'. John Prados, in a colourful and somewhat discursive CIA history, recaps and extends Weiner's inquiry, focusing on its directors (the 'ghosts') and contending that its post-9/11 excesses have further compromised its core functions, as well as its ethical standing. Prados characterises former CIA director George Tenet as a 'failed exorcist' of subversive agency ghosts – the horror-story metaphors get a little strained – who wanted to bring the CIA out of the Cold War shadows and create a new bond between it and the American people. Intelligence failures on 9/11 and Iraq derailed those plans – 'the demands of world events and the pressures of zealots to whom [Tenet] owed responsibility drove him to take the CIA beyond the pale and then betray principles in defending improper actions' (p. 312). According to Prados, the agency has essentially reverted to evading scrutiny and responsibility for its transgressions ever since, its status complicated by President Donald Trump's fraught relationship with the US intelligence community.

David Omand, a former UK intelligence and security coordinator who served as director of the Government Communications Headquarters (GCHQ) in the 1990s, and political scientist Mark Phythian, offer some guidance. While they are hardly as innocent as Henry Stimson, the US secretary of war who famously intoned that 'gentlemen do not read each other's mail', neither are they as cynical as Cold War-era intelligence professionals who regarded the Carter administration's effort to subject clandestine activity to the rule of law as naive and silly. In fact, the authors quote with approval the conviction of Stansfield Turner, Carter's director of central intelligence, that 'there is one overall test of the ethics of human intelligence activities. That is whether those approving them feel they could defend their decisions before the public if the actions became public' (p. 11). The book is inventively structured as a dialogue between a seasoned high-level practitioner and an objective scholar, and the two interlocutors ultimately agree that the just-war concepts of just cause, proper intention and authority, proportionality, reasonable prospect of success, discriminateness and necessity should apply to intelligence. Of perhaps overarching philosophical interest is the authors' conclusion, premised on the assumption of an open and democratic society, that the primary function of contemporary intelligence agencies is to serve 'protecting states' (as opposed to the 'secret states' of the nineteenth and early twentieth centuries) by supporting law enforcement in detecting and preventing serious crime (p. 227). This quite practical extension of their relatively idealistic but well-informed views seems to point to a plausible way out of the darkness that so concerns Prados.

Under Surveillance: Being Watched in Modern America
Randolph Lewis. Austin, TX: University of Texas Press, 2017.
$27.95. 267 pp.

**Beyond Snowden: Privacy, Mass Surveillance, and the
Struggle to Reform the NSA**
Timothy H. Edgar. Washington DC: Brookings Institution Press,
2017. $21.99. 276 pp.

For all the hand-wringing that the National Security Agency's (NSA) intrusions on Americans' privacy have provoked over the past few years, there have been relatively few journalistic or sociological accounts providing a nuanced picture of day-to-day surveillance under a US security apparatus and corporate leadership that have become drunk on it in one form or another. Randolph Lewis, a professor of American studies at the University of Texas, offers a warmly conversational treatment that is also searching and literate. With regard to widespread surveillance, he says at the outset: 'You might even think it has little impact on the functioning of a healthy democratic culture. This book will suggest otherwise' (p. 11). Along the way, he does observe that ambivalence conditions a degree of tolerance for surveillance in the name of security and the greater good, noting that:

even someone who shares the skeptical views of Edward Snowden might ponder the upside of surveillance culture and wonder if a technological system designed to capture our buying habits and assess our terroristic potential, to control our borders and monitor our parking lots, might serve more humane and hopeful purposes. (p. 77)

But he fears too many such concessions could yield the extreme case in which each individual can covertly monitor some others:

Dully obsessed with our seemingly limitless gaze – neither satisfied with our digital voyeurism nor able to give it up – we'll simply be *brooding* over our own little kingdoms of insecurity, struggling in vain to remember what privacy, security, and community felt like before the advent of the plastic all-seeing eye. (p. 200, emphasis in original)

Timothy H. Edgar, a former American Civil Liberties Union lawyer and National Security Council director for privacy and civil liberties, furnishes a more technocratic, but far from unenlightened, viewpoint. He believes that the Snowden revelations did prompt the genuine institutionalisation of privacy and civil-liberties concerns into US government surveillance programmes, and acknowledges that many US intelligence professionals tasked mainly with collecting information take these concerns seriously. But, he says, 'there is much more to do' (p. 10). While Edgar duly tenders policy recommendations, he also concludes that the traditional checks and balances afforded by the separation of powers are not, in practice, enough. Congress, which 'confronted the issue of NSA surveillance only because it was forced to do so' (p. 103), remains a passive-aggressive obstacle. Even a competent and conscientious executive branch, inevitably consumed with the quotidian pressures of executing policy, will be prone to err on the side of expediency. And judges, especially those on the Foreign Intelligence Surveillance Court, need to be better informed about how government surveillance works. In the end, says Edgar, only 'active pressure by an informed public' can ensure that privacy and individual liberties are protected (p. 112). The Trump administration, manifesting a lack of concern for both, and an inclination to politicise the process of generating intelligence, has made that lesson all the more urgent.

Closing Argument

Post-withdrawal Iran

Clément Therme

I

After the United States' withdrawal from the Joint Comprehensive Plan of Action (JCPOA) – the Iran nuclear deal – in May 2018, Iran's role in the Middle East has become even more uncertain. Despite the blow of US abrogation, Tehran remains inclined to continue adhering to the deal. But there are in fact two courses open to Iran – one conciliatory, the other provocative. The first would involve Iran's integration into the global economy, whereby it would pursue membership in the World Trade Organisation and assume a greater role in regulating the international oil market, potentially to the benefit of its neighbours. The second would centre on advancing Iran's existing regional foreign policy, and in particular its military interventions in the conflicts in Iraq, Syria and Yemen.[1]

Domestic popular opinion appears to favour the first approach of normalisation. Voters elected President Hassan Rouhani to a second term primarily to enable him to realise his promises to improve the daily economic life of Iranians. The security apparatus did not intervene in the electoral process as it had done in 2009, and his majority of 57% against his conservative opponent Ebrahim Raisi's 38% was higher than expected. After the results were announced, spontaneous outbursts of elation erupted from crowds all over Iran's major cities – even in Mashhad, Raisi's hometown. The Iranian people, then, want a return to the reform and

Clément Therme is Research Fellow for Iran at the IISS.

Survival | vol. 60 no. 6 | December 2018–January 2019 | pp. 231–240   DOI 10.1080/00396338.2018.1542823

detente agenda of the reformist president Mohammad Khatami, who was in power from 1997 to 2005. But because the hardline judiciary is preventing Rouhani from applying his reform agenda to civil liberties, his primary focus is on the economic dimension. With an eye to recalibrating the balance between the economic interests of the country and its revolutionary ambitions, Rouhani ran not only on promises of domestic reform, but also on a record of diplomatic moderation vis-à-vis the Gulf states (especially Saudi Arabia).[2] But Supreme Leader Sayyid Ali Khamenei and the Islamic Revolutionary Guard Corps (IRGC) have primary authority over regional policy and are resistant to Rouhani's designs.

Iran's trade relationships could be playing a small role in sustaining the possibility of detente. Iran's largest trading partner in the region – second only to China overall – is the United Arab Emirates (UAE), accounting for $16.8 billion in trade last year, an increase of 21% over the previous year.[3] This has leavened the UAE's security-oriented approach to Iran. Turkey, Iran's second-largest regional trading partner at $10.7bn, has shown a readiness to help European companies bypass American unilateral sanctions against Iran. Iraq ($6.7bn) remains a very important market for Iranian non-oil exports.[4] Trade with Afghanistan is also significant in that most of the trade is in non-oil commodities. In addition, Oman is well positioned to increase its trade with Iran, especially in the energy sector, which should reinforce its incentive to maintain its traditional diplomatic role as a neutral broker by sponsoring a negotiating channel between the United States and Iran.[5] Iran's November 2016 agreement with OPEC to cut oil production to buoy prices has enabled Tehran to project the image of a sound and reliable OPEC partner. US President Donald Trump, however, is pushing Saudi Arabia to offset reductions of Iranian oil exports after US sanctions against the Iranian energy sector take hold in November.

Other factors, however, have dampened Iranians' appreciation for detente's upsides. Inside Iran, a major one was the death of Ali Akbar Hashemi Rafsanjani in January 2017. He represented the pragmatic face of an ideological state. The 'godfather' of Iran's so-called moderate faction, Rafsanjani was one of the main supporters of an economic opening towards Europe and of the normalisation of Iran's relations with Arab countries in general, and Saudi Arabia in particular. His political network was behind the election of both Khatami and Rouhani, both of whom favour more constructive relations with Iran's Arab neighbours. Rafsanjani also sought enhanced economic relations with Europe to decrease Iran's growing economic and political dependency on China and Russia.[6] This position became even more pronounced after Rafsanjani's defeat by Mahmoud Ahmadinejad in the 2005 Iranian presidential elections, and was arguably vindicated by Rouhani's election.

Rafsanjani espoused the concept of '"depoliticisation", whereby "expertise" firmly supplanted "commitment" or ideological preferences'.[7] Powered by this concept, Iranian technocrats increased their influence and became a political elite, moving Iran away from purely revolutionary ideals towards a pragmatic focus on technological development and national interests. This new orientation was at the centre of the rapprochement between Iran and its Arab neighbours. When Rafsanjani passed away, though the rulers of Saudi Arabia remained silent, his family received official messages of condolence from Bahrain, Kuwait, Qatar and the UAE.[8] He embodied reassurance for Gulf states wary of the ayatollahs' revolutionary zeal. At the same time, Iranians perceived Rafsanjani as a protector of Iranian national interests.[9] His death has left Rouhani without a pre-eminent political sponsor, and made him more vulnerable to Iranian factional politics in general, and the conservative religious establishment in particular.

II

Nevertheless, despite temptations to disavow the JCPOA over what by international consensus was a disingenuous and invalid withdrawal on Trump's part, Tehran appears intent on sticking to the JCPOA for now. Its reigning hope is that a European rescue, however improbable, is in fact viable. The central question is of course whether European countries seeking to bolster Iran through trade relations can withstand US sanctions; in the long term, the answer is probably no. Yet there is a small chance that they will be able to thwart sanctions, and conciliatory Iranian behaviour would enhance that possibility.

Most European governments support Rouhani's desire to increase bilateral economic cooperation and thereby empower Iranian civil society. But at this juncture, for Rouhani to succeed in doing so, Tehran would have to demonstrate a high degree of international rehabilitation. One possible way of reaching this high bar would be Iran's full compliance with Financial Action Task Force (FATF) requirements. Based in Paris, the FATF is a respected and influential 37-member intergovernmental organisation formed at the 1989 G7 summit, charged with combatting money laundering and terrorist financing by way of a rigorous peer-review process. Iran has been on the FATF blacklist since 2008, mainly due to its financial relationship with Hizbullah, the Lebanese Shia militia and political party which the United States and some European governments consider a terrorist group. Fruitful negotiations between Tehran and the FATF in June 2016 led to the acceptance of a 12-month action plan by Iran. In June 2017, because the plan had been fully implemented by Iran, the FATF decided to continue to suspend its call for countermeasures for one more year. This extension was enacted once more in June 2018, effective until October 2018.[10]

Iranian compliance with the FATF is controversial within the Iranian government, however. Rouhani and the elected government believe the economic development of the country and the fight against money laundering and financial opacity should be the top priority. In turn, the FATF is a political tool for fighting corruption and improving the economic and financial efficiency of the country. But the religious leadership sees the FATF as an insidious colonial arrangement designed to compromise Iranian independence and its capacity to support revolutionary groups in the Muslim world. Thus, it is in Iran's national interest to preserve the identity and the ideals of the Islamic Revolution by rejecting the FATF.

There are indications that the religious leadership may be relenting, and that a dispensation acceptable to the FATF could arise. In August 2018, the Guardian Council, which had previously blocked four bills related to the FATF initiated by the parliament, approved a bill to amend the law on the FATF, committing Iran to a national action plan for addressing its shortcomings in combatting money laundering in order to be removed from the

FATF blacklist.[11] To show sufficient good faith, however, Iran would need not only to enact structural reforms of its banking system in line with the most advanced international standards, but also to end its financial and operational support for proxies in the Middle East considered by many to be terrorists. It would also have to adopt a higher degree of transparency in order to address international concerns regarding money laundering.

The probability that such a scenario will materialise remains low for two reasons. Firstly, there is no solid consensus in Iran to change its regional policy for economic gain. Secondly, the Trump administration's anti-Iranian attitude is not based on factual analysis, but on ideological and emotional impulses. That said, European countries could function as mediators between Iran and the United States, and between Iran and Saudi Arabia. The murder of Saudi journalist Jamal Khashoggi by Saudi intelligence operatives in October with the suspected sanction of Crown Prince Muhammad bin Salman Al Saud (MBS) has reduced Riyadh's – and by extension Washington's – political capital in the region; could disrupt the United States' aggressive strategy for confronting Iran and enlisting Saudi Arabia's cooperation on oil prices; and may for a time make both governments marginally more susceptible to diplomacy.[12] But conservatives inside Iran (the IRGC, the Justice Department, the Supreme Leader's Office) will still challenge Rouhani's narrative of Iran's peaceful economic rise.

III

The greatest impediments to Iran's international reintegration are not hidebound Iranian conservatives but rather hidebound American ones – in particular, National Security Advisor John Bolton, Secretary of State Mike Pompeo and Trump himself. In announcing the US withdrawal from the JCPOA last August, Trump demonstrated his ignorance of Iranian nationalism and notions of regional eminence – which long predate the 1979 revolution – by using the term 'Arabian Gulf'.[13] While his compunction to avoid the label 'Persian Gulf' may be explained by the administration's cultivation of a strong relationship with Saudi Arabia, the president might have had the diplomatic courtesy simply to say 'Gulf'. More broadly, he invoked the Iran of the early revolutionary years, when it was at war with

Saddam Hussein's Iraq (1980–88), failing to take into account the socio-cultural transformation of the country over the last 38 years.[14]

Furthermore, Trump's withdrawal of the United States from what is a popular agreement in Iran has allowed Iranian hardliners to portray the US as a treacherous country itching for war, in line with Khomeinist propaganda. Khamenei stated that Trump's ill-informed, tone-deaf attempt to send Iran back to where it was 50 years ago was a demonstration of his 'mental backwardness'.[15] Trump's anachronistic misapprehensions about Iran may, ironically, cause it to regress back to the elementary anti-Americanism of the first post-revolutionary years. Iranian officials across the political spectrum read Washington's focus on issues related to but not directly covered by the JCPOA – in particular, its ballistic-missile programme – as a mere pretext for engineering not only its behavioural change in the region, but also regime change in Tehran.[16]

They are probably correct. Even if the Trump administration's intention is not to provoke a military confrontation with Iran, the action it is contemplating could render that consequence more likely. For instance, if Washington imposes new sanctions on the IRGC, Tehran could place the US Army on its list of terrorist organisations. Brigadier General Masoud Jazayeri, spokesman for Iran's armed forces, has noted that 'hundreds of thousands of American forces are present in the region' and warned that if US forces overreach in the region, especially in the Gulf, Iran will confront them. Popular domestic opinion is likely to support that kind of response. The Iranian people perceive a striking difference between the current and previous US administrations. Barack Obama, when he was the US president, drew a clear difference between the population and the regime, quoting Iranian poets such as Hafez in his New Year address.[17] In contrast, Trump's caricaturing of Iran as a 'rogue regime'[18] and his tight embrace of Saudi Arabia – now revealed to be emphatically roguish itself under MBS – has induced Iranians to close ranks and embrace a common nationalism more snugly, even if they increasingly reject theocracy.[19]

At least by default, Iranian and Saudi efforts to increase Gulf stability seem more likely to succeed if they do not involve the United States. Even then, they will be compromised by an Iranian population disenchanted with perceived American prejudice, misunderstanding and perfidy. In the absence of formal bilateral diplomatic relations, regional groupings and unique cultural interests can provide opportunities for constructive diplomatic dialogue. The November 2016 Saudi–Iranian OPEC pricing agreement, for instance, resulted from Iranian and Saudi pragmatism. So did the March 2017 agreement allowing 85,000 Iranian pilgrims to journey to Saudi Arabia in 2017. When Iran and Saudi Arabia prioritise their national interests over security concerns or revolutionary ideals, they can sometimes find common ground. The opening of an Iranian interests section in Jeddah could be the first step towards a more systematised reduction of tensions between the two regional rivals, notwithstanding the United States' retrograde Iran policy.[20] European capitals committed to sustaining the JCPOA and engaging Tehran may be able to facilitate this to the advantage of all concerned – except, perhaps, Washington. While Saudi Arabia is not at present seriously interested in detente with Iran, such an eventuality would not be inconceivable if Iran were to reorient its regional policy towards socio-economic development and away from geopolitical intrigue.

Notes

1   See Alex Vatanka, Sanam Vakil and Hossein Rassam, 'Response: How Deep Is Iran's State?', *Foreign Affairs*, vol. 96, no. 4, July/August 2017.

2   See, for instance, Dina Esfandiary, 'Why the Outcome of Iran's Election Does Matter', *Washington Post*, 19 May 2017, https://www.washingtonpost.com/news/democracy-post/wp/2017/05/19/why-the-outcome-of-irans-election-does-matter/?noredirect=on&utm_term=.75e156f670e8; and Vali Nasr, 'How Rouhani Won in Iran', *Atlantic*, 22 May 2017, https://www.theatlantic.com/international/archive/2017/05/iran-election-rouhani-shia/527577/.

3   'Iran's Non-Oil Trade with Persian Gulf Arab States Increases over 16%', *Financial Tribune*, 1 July 2018, https://financialtribune.com/articles/economy-business-and-markets/88956/irans-non-oil-trade-with-persian-gulf-arab-states.

4   'U.S. Sanctions Crushing Blow for Iran's Exports to Iraq', *Al Bawaba*, 9 August 2018, https://www.albawaba.com/news/us-sanctions-crushing-blow-irans-exports-iraq-1171162.

5   'Oman, Iran to Boost Investments', *Oman Observer*, 13 August 2018, https://www.mofa.gov.om/?p=7458&lang=en.

6   See Clément Therme, 'The Islamic

Republic After Rafsanjani', IISS Voices, 12 January 2017.

7   Eskandar Sadeghi-Boroujerdi and Siavush Randjbar-Daemi, 'Serving the Leviathan', *Jacobin*, 18 January 2017, https://www.jacobinmag.com/2017/01/iran-rafsanjani-ahmadinejad-khamenei-reform.

8   See Hadeel Al Sayegh, 'Some Gulf Arabs Commiserate over Iran's Rafsanjani, Saudi Silent', Reuters, 9 January 2017, http://www.reuters.com/article/us-iran-rafsanjani-arab-idUSKBN14T159.

9   Henry A. Kissinger, 'Iran Must Be President Obama's Immediate Priority', *Washington Post*, 16 November 2012, https://www.washingtonpost.com/opinions/henry-kissinger-iran-must-be-president-obamas-immediate-priority/2012/11/16/2edf93e4-2dea-11e2-beb2-4b4cf5087636_story.html?utm_term=.2ac2bd346ebe.

10 John Irish and Matthias Blamont, 'Anti-Money Laundering Body Gives Iran Until October to Complete Reforms', Reuters, 29 June 2018, https://www.reuters.com/article/us-iran-sanctions-fatf/anti-money-laundering-body-gives-iran-until-october-to-complete-reforms-idUSKBN1JP34N.

11 On the Iranian financial system, see Rouzbeh Parsi, 'Great Expectations: The Iranian Economy After the Nuclear Deal', International Policy Analysis, Friedrich Eiber Stiftung, December 2016, p. 15, http://library.fes.de/pdf-files/iez/12987.pdf.

12 See, for example, David E. Sanger, 'Khashoggi Disappearance May Disrupt Trump Administration's Plans to Squeeze Iran', *New York Times*, 16 October 2018, https://www.nytimes.com/2018/10/16/us/politics/khashoggi-trump-iran-sanctions.html.

13 'Transcript: Trump's Remarks on Iran Nuclear Deal', NPR, 13 August 2018, http://www.npr.org/2017/10/13/557622096/transcript-trump-s-remarks-on-iran-nuclear-deal.

14 Abbas Milani and Larry Diamond (eds), *Politics and Culture in Contemporary Iran* (Boulder, CO: Lynne Rienner, 2015), p. 299.

15 See Clément Therme, 'Donald Trump, a New Advocate for Iranian Nationalism and Islamist Hardliners', *Conversation*, 8 November 2018, https://theconversation.com/donald-trump-a-new-advocate-for-iranian-nationalism-and-islamist-hardliners-86793.

16 See Steven Simon and Jonathan Stevenson, 'Trump's Dangerous Obsession with Iran: Why Hostility Is Counterproductive', *Foreign Affairs*, 13 August 2018, https://www.foreignaffairs.com/articles/iran/2018-08-13/trumps-dangerous-obsession-iran.

17 See President Obama's 'Nowruz Message to the Iranian People', 19 March 2015, https://www.youtube.com/watch?v=pZoMIS3cFRA.

18 Rhys Dubin, 'Iran's Not a Totally Fake Democracy, Study Says', *Foreign Policy*, 19 October 2017, http://foreignpolicy.com/2017/10/19/irans-not-a-totally-fake-democracy-study-says/.

19 See, for example, Thomas Erdbrink, 'Long Divided, Iran Unites Against Trump and Saudis in a Nationalist Fervor', *New York Times*, 26 November

2017, https://www.nytimes.com/2017/11/26/world/middleeast/iran-nationalism-saudi-arabia-donald-trump.html.

20 'Iran Plans to Open Interests Section in Saudi Arabia', Press TV, 5 August 2018, https://www.presstv.com/Detail/2018/08/05/570228/Iran-Saudi-Arabia-interests-section-Qassemi.